One Day on the Gold Line

A Memoir in Essays

Golden
Foothills
PRESS

Carla Rachel Sameth

Published by Golden Foothills Press
Pasadena, CA 91104
www.GoldenFoothillsPress.com
goldenfoothillspress@yahoo.com

(Originally published in 2019 in softcover and hardcover in a first edition in a prior version by Black Rose Writing in the United States of America.)

ISBN 978-1-7372481-1-8

Cover photo: Stock Photo ID: 605957462, "Sunrise at railway station in a
    beautiful morning." www.shutterstock.com
Author photos, bio & back cover: Hilary Jones
Cover design: Thelma T. Reyna & Kevin Poythress
Interior design: Thelma T. Reyna

Music credits:
"Ooh Child" by Stan Vincent © 1970 Frantino Music and Kama Sutra Music Inc.
    All rights administered by Sony/ATV Music Publishing LLC, 424 Church
    Street, Suite 1200, Nashville, TN 37219. All rights reserved. Used by
    permission.
"All I Really Need": Words by Raffi, D. Pike, B & B Simpson. Music by Raffi.
    © 1980 Homeland Publishing. Used by permission.
"You'll Sing a Song and I'll Sing a Song": Words by Ella L. Jenkins. Used by
    permission of Ella Jenkins and Ell-Bern Publishing.
The publisher and author apologize for any omissions in the music credits. If
    contacted, they will rectify these at the earliest opportunity.

Printed in the United States of America

Praise for
One Day on the Gold Line

"The well-crafted essays of *One Day on the Gold Line* kept me riveted. Carla Sameth tells deeply moving personal stories about overwhelming yearning and love that make you frighteningly vulnerable, finding the courage to face the worst, losing the person you were in your youth and discovering her again. This is a truly beautiful book."

—Lillian Faderman
Author, *Naked in the Promised Land: A Memoir*

"There is so much to admire in these warm, funny, and deeply human tales of love, sex, motherhood, and other adventures. Carla Sameth never gives up on herself, and her readers will never give up on her."

—Héctor Tobar
Author, *Deep Down Dark: The Untold Stories of 33 Men Buried in a Chilean Mine and the Miracle That Set Them Free*

"Carla Sameth's writing is poignant, powerful and needed."

—Shonda Buchanan
Author, *Black Indian*

"Race, class, drugs, sexuality, otherness . . . twenty-first century American hot-button issues are on full display in this brave, gritty, unflinching memoir. …Sameth navigates dangerous cultural trends tearing at the fabric of her non-traditional family. [She] shows that a family is not an abstraction, but a tribe that overcomes threats only when those threats are faced head-on. This is a 'feel-good' book… because of its clear-eyed, truth-telling love."

—Sue William Silverman
Author, *How to Survive Death and Other Inconveniences*

"A beautifully written memoir . . . notable for clarity and originality. A sharp wit and defiant humor run through this book, giving it an upbeat energy."

—Kathryn Rhett
Author, *Survival Stories: Memoirs of Crisis*

"Carla Sameth has seen it all—and she's the perfect guide to show us the poetry she found. Like motherhood itself, *One Day on the Gold Line* will break your heart in all the right places and put it back together a little differently."

—Ariel Gore
Author, *We Were Witches*

"A stunning read. Sameth pulls no punches as she tracks the highs and lows of queer family-making. . . . Sameth has found the courage to break the mold, and ...tells the story of how she did it—with grit and recovery, laughter and unflinching self-investigation."

—Aimee Carrillo Rowe
Author, *Power Lines: On the Subject of Feminist Alliances*

"Set in California, in the context of Black Lives Matter, same sex marriage laws, and publication of *The New Jim Crow*, Sameth's narrative is a riveting story of resilience—of what happens when what we hope for, and what we get, stand in stark, though sometimes beautiful, contrast."

—Marcelle Soviero
Editor-in-Chief, *Brain, Child*

"A splendidly raw and witty memoir-in-essays . . . eloquently laced with dark humor. Carla Sameth exquisitely confesses the flinching sacrifices and immeasurable rewards of motherhood."

—Melodie J. Rodgers
Editor-in-Chief, *SOREN LIT*

REVIEWS

"Carla Sameth's aching desire to become a mother, followed by the life she experiences once that dream becomes a reality, will crack your heart open with pain and joy. Sameth's writing is honest, beautiful, and hits a balanced note of revealing her often-naïve, younger self with a wiser reflective and compassionate narrator self...."

—Cassandra Lane
LA Parent

"A book that drew me in from the beginning. . . . Sameth is honest in her story of challenge and loss as she tries to achieve a picture-perfect family. She moves the reader from one crisis to another with a steely spine. . . . *One Day on the Gold Line* is beautiful, raw, and poignant and a good reminder of how we can be both vulnerable and strong at the same time."

—Christina Consolino
Literary Mama

"Writing against fantasies of ideal motherhood, Sameth's book presents a brutally honest and much-needed account of family-building and parenting in the twenty-first century."

—Robin Silbergleid
New Pages

"Sameth was determined to have her baby by any means necessary and, as he grew, strove to create a nurturing family. The traumas inherent in her efforts, as well as her fierce maternal love, are the grist of *One Day on the Gold Line*."

—Alison Ernst
Brevity

One Day on the Gold Line

A Memoir in Essays

Carla Rachel Sameth

1/6/2023

Dear Courtney,

Thank you for being a part of the journey!

With love and respect,

"Singing Mommy"

Carla

To my son—love you to infinity

Author's Note

While I navigated personal and family challenges depicted in this memoir, it was difficult to find books that mirrored my nontraditional family's life journey, or that looked like ours: multiracial, blended and unblended, led by a single parent who happened to be Jewish and queer, who'd experienced miscarriages and police brutality, whose son fought racism and drug addiction. I hope this memoir offers some solace and solidarity and finds its way to someone who also seeks to see some part of themselves reflected in what they read.

The story I tell here is my "truest truth." Because our individual memory is imperfect, I've relied on my writings over the years; journals; videos; letters; conversations with family members, friends, colleagues, and old classmates to help me flesh out the memories I have summoned. The dialogue and scenes were reconstructed to the best of my ability. Events were compressed or reordered as needed to fit the story lines. The names of some people and places were changed. Also, trauma can cause further fragmentation of memory, making it more elusive; so sometimes writing in alternative forms—such as several of the essays in this book—helps one to excavate this material.

While a lot has happened in the world, in my world, in all our worlds, since this book was first published in 2019 by another press, I have opted to keep this story as it was originally written because that's how I lived it before any of us knew the events that would take place.

—**Carla Rachel Sameth**
Pasadena, CA

Introduction
by Gerda Govine Ituarte, Ed.D.

I first met Carla Sameth in 1994, when I served on the board of the Pasadena organization Women at Work. Carla ran programs that furthered the organization's mission to improve women's economic and employment opportunities. In later years we reconnected as writers and as mothers who had suffered loss.

In 2016, I founded the Pasadena Rose Poets and asked Carla to join our efforts to make poetry accessible and available in unexpected places. Through this literary project and many others, a sisterhood built on words developed between us. I am continually awestruck by Carla's ability to pull poetry and prose from the deepest parts of herself and hold them up to the light.

In her award-winning memoir, *One Day on the Gold Line*, Carla displays incredible courage as she writes her truth while naked to the world, even when discomfort and insecurity ride her shoulders. Stronger still were her determination and intentionality, woven with grit and humor, in the midst of ancestral whispers.

Carla writes as a way to save her own life, make sense of her world, and leave vulnerability in the dust. She refuses to let shame stop her from writing her truth. She wrote the book she would have liked to have read as she faced formidable challenges as a queer single woman and mother helping her son navigate the dangers of growing up Black in America. She hopes this memoir helps readers find their own courage and resilience and feel less alone in their own struggles. Through daring to tell her story, Carla proclaims, "This is my journey, and I invite you to come along."

Delving into Carla's story, we witness the numerous ways to dance with survival. Carla seeks to create a safe and nurturing home for her and her son while she battles defeat, upset, and trauma. As a Black/Puerto Rican woman from the US Virgin Islands, mother, and diversity specialist who has fought to address issues of equity, I've seen firsthand the destruction and impact of racism on individuals and families. But Carla does not allow herself to come up empty, even as she contends with her son's struggle with addiction. By digging deep, she finds the courage to keep going. Writing and motherhood are the essence of her existence, the well of her strength.

Carla in her uncensored voice describes experiences shared by those whose identities do not conform to societal expectations. She originally imagined that for her son, having a queer single mom, being Black and Jewish, or being part of a blended family would make his life richer. But the reality was much harder. There is a power in her story that lingers after the reader turns the last page. These linked essays create a bigger, richer, and deeper story. Together they are greater than the sum of their parts. She takes us on a wild ride through contemporary parenthood infused with the magic of her words.

Gerda Govine Ituarte, EdD, is a poet; a diversity, equity, and inclusion expert; and the founder of the Pasadena Rose Poets in Pasadena, CA.

Table of Contents

The Burning Boat

That night on the ferry from Italy to Greece, I felt I was performing a sort of tashlich, the Jewish New Year's tradition of symbolically casting off sins and regrets of the previous year in the form of bread crumbs tossed into flowing water. Earlier that evening, the warm ocean night had wrapped me in a peaceful feeling of embarking on something new while leaving behind my recent losses, as if I had tossed them into the ocean.

It was 1991, and I was thirty-two years old. I was fighting to recover from what felt like the biggest loss. I had been engaged and living in San Francisco when I accidentally got pregnant. I dreaded having another abortion. The first one, two years prior—while in another doomed relationship—had felt necessary. But it had left me sunk so low that I was like a poster child for the anti-abortion movement. This time around, not realizing I was pregnant, I had been taking medication that could harm the fetus. After much research and agonizing indecision, I terminated the pregnancy. When my fiancé and I split up, I lost hope of having a baby in the near future and in the dreams I had for a lasting relationship. The quicksand of unrelenting regret threatened to swallow me up again.

I had made a new plan. Go away on a magical trip overseas—Europe, Greece, maybe Turkey and Israel. Then return and buckle down to the serious business of job, house, and baby—but on my own.

◆

A noise broke into my dreams, ending the blissful quality of my sleep. *Drunken sailors*, I thought and rolled over, hoping to recover my dream. The pounding and shouts of "Wake up, get out!" in broken English continued. Groggy, I tried to sit up. I staggered out in my pajamas, no bra. Passengers had fallen asleep curled up against one another, languid, cozy, on top of blankets strewn about them, children sleeping on parents and dogs sprawled in between. On the ship deck the idyllic scene had shifted to chaos. Dozens of sailors tried to climb the mast of the ferry, fighting with some kind of mechanism to lower the lifeboats, clearly something they had never had to do before. Other sailors stood looking agitated, puzzled, waving their arms and shouting orders in Greek. Families and lovers whom I had envied the night before seemed frenzied, panicked. Children and parents clung together—some cried, some held babies. Dogs ran the length of the deck barking or huddled with the children, whimpering. The sailors managed to lower the lifeboats, which dropped one by one into the water with loud, messy splashes.

Sailors shuffled women and children onto the lifeboats. Some couples refused to be separated. Strangest of all were the dogs: some men remained on board while the dogs went on the lifeboats.

I ran back to my cabin and grabbed my Grandma Stella's silver etched ring from Mexico. She had given it to me when I was in my twenties and was suffering from the aftermath of a breakup, and I'd told her, "Now we are engaged, Grandma." That ring was one thing I'd hung onto over the years. Something enduring and unusual for me, because I hadn't lost it yet. Running my fingers over the etching, I felt something familiar, which added to my oddly calm demeanor, though my extraordinary grandma had not been known for her nurturing.

On deck, an Italian man attempted to comfort both his wife and me, though I was dry-eyed. Like me, all the usually elegant Italian women were braless, but the men must have gone to bed with their Italian suits pressed and ready to jump into, because that's how we saw them now. They were beautifully and immaculately dressed, not a wrinkle.

I was hustled along into a lifeboat by momentum. No one stopped to ask if I wanted to be saved, but I got in, obediently. In my lifeboat people were crying and crossing themselves. A German woman insisted desperately to herself, "My husband—he is still on the ship. But he is a good swimmer."

A lifeboat in the middle of the ocean. In the middle of the night. Complete darkness as we drifted away from our ferry. I wondered if our ship was sinking with the remaining passengers and our belongings. Would these few people around me in my lifeboat be the last ones I'd see? I didn't know them, had barely spoken with anyone on this trip. Who besides my family would feel pain at my going? Would my ex-fiancé feel any regrets? Had I left anything undone? I imagined my parents and my siblings, and I felt a prick of sadness for them; after all, I would hate it if one of them died.

I was no longer afraid. I had been more frightened the day before, when I was in Bari, a steaming, dangerous port.

Instead, a relief washed over me, as I no longer beat myself senseless with self-blame, regrets, ruminations. Instead, I thought, *I've led a good life.* At thirty-two, I'd experienced a lot.

I remembered the love from Henry, my safe, longtime Filipino boyfriend from my twenties; my family; my friends; the places I'd traveled, the magic of Chaco Canyon. Finding my muscles in Simpson

Meadow. And now here—the middle of the Mediterranean—what better place to go? Besides my family, a few close friends, who would miss me?

I wanted to believe that Henry would mourn me. I remembered how he first got my heart when we saw a lonely older person pushing a cart down the street. It's so sad to grow old alone, we agreed. And then he said, "I know it's too soon to say these words, but I'd like to grow old with you." Henry used to beg me, "Just have the kids, and you can go off and do your thing. I'll support you through medical school. I'll say, 'Mommy had to work,' and I'll take care of them."

I had always thought I could just check in when I was ready for children, and Henry—or someone like him—would be there. That didn't happen. Instead, I broke his heart when I fell into the seductive orbit of a Nicaraguan man with six kids. Now, several years later, I was alone. Henry, too, was part of the collateral damage from decisions I'd made, addictive love I'd run with—part of my tashlich. Regret seeped in and undercut the brief serenity and gratitude I'd felt a few moments before.

I glanced over at the one other woman not crying. She rocked her baby and sang softly, eyes locked with her infant's. No room for anyone else. Magic. I gasped as I realized how much I wanted that. I remembered having had that life inside me, how I'd already felt like a mother. "No!" I said out loud, and then the boulder inside me that kept the tears in rolled out, and I wept. I was not ready to die without having had a baby.

With the first light of dawn and a striking sunrise, I started to think that I should have grabbed a camera instead of the ring. People seemed to have fallen silent—for how long? A large ship pulled up. They threw down a ladder, and we climbed in.

Passengers on our rescue ship moved over, made room, and offered us food. We found out what the problem was: engine fire. Apparently engine fires are the biggest potential danger on passenger ferries like ours. Everyone assumed their cars and belongings were gone, and we were just happy to be alive. The honeymooners didn't see a bad omen—their life going up in flames. Instead they saw a new beginning.

And I decided to do the same.

Simpson Meadow

Alone, buck naked on the warm, flat boulders by the middle fork of the Kings River, I felt the smoothness of the rocks, the hardness of my muscles, and the soreness. No exhaust fumes or car horns. My body's pungent odor blended with the scent of pine and the inviting aroma of fresh-baked bread from our makeshift kitchen. A cool breeze lightly caressed me. I was twenty years old. I had no idea what I was doing out there. I was part of the first all-women backcountry trail crew at Sequoia and Kings Canyon National Parks in California's Sierra Nevada mountains; the year was 1979.

The night before we left for the backcountry, my two crewmates, Eva and Michelle, had brought me to a little hidden bar down a desolate road and halfway up the mountain on the 180 between Grant Grove and Trails End. Eva and Michelle were locals from Three Rivers: tough, über-confident and self-reliant nature girls. They'd had experience working in the backcountry before. I found out later that the inclusion of women on backcountry trail crews had come about only as a result of Michelle threatening a lawsuit. By putting us all on one crew, those in charge of Sequoia and Kings Canyon National Parks probably hoped to prove that women could not handle working together in the wilderness.

We were in a sweaty bar packed with swaggering, voluptuous cowgirls and other regulars hanging about. A rusty cowboy bar filled with lesbians, sawdust on the floor, and not like anywhere I'd ever been. I imagine it was called something like the Tie Me Up.

"Damn!" I shouted out to my new backcountry crewmates. "Where are all these women coming from?"

"They come from all over the state when she plays," Eva said and winked, pointing at the woman perched on a stool with a guitar.

We were also there to see her. She was famous—the only female helicopter crew member. She sang out there once or twice at the start of every summer.

"Is she flying us down to our camp?" I shouted to Eva above the noise. She smiled and shook her head no. The singer's voice was strong and tough, but her lyrics were sweet, and all that combined with her sturdy helicopter-crew cowgirl look mesmerized me.

Just as I was settling in, it was time to head back to camp. I wasn't sure when I'd ever get to a place like this again. We drove back to our camp at the base of the Sierras.

The next morning, I awoke to loud sobbing outside my tent. A few minutes later, I met our crew leader, Laurel. Big, dirty tears streamed down her face. She looked mad at being discovered. A small crowd of maintenance men and ranger types were standing around. Gawking.

She blew her nose loudly. "I miss him so much, my Buddy! We ain't never been apart!" Snot dripped from her nose, and her straggly, dirty blond-brown hair was a mess. Her hands shook as she reached into a tobacco chew bag.

Eva walked over for a better view and stared hard at Laurel. "You're crying for your boyfriend? Really?" she said with disdain. Yesterday Eva had bid a cheerful good-bye to her college boyfriend from Fresno and was already back with her summer man, Jack the Packer. Eva was tall, almost rangy, but with curves; she had wavy shoulder-length blond-brown hair and glistening green eyes. She walked with a certain ultra-sure-of-herself swagger and a half smile that seemed to hint she had a joke she might share with you, but you could never be quite one hundred percent sure she liked you. I immediately sensed she was the type of person I'd strive to have like me. Jack the Packer was substantially older and stood in deep contrast to her college boyfriend, who was closer to our age, very friendly, almost goofy. Jack was an absolutely no-nonsense kind of seasoned outdoor man. Only later would we see his eyes crinkle on rare occasions and usually when looking at Eva.

"No! It's my dog!" Laurel yelled out indignantly. "Yuh think I'd be crying out for some man?" Laurel half-snickered, half-sniveled, while managing to shove some chewing tobacco into her mouth. Eva and Michelle just stared in horror at this woman who had been put in charge of us.

"I don't imagine they'll last the summer," I heard one guy say.

"I was betting on them turning into a buncha lesbians," I heard another man comment.

I was embarrassed by Laurel. Repulsed. I saw a couple of guys looking uncomfortable, not saying anything, and decided that they were the decent ones. One of them smiled shyly and reached out a hand. "Eddie Rodríguez—nice to meet you. Good luck!"

Later that day, the four of us—Eva, Michelle, Laurel, and I—were flown into the backcountry by helicopter. Simpson Meadow is not known for drop-dead beauty, like Yosemite. And just to get there requires going over several mountain passes and some of the roughest and most isolated terrain in the National Park system. You can get lost out there (which I almost did that summer). You'd wind up a part of the natural ecology, bones sucked dry, and anything left getting recycled into the ground to feed the next generation.

I had only taken this summer job for the money, but I breathed in deeply as we looked down at a river snaking through a valley surrounded by steep gray and white granite walls. Surprisingly moved, I watched as we passed rich green areas densely populated by pines.

Originally I had hoped to spend the summer working with an economist on the Blackfeet Indian Reservation, writing about the effects of mining on the tribe. I didn't take that internship, though. It was unpaid, and my parents had made it clear that summers were for earning money for college. So I begrudgingly accepted the well-paid position I was offered on the backcountry trail crew in Sequoia and Kings Canyon National Parks. A position that most would have died to have been offered. And later I would look back and realize that it was a once-in-a-lifetime experience. I had previously participated in internships with the Student Conservation Association—one in the Grand Canyon, one in Chaco Canyon—and later landed a National Park Service job at a strange little place called Gran Quivira, now part of the Salinas Pueblo Missions National Monument in Mountainair, New Mexico. In Mountainair, I'd had to fend off rattlesnakes, knife-wielding self-labeled *pachucos*, and Holy Rollers. I hooked up with an older ranger boyfriend (he had twenty-seven years to my eighteen), mostly for the protection of being with someone. I wasn't that into him, but the following summer I told him, "If you pierce your ear, I'll go with you to Idaho." I wanted a boyfriend with a pierced ear, and I didn't have my summer plans firmed up. So he pierced it, and off we went to Salmon, where I had a series of strange jobs, including one on a type of chainsaw-massacre US Forest Service crew on which I actually learned to use and clean a chainsaw and to cut down trees infected with mistletoe. Now here I was, soaring over Kings Canyon on my way to a backcountry base camp where I would spend the summer.

A short time later, our helicopter pilot pointed to a seemingly straight-up series of switchbacks. "There's the Bitch. Look at it and weep, ladies!" he said. The Bitch needed repair, he told us, and who better to do it than the inaugural All-Women Backcountry Crew of Sequoia and Kings Canyon?

I asked why the trail was called the Bitch, and, as the pilot went on to describe it, I began to understand. "Oh, it's just a little old 4,000-foot-altitude climb up to Granite Pass from Simpson Meadow. Over five miles where there's no water, and hard as hell climbing up to that first plateau. Eight miles straight up to the top. You gotta be a bit crazy to go out to

Simpson Meadow and climb the Bitch, so you won't find too many hikers out there. Not to mention the rattlers and bears that call Simpson Meadow home."

The Bitch was where we would begin each morning and work our way down. *Shit*, I thought. I'm actually scared of snakes . . . the sound of that rattle.

I have since read various narratives that describe our base camp something like this: "You follow a sparsely vegetated, lengthy trail up through the middle fork of Kings and arrive at Simpson Meadow. It is more than a mile long, covered with long, lush grass in some areas and surrounded by intimidatingly tall, elegant pines."

When we landed at Simpson Meadow, I saw a few odd spots of color, spring wildflowers hanging on into early summer—tiger lilies, asters, and shooting stars. The canyon was majestic and daunting on the day we were dropped in by helicopter, but Simpson Meadow itself looked almost homely. No lush green. This was where we would make our base camp. A wood corral sat alone, as if abandoned, with a big white salt block inside. "It's for the horses. They'll be here with Jack," Eva explained. I'd already been told that our supplies and food—whatever we wanted, from steaks to alcohol—would be packed in by Jack the Packer or flown in the same way we'd come. Later Eva would take a lick of the salt block on a dare; I'd find she'd do most anything on a dare.

Growing up in Seattle, I'd camped with my family all my life, but I didn't know how to set up a tent by myself. Michelle offered to help me. Eva had already set up hers and was off splitting wood, making the loud, steady, confident noises of someone who knew how to use an ax.

Everything smelled good—the wood, the air, even my sweat.

"Hey, are you the city slicker?" Eva said as she walked back from splitting wood.

"Not exactly," I muttered, but I was intimidated by these girls. They were annoyed with each other and with our leader. Each of them was convinced that she should have been made boss. Eva was super coordinated and good at everything, including academics. I'd already learned she had graduated more than a year early from high school. She was musically talented and could sing and play various instruments. She was carving a dulcimer, something her Fresno woodworking boyfriend had started her on. She always seemed to be confident in her relationships with men and to have little respect for most women. And I wasn't changing that feeling; I knew she was already disappointed that I wasn't better at doing the outdoor work that she and Michelle seemed intuitively good at figuring out. They weren't happy about working on an all-women trail crew either.

Unlike Eva, Michelle's appearance and manner were simple and straightforward, and I never felt that I had to do anything more to earn her respect than working hard and being the best person I could. She was short compared to Eva, with truth-telling clear blue eyes and blond hair in a straight, shoulder-length cut. This in contrast to Eva's certain come-hither look, as well as a standoffish "I might actually be way too cool for you" manner that Eva seemed to affect. She was the pushmi-pullyu, and Michelle was all there, solid, loyal—if she decided you were trustworthy and a friend.

I didn't know how to do much of anything beyond grunt labor, but at least I had endurance and tenacity. Hammering a nail, using an ax or a pick, I thought I could do that stuff, but I felt lame and inept with this group. I had gotten this job mainly through my skill at filling out applications. I could weed, mow lawns, dig ditches . . . but building something or balancing on a shaky log to cross a river had never come naturally. Now that I'd started college, I was beginning to think that unskilled labor might someday get boring.

"Well, I worked last summer for the US Forest Service," I offered up. "On the chainsaw crew." Another job I'd landed only because I was good with application forms.

I considered myself lucky that I hadn't accidentally ripped my arm apart with a jagged cut from my chainsaw. I just liked a challenge—the idea of learning how to do stuff that didn't come naturally to me, like auto mechanics and construction work. When I was young, I had loved playing tackle football in the local park back home in Seattle. Even after a neighbor boy's knee went into my face and gave me a massive bloody lip, I lived for rushing. In fourth grade I was the best girl baseball player at my rough elementary school. (Back then they called me "Sammy Boy," and I fought against bullies with my three "boyfriends." We were a regular United Nations gang of four—German American, African American, Japanese American, and me, Jewish.) By the sixth grade, however, I was always the last picked for teams. In college I'd decided to show I was tough by going out for the women's rugby team. I don't know why, except that I was—and still am—a tenacious and fearless rebel. Unlike the other members of the rugby team, I had never played organized soccer, I wasn't particularly fast, and I certainly wasn't athletic. My first year I played the hooker position on the rugby team at University of California, Santa Cruz, and barely escaped injury. Many years later, at fifty-four, I considered playing rugby again. Today, I wonder who that person was who was ready to do that. I long for a body and soul that are firm and ready for adventure. When I am timorous and afraid, the strong, tough Sammy Boy part of me goes walkabout, a complete stranger.

"First things first. Where's it going to be?" Michelle was pacing around, looking for some kind of right spot. I assumed it had to do with pitching a tent. She looked over at me and smiled. "The shitter. We build the throne, you know?" she said.

Eva came over, Laurel trailing behind, trying to look leaderly. "It's a competition we have going on," Eva explained. "Every summer, each crew tries to build the best outhouse, and of course the guys want a throne to sit on."

"So do I," Laurel said. She appeared serious.

Eva looked at Michelle. Then at me, and she winked. "Let's do it then!" What happened next was about an hour of debate that I didn't entirely understand about which spot was best. Once the three of them agreed (I was going along for the ride), they began discussing the ideal setup. This is what I remember: We all said we wanted stability, and there would be two main boards over a trench. But after that there was a lot of shouting, drawing in the sand, and reminiscing about the best outhouse each of us had ever experienced. I had never built one before, but I knew that friends of my parents had built a fancy redwood double outhouse on Lasqueti, a small island off Vancouver. Schoolteachers like my dad, they had moved to Canada with their two sons, essentially homesteading out of fear that their sons might someday be drafted for the Vietnam War. What impressed me most about their rural existence was the luxuriousness of that two-seater.

Jokingly I suggested that we be suspended above the trench so that no one's butt came near the shit. "Hey, she might be onto something," Michelle said. "Why not use the corded rope so that we squat and hang onto it?" I remembered the bunny rope tows and going down ski slopes between my dad's legs in the days of wood skis and lace-up boots. Yeah, kind of like that; we would build it so that your feet would be planted, your butt hanging over. We quickly went to work. I was good at digging the trench, and in no time we had a state-of-the-art shitter. Laurel insisted on trying the new throne out immediately, and we all moved tactfully away.

Suddenly we heard screaming. "Shit, aah! Help!" We went running over to where we'd left her. Laurel was hanging suspended upside-down, head toward the shitter, which smelled like it had been used. I started to giggle: at first all you could see were Laurel's boots, and she looked like the witch from *The Wizard of Oz* when Dorothy's house landed on her. As glanced over at Eva and Michelle, I could see I wasn't the only one thinking about the witch's shoes. They were already busy helping her get upright again. They quickly studied the flaws in their design and made the necessary modifications while Laurel stood by cursing.

Just then I remembered that I did have something to offer. "Hey, we built a sauna one summer where I went to camp," I announced to Michelle.

"Oh, yeah?" She looked interested. "Let's do one here—what's it take?"

I couldn't really remember the specifics, since I didn't actually build it, but I tried to sound sure of myself. "Plastic covering, some kind of wooden structure, fire pit to heat rocks, and a watering can to dump water on them." There was a river running alongside the meadow; we could hear its soothing presence in camp. "That's where we'll jump in after—first the hot, then the cold."

Michelle was already walking around, looking for a good spot. "Eva, get over here—we're going to build a sauna." We couldn't see Laurel; she was off in a tent worthy of a crew leader, and we imagined that inside she was weeping for her dog again.

Michelle moved quickly. She pulled up branches and cut off long, pole-like limbs, and in no time she had built a wooden structure. "We've got the tarp already," Eva said and brought it over. We went to the riverbed and gathered rocks and then dug out our fire pit. I was proud that my Canadian Jewish summer camp experience, which had taught us kibbutz ideals, labor history, and socialism, had given me something else useful as well.

That night we took our first sauna. Laurel joined us. Of the four of us, our crew leader seemed the most uncomfortable being naked. Who could blame her? She wasn't a pretty sight. Beer belly, greasy hair, a sort of trailer trash look, she forever soured me on San Luis Obispo, where she'd gone to school. Eva stretched out with a contented sigh. Her body was long and toned, and her breasts looked really good just sitting there. I tried not to stare.

"You're going to need this after climbing the Bitch every morning," Laurel announced.

"As if you've been there," Eva said disdainfully. "It's not such a big deal. We built some water bars up there last year. It's ugly. What's the point of spending a summer repairing a five-mile trail no one goes on?" Water bars I knew about—the way water is diverted by placing wood or dirt across the trail to prevent erosion. I had grown up hiking over them, but I'd never actually built one.

The next morning we all started out. We would pack in our water, knowing there wouldn't be any on the way up the Bitch.

"You ready?" Michelle asked me encouragingly, watching me stare at the trailhead. "Just keep looking down and around, since there are a lot of rattlers out there."

It was dusty and already warm. My legs were long but not particularly strong. The first morning I felt nauseous after thirty minutes of going up switchbacks, but I pushed on and stayed toward the front of the line, right behind Eva. I felt Michelle behind me, and I found this vaguely comforting. "You okay?" she asked every so often.

"Oh, sure. My family used to climb up mountains to glacier lakes on the weekend!" I tried to sound confident, but I was panting and could barely get the words out. I wished there was such a lake to jump into right then; I'd loved swimming in those cold Washington waters after a rigorous climb.

Laurel took up the rear, stopping once in a while to slurp water and spit out tobacco. After less than an hour, I was sweating and breathing hard, but my legs were becoming like tight machines. I knew I could keep pushing, but this time there would be no reward at the top, no cool lake.

By the end of that morning, after our first climb up the Bitch, I could barely move. The first days were hell, but I didn't give up. Being stubborn was the one thing I had going for me. During the first week it took us about three hours every day to get there. We would shed our work shirts, then our tank tops, and by the end of the week we worked only in our shorts and bras. My legs were already getting stronger and browner.

We were working on a reroute of a trail, and I felt good being able to just dig in and feel like I was accomplishing something. But being around Eva and Michelle was stressful—the unsaid, the subtext, and the more obvious squaring-off competition. And though we had no big conflicts at that point on our crew, when there was tension, Eva and Michelle insisted that men's crews were simpler, that women complicated things with their emotions, lack of confidence, and illogical thinking. Eva and Michelle identified with the more stereotypical male traits. I felt uncomfortable with this disdain for women; I had grown up seeing myself as a feminist. I was given Robin Morgan's groundbreaking women's lib anthology *Sisterhood Is Powerful* for a bat mitzvah gift (I was the first girl to have a bat mitzvah at our temple) and took an independent women's literature class in high school from a lesbian teacher who was in the socialist feminist group Radical Women. But otherwise I admired Eva and Michelle and wished that I was more like them.

Michelle and Eva were not happy that we had been assigned only unskilled grunt labor, like "brushing"—digging up and moving rocks, fixing trails, and making water bars and step-ups on the Bitch. They thrived on challenge; they were wired to build complex bridges. I discovered they had a feud going between them that had begun in elementary school and flared up whenever they worked together. They competed in everything and fought over who would teach me how to split wood. After an afternoon of almost breaking the ax a few times, though, I was proficient and loved to take my turn adding to our woodpile. I fantasized that my arm muscles would soon be as big as Michelle's and Eva's.

Down at our base camp by the river, we moved dirt around and built an area we called the Beach. We were paid for working six days a week, with the sixth at the overtime rate of time and a half. We each took turns staying in camp one day, washing clothes, cooking dinner for the group, splitting wood, getting the sauna ready, and watching out for bears. I loved our rotating in-house day assignment. I went for walks, made bread, fixed dinner, read, wrote, and lay naked out on the rocks. Eva was always productive, working on her dulcimer or carving something new. Michelle and Eva were carving wood hair barrettes. I wanted to learn how to do this, but my small motor skills were not great, and I was afraid of being embarrassed. They showed me how to use a knife to carve a wooden hair stick and barrette without cutting myself and how to sand it smooth.

Though Laurel had been named boss, no one, not even I, believed in Laurel's legitimacy. Laurel seemed to look at me early on as the fuckup of the group. I wished somehow I could change my personality, my upbringing, the role model of my acutely unconfident dad, who always asked for help. I knew I wasn't dumb, but I couldn't seem to do too much by myself without guidance. I have inherited a certain doggedness from my dad, though, a refusal to give up even when that seems the sensible thing to do.

One day, when Laurel was scheduled for the in-camp stint, she announced she wasn't sure that she'd have supper ready for us. "I've got female problems. I'll see if I feel like cooking anything," she informed us.

The next day Laurel told us that she was staying in camp indefinitely. "I'm sick and gonna have to get my stuff taken care of," she said, then glared at us, as if daring anyone to protest.

Laurel was flown out at the end of the week. Supposedly, she had some sort of vaginal or urinary tract infection. We knew she just couldn't be away from her dog anymore. A temporary trail crew leader, Joel, came out to join us for a part of the summer. Then a bridge crew of four men showed up just as the rain began coming down. For a week it rained constantly while we huddled inside of a hastily erected big tent. Joel pulled out a fiddle, and we square danced for days, waiting for the rain to slow. Finally, it stopped, and by then the bridge crew was called back to base camp.

On the trail, Michelle and I started to get to know each other. She told me about Richard, the man she constantly admonished. "Richard, where are you, darn it?" she would say as she pulled out his small, crinkled picture from her wallet—all that remained of him.

"Nice cheekbones," I noted. He was dark and mysterious looking.

"It's the Cherokee in him. Met him the first night I arrived at the Moonie compound." Michelle smiled. "I was wandering around Oregon, lost and hungry. Some women who were *really* friendly invited me to dinner," she said sheepishly. "I guess I'm just not very smart about this stuff. I had never heard of the Moonies before that." She was referring to what most of us viewed as a creepy brainwashing cult from the 1970s that used to prey on youth. "Moonies" came from their leader's name, Sun Myung Moon, the founder of the Unification Church.

Michelle continued, "Richard found me. His black, black eyes—I mean, they *knew* me. By the next night, I realized he was right—we had to escape the Moonies. Anyway, I'd have gone anywhere with him by then."

But soon after they fled, he had simply disappeared. I had never before met someone who was part of a cult, but it seemed like Michelle had escaped just in time, before her eyes became glazed with unreasonable happiness. Now, instead, they had the sadness of missing someone.

Four weeks went by. I worked slowly and steadily. My arms were not prone to show muscle, and I had blisters, but my legs were becoming hard. "You turned those skinny legs into muscle now," Eva said and whistled at me.

I also liked the way my breasts felt hot and firm under the sun. My stomach had lost some of its roundness. When I swung my ax and hit my target, I remembered being tough Sammy Boy—the inner-city fourth-grade "tomboy" (as they called us back in the day)—who had fought off anyone messing with me or my buddies.

That summer, in an effort to convince them I was once tough, I told them my old nickname. They decided to start calling me Sammy Boy too. But they also still seemed to see me as the city gal.

I was afraid of Eva, but I was also attracted to her in some way. I wanted her to like me, to be impressed, to focus all of her attention on me. Michelle was the one who became my fast sister-friend. I have two actual sisters, and I'd always naturally sought close woman friends.

Michelle told me over and over again, "Don't trust Eva; I've learned." I never really heard the entire story of their complicated lives together, why Michelle believed Eva would bring such danger and betrayal.

I tried to steer clear when Michelle and Eva started sniping at each other. My loyalty was to Michelle. It was Michelle who waited behind with me and instructed, "Do it like this—don't be afraid" when we took hikes and had to jump over rocks up a stream.

One day four medical students from Georgetown University showed up, faint, hungry, and blistered. "Uh, hello . . . ladies?" one said. Perhaps they were hallucinating—finding wood nymphs who cleared trails wearing just bras and shorts. One of them had bright blue-green eyes, but they were safer looking than Eva's. "Maybe we finally died, and this is Heaven?" he asked, winking.

"You guys are more than welcome to eat with us; we have too much," we told them. They had disgusting freeze-dried food. Our fresh food had just been flown in.

First we directed them to our swimming hole and the Beach. Then we fed them a real meal: steak, salad, corn, potatoes, homemade bread, and, of course, beer and whiskey.

After dinner, the music started. Eva and Michelle were both musical, and I sang along with everyone else. Eva and the best-looking doctor harmonized on an Irish song he taught her. She showed them the dulcimer she was making. Eva stayed up all night flirting and playing duets with the good-looking doctor, who I believe had packed in his own instrument. I had my eyes on him too . . . and on her. But I wasn't going to try to compete with Eva. And I sensed that I could win with her only by rejecting her. I had already begun to respond to the allure, the magnetic, even addictive quality of the unavailable or the uncertain in relationships.

During the day, walking up the Bitch, Michelle and I had begun to share nuggets of our lives. Michelle often sounded troubled when she spoke about Eva. "Eva is not who you think," she said repeatedly. "She really hurt Carmen. Carmen left everything—her family, her community—to live with Eva in Three Rivers." I had already heard some of this "Juliet and Juliet" story from Eva. At age thirteen, Carmen and Eva had fallen in love. Carmen was from Woodlake, California, a town of Mexican farmworkers. Eva was from a wealthy—if pretty unconventional—Swiss German family living in a sprawling farmhouse in Three Rivers.

"Carmen won't talk to Eva now," Michelle told me. Carmen sounded like my idea of beautiful—long, dark hair and deep eyes, caramel-colored skin, and a strong character. I tried not to look too interested as she described Eva's ex. "Carmen told Eva that she can't be with anyone white—that represents the oppressor." Michelle offered me fragments. "Eva's family, they're all the same way. She'll tell you they are Buddhists, but they probably treated Carmen more like help. And she stayed. She was so in love with Eva, and she didn't want to go back to her family."

Eva's version of the Carmen story was different. "We were young; it was puppy love. We grew apart. I was headed for college, and she was not academic. She just couldn't seem to get over me." Eva shrugged when she told me the story later, suggesting that this was a common problem for her: people getting too hung up on her when she was ready to move on. Me, I was just jealous that she'd had a real relationship with a girl—and at thirteen!

One night, there was a huge full moon silhouetting the mountains, a river lullaby, and a sky full of stars. Just around the time I started to think about going to sleep, Eva came over to see me and offered me a swig of Jack Daniel's.

"Heya," she said in her faux drawl, "want a massage?"

I was surprised, but I liked the idea. "Sure, what the heck."

"Lie down there," she commanded and sat on my butt as I lay facedown. She started rubbing and scratching my back. "Oh, you are way too tense. What's wrong, haven't been touched lately?" She applied more pressure with one hand. I shivered, but I wasn't cold. Her other hand had a life of its own, its touch soft and sensual and masquerading as calming, but it woke me right up. Under her firm and confident hands, I began to relax and make contented sounds: "Ahh, ohhh, that feels great." She leaned around and on top of me, her body long and muscular, an arousing weight. "Oh, you feel good," she said.

I was willing her to move those hands down my sides and past safe territory, but I couldn't tell if she was being sexual or if I was just feeling that way. Sometimes even now somebody has to get right in my face for me to know that things are going down that way. And even then, I wasn't completely sure when she slid her face down next to mine and she kissed me. (Was that really a kiss . . . and then was she really sucking on my nipple?) She looked at me with a funny half smile and helped me flip over onto my back with her kiss, which was surprisingly soft—first on my lips, then on my breast, then harder. She was running the show, but I couldn't stop my body from leaning into hers. "Don't stop," I said, gasping, in between loud breaths. She paused, as if she knew she was torturing me. I sighed. Leaned back. her hand was running down and around, everywhere but where I desperately wanted it, and at the same time I wanted to make this last forever. I loved the fact that her hand was not sitting on fat flesh but on fairly hard stomach and thighs. "Yup, you do have muscles, city girl," she whispered hoarsely. Her hands moved confidently between my legs, stroking, and then, because I didn't want the feeling to stop, as sometimes happens, the moment passed. I leaned into her, pulled her around and moved down her body, touching, kissing, and listening to her groans as she fully let go into the moment. And then I wondered, *Where did it go?* as my orgasm slipped away. Eva didn't know I hadn't come, didn't ask; she cuddled into me and said, "Let's sleep now." Spooning me, she was soon snoring softly. I was awake most of the night but finally started to fall asleep just before I heard her get up and leave the tent. Noises drifted in as she made the fire and started the day.

"Hey, Eva, can we talk a sec?" I asked her later, when we were alone for a moment.

"Come back tonight," she responded, her only sign of affection a slap on the butt.

I have often fallen in love easily, and I've always wanted to think the other person feels the same way. An orgasm or a really romantic song has a way of doing that to me—causing me to skip over a huge territory of unknowns to believing in true love and happily ever after. The second time with Eva, instead of holding back, I let her pin me down and bring me to orgasm. I realized that I needed to take what I could get when I felt it. I wouldn't stop the feeling. Often, I couldn't and didn't want to stop myself, and I gave in to the trembling, wave after wave rocking my body. River sounds drowning out the loud half cries, half sighs. But it wasn't a given for her that she'd come. It usually was for me, with her. "You're just sooo darn easy . . . so irresistible," she said. With her, I was.

We moved into one tent, without any discussion. I was already wondering what it would be like to have an actual girlfriend. The alarms that shrieked, "She's not girlfriend material!" were on "silent" in my head. Maybe not my type—I was leery of anyone with WASPish features—but there was something about her. And she really was fearless. And cocky. Unlike me. This was both intimidating and alluring. She wasn't always ready to make love. "Let's just sleep, cuddle," she'd say, as if she knew withholding would keep me under her control. I didn't know what I was doing for her exactly. I knew only that I wanted more of her, and I'd begun to imagine that we had a relationship—though hidden in the daytime. It would be my first real relationship with a woman. At that time I knew I was interested in seeing what that would be like. But I also knew that to keep her, I had to be less available. I'd pretty much found the kind of woman who was like the kind of men I tended to get hooked on. Intense, confident, not truly accessible. Her body mirrored this feeling, elusive to capture, taut, muscled, smooth, and emitting an almost imperceptible, sweet, patchouli-like smell. So subtle with a hint of sweat. I felt her hardened muscles when she leaned into me or I held onto her. Her breasts were the only soft part of her body, and I liked to imagine that with her toughness came a certain vulnerability.

At that time, I'd had only one real sex-with-a-girl experience — with my best friend in the last year of high school just before we graduated. I remember being very into it, but the memory gets mixed up with a bottle of Southern Comfort we drank just before we did it in the back seat of her parents' old Mercedes. Before that time, I had only been looking; I was usually too uncertain to really flirt. But I had thought about it a lot, ever since I was about eleven and a Girl Scout counselor told my cousin Janice and me not to lie so close together. "They thought we were going to queer off," Janice had said.

As we hiked up the Bitch each morning or hung out together in base camp, Michelle continued to caution me or complain about Eva, but I didn't tell her what I was doing with her rival. Even though Eva and I kept our relationship confined to our nights together, I worried about Michelle feeling alienated. I couldn't tell if Michelle sensed the tension, the electricity at times between Eva and me. Once or twice, Michelle had seemed to notice some kind of guilty look of complicity, perhaps that she was interrupting something when she came upon Eva and me talking intensely or when we'd just broken away from a hidden embrace. Michelle didn't ask me about my relationship with Eva, nor did any of the visiting (male) workers who passed through, even though I caught some leering, suspicious, even curious looks from them.

Whenever Eva reached over for me, in reality I was almost always available. When she turned away from me, I was wide awake, my body buzzing, wanting her. But then she would hold me, and we would fall asleep, spooning. When I woke up, she was almost always gone, already starting the morning chores, lighting the fire.

◆

Eight weeks into the summer we were halfway down the Bitch, working in our shorts and bras, repairing water bars and building new ones so that when it rained the water would run off the trail. We were clearing off trails that we were not sure would ever even be used. It was an endurance test of some sort, and we were all in sync now—*we* were working the Bitch, instead of the other way around.

One afternoon Jack the Packer came through with our supplies, his crinkly eyes fixed on Eva. She stared right back at him with her catlike smile and went off with him and his horses. She had told me she loved learning his horseshoeing tricks and other trade secrets. But I was not happy with her facility for moving from one tent to another, and I had no desire to compete with a grizzly-faced, smelly old packer. I just could not see the attraction. Even with the crinkly eyes.

I didn't even get a chance to ask her, "Will you be staying with me tonight?" She made it clear when he arrived that her place was with him. "Gotta go help Jack with the horses; he's had a long trip and brought us everything we want. He's great, isn't he?" she called out to me after we'd helped with the unloading.

He set up his neat little bedroll a respectful ways away from us. Later, Eva put up a tent of sorts around them. I told myself that this was why I still kept my armor on with her and didn't ever share how much I liked her. Mad, back in my own tent, I planned to be done with her.

But after Jack the Packer left, Eva quietly climbed back into the tent with me, and eventually I responded to the insistent stroking around my body. I imagined there was some kind of unspoken apology when she made love to me that night, that her feelings for Jack and for me inhabited two vastly different camps.

The next morning I was a wreck. Luckily, it was my in-camp day. I told Michelle I needed to talk with her, and I unloaded the whole story of Eva and me. "I know you warned me. I'm sorry; it just happened," I said. I sobbed and pleaded with her to understand.

Michelle shook her head and hugged me, muttering, "Oh, Eva, Eva, why do you do this?" Michelle and I started sleeping outside, side by side without a tent, under the stars, which were brighter and clearer than anything I'd seen before. Sometimes that was enough to distract me from my longing for Eva's strong hands and teasing laugh.

I still went to Eva's tent a few more times, but it was impossible for me to sleep. And it was difficult to do this discreetly; we were still not out to the rest of the backcountry crews who would come through off and on over the summer. After we'd fooled around, I would go back out to lie down next to Michelle, even when Eva urged me to stay. Before I left one night, I told Eva, "Your people made lampshades out of my people." I was thinking like her Mexican girlfriend, Carmen: we came from different backgrounds, and I couldn't trust her not to betray me, so I fell back on blaming her ancestors and told myself she wasn't for me. Eva seemed unfazed by my characterization of her as a racist; she saw herself as strong, sexy, and desirable to any ethnicity and gender.

Except for Laurel, our original crew leader, the rest of us survived the summer, and we rode out on horseback over the many mountain passes. Jack the Packer headed the group, and Eva spent the two nights on the trail with him. Her Fresno State boyfriend met her at the park entrance. Jack made a hasty exit when we arrived at park headquarters. I felt one more jolt of hurt at the casual good-bye Eva gave me in front of her boyfriend. But later she hugged me and whispered, lips brushing against my ear, "Sammy Boy, I'll miss you—meet me in San Francisco."

◆

The Bitch was relentless and unforgiving. That summer, our bodies became part of its rhythm. I learned that I could push my body as hard as I needed to. I discovered the sensual side of Simpson Meadow: her hidden waterways, a nighttime laced with stars in a darkness undiluted by city lights, and the music we made to the sounds of the river and the wildlife. I learned what it was to be a sexy woman who could swing an ax. I had my first girlfriend, and I learned that I wanted more, someone I could be with out in the open, who might stick around, a soul mate even. But I survived Eva, and I survived the Bitch. Many years later I calmed myself by thinking about being on that flat, smooth rock, sun beating down on my naked, muscular body. I remembered what it felt like to spend a summer pushing myself to be stronger and less afraid. At times this memory helped me find some hidden reserve of Sammy Boy and push through whatever obstacles threatened to take me down. And for a moment I remembered the strong me who walked out of Kings Canyon at the end of that summer in 1979.

◆

We were the last all-women backcountry trail crew in Sequoia and Kings Canyon. The next year, Eva and Michelle each got placed on a crew with men, which built bridges and more complex trail constructions.

Eva and Jack the Packer went back to Simpson Meadow later for a short project. Rumor has it that they ran into a bear—a really big one. They killed it, cut it up, ate a little, and buried the rest.

And the Bride Wore Demerol

On November 13, 1993, I got married for the first time. I had been engaged to Larry for only about six months, and we had already lost three pregnancies by the time we tied the knot. Larry and I didn't know each other well, but we had worked together at a labor union years before, and I was a sucker for his deep, resonant voice and phrases like, "I'd like to grow old with you," or Larry's golden line: "Wanna have my baby?" Our main goal was to have one, but we convinced ourselves that we were also in love.

Just before a big occasion like a wedding or birth, everyone likes to share their stories, and two days before my wedding, a work colleague treated me to his: "So one day before my wedding, everything was all set up perfect—caterer, seating, band—my wife had it all organized. Nothing could go wrong. And then I bit down on a hard candy and *ow!* Lost my tooth. Went to my wedding on Novocain with a missing tooth."

I felt smug. Nothing like *that* was going to happen before my wedding. Everything was arranged—perhaps not perfectly, but under control, thanks to the last-minute appearance of a family friend who agreed to coordinate our do-it-yourself wedding. Some things, like my wedding dress, had been around long before this marriage was even conceived.

A couple of years before, I had moved from Los Angeles to the Bay Area to live with another man, my fiancé at the time. That was when my former boss at the labor union told me that his best friend, Larry, had a crush on me. I wasn't much interested in Larry, but I filed the information away until I returned to live in Los Angeles.

While still in the Bay Area, engaged, I had found an exquisite silk wedding dress—straight, form-fitting with a small train, lacy and embroidered—at a little shop in the beachside California town of Santa Cruz. "It's modeled after my great-aunt, who was an opera diva," the designer told me. I paid for exactly half of that dress and couldn't bring myself to give it up after I broke off the engagement. The shop owner agreed to hold it for a bit longer. Either I'd find some other wedding to wear it to, or I'd give it up along with my deposit. I had come in just under the wire with this wedding to Larry. I knew the dress would be perfect. The veil and headpiece were from Italy, and my hair was being done like Medusa's, with elaborate twisted braids by the hair stylist for En Vogue. I'd been growing my hair long for years in preparation for one wedding or another.

The night before my wedding to Larry, a friend came over and did a makeshift henna ceremony, not the complete, detailed hand painting but some "ritual" dabbing of henna on my hands. I'd wanted to have my hands painted as in the Sephardic Jewish custom prior to a wedding, symbolic of good luck. Family and friends come over, there is music and dancing, and the bride is painted with elaborate henna designs to ward off the evil eye. My family was too tired and practical to come over, except for my younger sister, Sheli. In addition to Sheli, my house was littered with friends who had come for the wedding. Everyone had to get up early to prepare for the ceremony; my friends had been drafted to help with floral arrangements and table decorations.

Larry and I were already living together, but the night before our wedding, he stayed at a hotel with his best man, someone I wasn't crazy about. He had asked me out once before Larry and I got together. I had hastily declined, and he had seemed disgruntled ever since. Perhaps he thought Larry shouldn't get someone he couldn't. In the world of labor unions and progressive politics, social circles can become incestuous.

That night I went to bed alone in the master bedroom while my friends slept in various spots throughout the house. Years later, I was wracked with guilt and remorse—how could I have let my friends sleep on the floor (a few of them) when I had that whole bedroom to myself? But I was certain it would be my last night as a single woman, alone. I was all about ritual. I'd even taken a mikvah, the ritual Jewish bath to render me pure and holy, days before with my feminist-spiritual rabbi, who had also supported me through the miscarriages. Larry had found a different rabbi who consented to marry us. Many rabbis will not marry an interfaith couple; Larry was Black and had been raised Southern Baptist. He had met Rabbi Neil in high school during an African American–Jewish youth experience group. Rabbi Neil had agreed to officiate for our wedding with the requirement that we go through the interfaith classes, have a series of meetings with him prior to the wedding, and agree to raise our children Jewish.

I was afraid I might be coming down with a cold, so before I went to bed, I took out a hot water humidifier and set it up. I moved it from the wood storage cabinet my older sister had made by hand when she returned from kibbutz and was exploring career options as a woodworker. I didn't want the water to stain the cabinet, as it was only on loan, so I placed the humidifier on the floor near my bed. Eventually, after an hour of tossing and turning, I drifted off to sleep as the soft little grunts of the humidifier and hot mist floated into my dreams.

At about 4 a.m., I was awakened to what sounded like rain on the roof. Rain is supposed to be good luck for weddings, but my wedding ceremony was outside. I leaped out of my bed to look out the window. My right foot hit the floor, and my left landed on the humidifier. A one-second pause. Then I screamed as I began to feel the first effects of the boiling water into which I'd plunged my foot. Sheli raced into my room from the next bedroom. "What happened?" she asked.

She saw me crying, screaming, frantic, glanced at my foot, then grabbed the phone by the bed and called the family patriarch: my brother-in-law. Yudie was once my camp counselor at the Jewish socialist summer camp I had attended in Canada that was run like a kibbutz. Many years later, he met my older sister in Israel, on kibbutz. Now he was the one everyone looked to for answers, whether for Torah interpretations (an adamantly secular atheist Jew, he was a scholar in all things Jewish) or for major decisions in crisis. He had initially been angry with me when I set out to have a baby, until he saw that there was a father in the picture. He had already planned my life differently, wanted me to go to law school (he'd help out), and then I could always someday adopt a child when the time was right, if I still needed that.

"Carla fell on a humidifier; she burned her foot!" Sheli stammered into the phone. "What do we do?

"It's 5 a.m. Put ice on it," Yudie said. He was practical and didn't like to be awakened. When I'd called him in the early morning after the first earthquake I experienced in LA, he had told me to go back to bed.

Sheli hung up and looked scared. She knew she was on her own and decided to take me to the ER. She grabbed our coats, found the keys, gave a hasty explanation to my alarmed friends, who were slowly awakening, and got me into the car. On the way to the Huntington Hospital in Pasadena, I started to feel waves of pain and cried out.

"So what made you first fall in love with Larry?" Sheli asked in an attempt to distract me.

"Oh, his voice . . . ow! I don't know, uh . . . ow!" I gave up trying to respond. Sheli dropped me off in front of the hospital and went to park. I staggered toward the admitting desk. Nurses walked by, but no one asked why I was there. "Sit down; we'll call you," one finally said in passing as my sister walked in.

I started to protest but sat down with my sister. The nurses were giggling. I saw them huddled together, looking at pictures. "Lord, she's so cute!" one said.

"Ow!" I called out loudly and stagger-hopped up to the desk again.

"I'm in pain. Can someone please help?"

The giggling continued. "Sit down, hold up, we'll be with you in a minute," a nurse said, detaching herself from her chortling coworkers. She looked annoyed with the interruption.

"Dammit, can't someone please help me?" I yelled. "I'm sure your baby is cute, but I need to get to my wedding." My sister looked embarrassed and tried to move me back to the seats as a few patients looked up, mildly interested. For 5 a.m., the Huntington Hospital ER was unusually quiet, I would discover later. The main depository for shootings, gang injuries, car accidents, domestic violence victims, and heart attacks, it's normally a hive of human misery. At that moment I was sure that there was nothing more important than my sharp, almost unbearable bolts of pain—which were shooting through my foot steadily now—and my upcoming wedding.

"Whoa, there. What's happening? Why don't you come on back?" A kindly, white-haired, bearded doctor appeared, put his arm around me, and led me behind the counter to an alcove that seemed to double as an exam area. "Sit down. What happened here?" he said as he pulled on gloves and took my foot in his hand.

A substantial-looking nurse materialized. "We was just about to do the intake, Dr. Thompson."

"No, they weren't; they were looking at someone's baby pictures," I said. I was bitter. I had no baby pictures to show. I was consumed with agony and self-pity inside my own little bubble.

"Let's just take a look-see here," Dr. Thompson said, unfazed, ignoring both of us. "So what happened? Did I hear you say something about a wedding? Hope you're not the bride." He gave a little chuckle.

My sister looked mortified. "Uh, yes, she is, actually, but she burned herself."

"Well, I can see that. I'm Dr. Thompson, by the way." He introduced himself as if we were at a social occasion. He looked closely at my foot, handling it ever so gently.

My pain was so severe that I became very quiet, almost catatonic, as I took in this doctor's calm, secure manner.

"She stepped in boiling water, a hot air humidifier," Sheli said. "Will she be okay?" She looked like she was in shock herself.

Just then I got hit again with a lightning bolt of hot, searing pain. "AHHHH!" I screamed.

"Today?" Dr. Thompson looked up. "I really don't see her walking to the altar today, I'm sorry to say." He shook his head and appeared sad, as if he, too, would be sorry to miss the party. Then he added, "I can't understand why people use those hot water humidifiers anymore. I've seen little babies burned . . ." Another sad shake of the head. Gentle eyes bored into mine as he held my foot. I twisted around again with the next shooting pain. "Hold on there, missy, I'm going to get you something for the pain."

"I have to be there at the wedding. There are hundreds of people," I managed to gasp.

"Big wedding then?" Dr. Thompson asked, conversationally. "Planning to dance?" The nurse just shook her head as if to say, "The crazy people we see coming through this ER . . ."

"Yes, yes, Jewish, African American, Latino—I have to dance," I said.

"Well, now, I guess we better get you over there. Nurse, let's get this bride some Demerol right now," he ordered.

"So you like to dance, do you?" Dr. Thompson continued. "I know there's a lot of that—what do you call it, the hora?—at Jewish weddings. And you said Latino, too. Salsa, right? So what kind of a band do you have set up?"

My pain rendered me as incoherent as if I was at the dentist trying to answer a question with a mouth full of cotton and instruments. But for Dr. Thompson, I'd try. "Yes, Billy Mitchell, an African American jazz band, plays Jewish music . . . and salsa," I blurted out.

"Well, how about that!" Even the big nurse looked encouraging now. She said, "You'll be feeling more like dancing in a few minutes" as she plunged the needle into me and pulled it out.

"Okay, so she can come back later if she needs another shot of Demerol before the reception. And get her a prescription for Vicodin—just in case," he addressed the nurse and my sister now. Then he looked at me. I was calmer, but tears were slowly sliding down my cheeks. I felt numbness and pain alternately, but no longer the all-consuming feeling of a foot on fire.

"Go easy on the champagne now," Dr. Thompson joked, looking around at his audience: me, my sister, the nurse. "Okay, let's wrap it up, then, and get her out of here. Be sure you come back and show me pictures." He smiled broadly at me. "You'll have to find yourself some nice white slippers; I don't see you getting into any high-heeled wedding shoes."

"Thank you so much, so much," I said to the doctor and everyone in my vicinity.

The nurses were all smiling now. "Getting married, yeah, yeah, get her to the church on time," one said. I guess my mom was right; everyone loves a bride. Even if she is rude and unruly.

As the pain subsided, I suddenly remembered Larry, my husband-to-be. I'd had my sister call him at some point. We were driving to the hair stylist now, behind schedule. "Sheli, what did Larry say?" I asked.

"Uh, I haven't been able to reach him yet."

"Did you leave a message at the hotel?"

"Yes, they, uh, said . . . well, maybe he checked out already."

A cautionary bell sounded in my head. My family had tried to locate him at the hotel unsuccessfully. Why wasn't Larry here with me where he should be? Yes, I had wanted to spend a traditional night before the wedding away from him, but now I was coming from the ER. Why hadn't he rushed over there to meet me? The thought went through my brain but didn't stay lodged tight in my usual wheel of rumination. I was definitely feeling the effects of the Demerol.

We arrived at the hair stylist and explained my condition. Then the phone rang. It was Larry. He had called the house, and they told him what had happened and where I was. "I can't believe it. Only you would do this," he said, mildly affectionate. "Are you okay?" He sounded loving, concerned.

"Where are you?" I demanded. "I was in a lot of pain, but I'm doing better now." Better was coming in steady waves of goodness, waves of reassurance that bordered on happiness, even euphoria, and shut out my anger at Larry for going on walkabout. He gave an odd explanation about why he couldn't be found at the hotel, which slipped away like water running down a slippery rock. I loved Demerol.

A short while later, my friend Terri joined us at the hair stylist's. A multitalented events guru, Terri was in charge of my makeup and the seating at the wedding. I had been consumed with doing the seating right. My mom and my sister's mother-in-law had insisted that it was important to have assigned tables. And there seemed to be the wrong number of guests at some tables. Or something. Terri said she'd handle it.

I looked at my younger sister, at the hair stylist, at my Medusa braids in the mirror, intertwined like snakes around my head. I looked at my face, almost fully made up, as Terri put on the finishing touches. "You knooooow," I said, a big smile on my face, "I think everything is going to be juuust fine."

Later, in the pictures, Larry and I looked like we were perhaps bride and bridegroom from a foreign country. I had a faraway gaze from the Demerol, and the Old World–style beaded Italian veil combined with my

Middle Eastern looks gave me the appearance of a bride who was meeting her groom for the first time. My friends had bought flat white Victoria's Secret slippers for me to wear with my burned foot; one guest thought this footwear was part of a Jewish ritual. Larry was tall, imposing, and handsome, dark skinned, with high cheekbones that made him look African, though he was from South Central LA. He wore an elegant blue-black suit and Moroccan yarmulke, a colorful, rounded skullcap shaped almost like an upside-down bowl.

My wedding day was not the first time I took Demerol, but it was the most memorable. They used to administer a sublime Demerol-and-Versed cocktail via IV for conscious sedation during procedures such as colonoscopies. That was amazing. Apparently one drug is given to relieve the pain and the other, to cause you to forget you ever had it. My brother, who is a lot like Mr. Spock from *Star Trek*, extremely logical and literal, says, "Then why give both?" If one allows you to forget the pain, his reasoning goes, then why give the other that doesn't let the patient feel it? I am glad my brother is not my gastroenterologist. Prior to my wedding to Larry, I had a lot of horrible procedures and ailments, including severe rectal pain and bleeding as well as the multiple miscarriages. So when I had to get the colonoscopy cocktail, I relished both the pain relief and the ability to forget everything, and especially the "everything is going to be okay" effect created by the mixture of the two drugs.

Many years later I heard that Demerol was a lot like heroin, and a lightbulb came on for me. I knew to stay the hell away from heroin. A massage therapist recently told me this about her experience with addicts: "When I do bodywork on heroin users, they feel crunchy, like their energy field is made up of broken bones." I have never tried heroin, but I have always extolled the virtues of Demerol. For those of us who live on a train going forward into future worries while simultaneously going backward into resentments and regrets, just to enjoy being on the train with no particular destination is a great relief. For someone who has ruminated her entire life, sometimes lost in a *Twilight Zone*–esque maze of what-ifs and pointless regrets, Demerol is a miraculous escape. And now that heroin is cheap and readily available (Demerol not so much), I have had at least one moment of considering the temporary reprieve it might provide. But a powerful deterrent is knowing that the feeling of "everything is going to be okay" quickly fades.

Heartbeat

Before we got married, the first time Larry and I had tried to conceive, I had gotten pregnant right away, no problem. I called Larry to tell him the news, and he told me his car had just been repossessed.

A few weeks later, I met my friend Lisa for lunch. While in the ladies' room, I suddenly felt wetness going down my leg. I looked down: bright red blood.

I had my second miscarriage two months later. The doctors told me there was probably nothing wrong with me, but I was scared.

I had seen Larry lose his temper once in a union negotiation, but it wasn't until sometime after my second miscarriage that he got that angry with me. He had disappeared one night and didn't call. When I questioned him, he screamed at me and raised his fist. But after it was over and he told me he would go to counseling, I felt comforted when he sang the song by the Five Stairsteps: "Ooh, child, things are going to get easier. / Ooh, things are going to get brighter."

Then, after almost four years of wanting to become a mother, six months later I was pregnant again. By the time I got the news of this fifth pregnancy—my third with Larry—I felt hopeful, but I was no longer telling people when I was pregnant.

Larry and I were renting a three-bedroom house in Eagle Rock that overlooked the San Gabriel Mountains. It was January 1994; we were married November 1993. We had been together for almost a year. At age thirty-three, I was feeling the passage of time. But something else too: a tiny shred of fear that I might not get another chance. And the two abortions I'd had prior to getting together with Larry sat boulder heavy in my stomach. I had reached my tenth week—the furthest I'd ever gotten without miscarrying. I knew from all the reading I had done that I should be hearing a heartbeat by this point. At my January check-up, I watched my doctor's face as he placed the stethoscope on my belly. "If we don't hear a heartbeat when you come back," he told me, "we'll have to think about the next step."

For two weeks I walked around worried that I was carrying a dead baby inside me. "There's nothing you can do," Larry said, cutting me off as I began to sift through my fears.

Back in the doctor's office, with my feet in the stirrups, I suddenly heard a sound. "Isn't that a heartbeat?" I asked. My baby's first one.

My doctor didn't look as happy as I felt. "I'm not so sure about the size of the sac," he said. "Come back in a week."

It was the night before my next appointment. Larry and I were arguing again. I ran outside. He pushed me toward the front door. He said he didn't want the neighbors to hear us fighting. He called me "bitch." He threw me down. I hit the cement.

I went to bed worried that the baby might not be okay.

The next morning, I woke just as the sun was coming up, eager to get to the doctor. I wanted to hear that heartbeat again. I tried not to think about the night before.

Larry was still dead asleep. I stretched my arms. That's when I felt it—a sudden jolt, as if a car had hit the house. Then came the rocking and shaking. We were having an earthquake.

I grabbed Larry and hung on. Finally, the ground stopped moving. "I need to check our wedding china," I said. It was still not put away. I climbed out of bed.

The room began to move again. Two pictures fell down. I heard glass shattering. I thought about the heartbeat.

The bed rocked again, but not as hard this time. I waited. Larry said, "I think it's stopped now."

I went first to the kitchen to see if the Mikasa was intact. "Hey, put your shoes on!" Larry yelled at me. There was glass on the floor.

We drank decaf and tried to get a radio station to come through.

From up on our hill, everything was still. I dressed for my doctor's appointment, which felt so important to keep. But suddenly I began to wonder what had happened down below. Many years before, I'd visited Mexico City after their big earthquake in 1985. The morning after the quake, my friend Ramón had headed to his job as usual, having slept through the worst of it. It was only when he stepped outside into the world that he understood the extent of the devastation. His office building had collapsed, colleagues dead.

Now Larry and I drove down the highway. The roads were empty, but I heard sirens streaming from all directions. Larry moved the radio dial for news, but I wasn't really listening. I had to know what had happened to my baby.

When I walked into the doctor's office, I saw file cabinets on the floor and papers scattered.

I put my feet into the stirrups. The doctor spread the sticky gel over my belly. He moved the Doppler around.

No heartbeat.

They sent me over to the hospital—Verdugo Hills, about twenty-five miles from the Northridge earthquake epicenter. I used to love the view from that hospital. It's where I always imagined having my baby, looking out over the hills while nursing after my delivery. There in the hospital where nobody wanted to be the day of the quake. Before the anesthesiologist put me under for my D and C, which would remove the fetal tissue from my uterus, I asked him, "How are you?" Some strange memory of politeness urging me on. He answered, "Terrible." And then I was out.

When I woke up after the D and C, it felt like a pole had been shoved down my throat. As I went down the elevator, pregnant women in various stages of labor stepped in and out. I looked at their bellies and sobbed. One of them got on, and our eyes met. She crossed herself.

Larry walked through the hospital with me but I cannot remember what he said or how he was doing; I was in another world. We went home. My cousins from the Bay Area called. An apartment building had collapsed where their mother was living near Northridge, and she was missing. They wanted me to help look for her.

For weeks people kept calling and asking how I was doing. Over and over I heard the question, "What was the damage?" It took me a long time to realize that what they were asking about was the Northridge earthquake, not my third miscarriage.

Mother's Day

It was Mother's Day 1995, the day I'd been dreading. I was not a mother, the thing I desired more than anything in the world. Yet I felt strangely calm. The day before had been one of the bad days. I'd yelled at Larry, "I can't take this rage!" while in a rage. Larry, raging, rose up in that way that frightened me, and I cowered, trying to hide under the fireplace ledge. I realized I needed to separate from him. Not just threaten to, but really do it. We'd been together since April 1993. Our entire time together had been spent focused on trying to make a baby.

What's happening to me? I wondered. Was it fear? Hormones? Prednisone? Prednisone was one of the many drugs I was taking for a confluence of autoimmune conditions that were thought to be causing me pregnancy loss after pregnancy loss. Prednisone made me hyper like a Labrador; some say it has a bit of a psycho effect. I didn't know if I was crazier from the drug or from having been pregnant six times with no baby to show for it, loss after loss. Or maybe the insanity stemmed from trying to have a baby with a man I no longer liked—from being married to someone who now disgusted and frightened me.

Progesterone was another substance I was taking. Each new treatment came with its own warnings, off-label uses, and possible side effects. They were all necessary, according to my reproductive immunologist. In fact, I was told that I needed more treatment, which could cost more than $30,000 a month (impossible for us). All this to have a baby from my own body, with my egg and my husband's sperm. Looking back many years later, I see it seems absurd—this blind adherence to a path that proved so destructive to my health and psyche. Especially when I'd always thought there were many possible paths to motherhood.

When he was thirteen, Larry and his sister had been sent away for a weekend trip with extended family. Their mother was ill and stayed behind. They returned and found out that their mother was dead. After she died, Larry and his sister moved in with their father. Larry's dad was hardworking and stern. He had a job as a night-shift custodian, eventually moving up through the ranks to supervisor. They never learned the cause of his mom's death. She had been a party animal, probably an alcoholic, cycling through a series of abusive relationships, one of which ended with her throwing grits at her boyfriend. I had heard that she was the favorite auntie of his cousins, but the chaos of constant moves and relationships might have kept her from being the mother Larry needed. He said that he had never even learned to clean his butt properly.

At age thirty, Larry made his way as best he could, eating odd meals at odd times, sleeping in odd places, going to bed with his clothes on. On this day, Larry sat in front of the television and ate leftovers. I had not filled his loss of a mother, nor had I become one. But it was Mother's Day. A double whammy. I had no baby, and no one was celebrating me. I longed to feel honored as having the heart and soul of a mother. I wanted the flowers, the card, the brunch, the recognition of my maternal being, acknowledgment of my unrivaled loss.

It seemed that Larry and I should have shared this sorrow, but I hoarded it as all my own. When we'd first started dating, Larry had won me over with the seemingly same driving need to have a baby that I had. His younger cousins were already having children, and he had felt old to not yet have a child. I had listened to his low, sexy voice and seen his shy, silent looks, convinced that perhaps still waters ran deep. I ignored the signs of uncontrollable anger, familiar to me from having grown up with a dad who had an explosive temper and huge guilt accompanying his outbursts. My dad had seemed the antithesis of a violent man, with his antiwar and ethical beliefs and his strong family loyalty. Larry, too, seemed to be a man imbued with commitment to social justice and, like me, wanted to create the family he didn't feel he had. But like my father, Larry was volatile, their tempers often leading to ugly words, and in Larry's case, sometimes to pushing, shoving, once even choking. And to my running, screaming, crying, picking up a fireplace poker and threatening to fight back. Just as I had jumped between my father and my sister when he had threatened to hit her with a plastic milk bottle. None of it made sense.

Looking back at my marriage to Larry, I believe that perhaps he was driven by history, trauma, and fear. Like my dad, he probably wanted to be the best person he could. Like them both, I, too, have been driven by this need of wanting those closest to me to fix what was missing or broken within me. And I was unable to step away from their brokenness but rather wanted to control it somehow. Yet, in so much of my life, I have found that one person's scars rubbing against another's can produce disastrous results.

◆

In reality, the house I shared with Larry was not a home. Our house had no routine, no regular meals. It was a lonely life. We rarely spoke. This was not the landing place, the peaceful hearth; there was no baby, nor was it the life I had imagined.

I was attending an abused women's group, and the women there were baffled as to why I would choose to have a baby with a man who hurt me. They were going through custody battles because they had made the same choices in the past. A former expert on violence toward women, I acted as if I facilitated that group. Yet I hadn't been able to tell them why I had to persist in my quest to have a baby with Larry. Still, I was determined to believe it was all possible—love, marriage, and baby—even if the danger signs existed before the wedding.

When I was close to thirty, I had run away from the security and comfort of my relationship with Henry, my Filipino boyfriend in Seattle, and I still lived with that regret. I missed the closeness and friendship that Henry and I had shared, and I hoped that, one way or another, we'd always be in each other's lives. I needed to have a baby with Larry before I could resume contact with Henry, because his subsequent marriage and children were reminders of all I had walked away from, what could have been, and I had felt it all over again with each pregnancy loss and each relationship breakup since the time I had left him.

Larry listened to the same music that Henry and I used to, slow soul, love songs of the seventies by groups like the Delfonics, the Stylistics, the Chi-Lites. These were some of the songs we played at our wedding. We had a Black jazz band that played Jewish music, big-band tunes, jazz, and salsa and a former DJ from *Morning Becomes Eclectic* (a National Public Radio show featuring world music) who played all the other songs we wanted. My usually cynical brother-in-law had commented about our wedding: "If only all of LA could be like this." I had found it much easier to create a wedding that brought all of the city's diverse and sometimes warring communities together than to create a peaceful marriage.

♦

A month before that Mother's Day in 1995, Larry and I had gone to see an infertility specialist, a Brazilian doctor whom we nicknamed "Dr. Doom." While he moved the vaginal probe in me, he complained about the overabundance of "faggots" at the World Cup and commented on how Larry looked like Forest Whitaker. Larry stood behind him making gagging gestures. I tried to signal him to say nothing; I didn't want to upset the doctor with the vaginal probe still inside me. Dr. Doom told us, without having read our voluminous medical records, that "people like us" should not have children or they might have problems. Who were "people like us"? Who had recurrent miscarriages? Who had some difficult-to-describe killer cells problem? We had learned the complicated immunological explanations from Dr. Beer, our reproductive immunologist.

Better to do surrogacy, Dr. Doom told us, as if that was simple. "Get your sister to do it for you," he suggested. The one who gave blood to me for one of the bizarre treatments, though she hated giving blood, just as she hated morning sickness? No, there was a limit to what one could ask.

After Dr. Doom removed the vaginal probe, he did a breast exam and said, "You have some kind of lump on your breast!"

"Uh, my breasts are cystic anyway," I told him, but we left thinking, *What is this?* I was the same age as Larry's mom was when she died suddenly. Larry looked shell-shocked, as if his life was going through some strange repeating spiral.

We walked out with instructions to get a mammogram and no clear idea of where we were headed. No baby. A marriage built entirely on trying to make a baby. A feeling of being less than desirable parents due to some deficiency of my stuff and his stuff and the intermingling that was causing killer cells.

You might think I was crazy—and I often was—to repeatedly revert to the feeling that I would simply dissolve if I couldn't fix our family. If I couldn't have a baby. All I know is that with each new lost pregnancy, my level of crazy, the medication and medical problems, and the financial debt just kept amping up.

I was like the team of nurses in a critical care unit that tried to force a tube down my dad's throat while he lay squirming beneath them; they barely noticed his wild panic and distress. It's as if they were plumbers with a job to do, get that snake through the tube, their focus interrupted only by my insistence that they stop hurting my father. But they were undeterred.

I was relentless: we would create the perfect "We Are the World" family.

But my tenacity was no longer an asset. My unstoppable desire to have a baby, to grow a family no matter the cost, was destroying my body and soul.

Walking around on our steep street the day before Mother's Day, I had heard chattering birds and smelled jasmine. I'd smiled at a little boy imitating his father, who was also really just a boy. I had allowed myself to notice these things, to be strangely and gratefully detached from my self-absorbed misery, to let myself feel a rare caress—sunshine.

But now it was Mother's Day, and there was no card awaiting me, no flowers, no breakfast in bed—no child. I sat in the bedroom feeling sad, knowing I might not see anyone I cared about today. My sadness bored me. Ennui and self-pity enveloped me. Why would this dreaded Mother's

Day be different from any other day? Like everything else I still insisted I might control through feral and misguided tenacity, I believed that Larry and I should endure this day together. I'd assumed he'd go to the movies with me, but he sat in the living room watching television; he didn't want to talk to me or even sit beside me. Where was the husband from our wedding invitation, "My Beloved, My Friend"? The hope, the precious love from almost a year-and-a-half ago seemed far away. I did not ask myself what shame, what wretchedness, Larry wrapped his body in. That his mother was dead and what other meanings Mother's Day might have had for him—his own sense of failure, not being able to produce a baby like all his younger cousins—this is not what I was thinking about. I was only able to see my own suffering.

Why didn't I just get in the car and drive away? I stayed. My internal broken record half-whining, half-ranting: *Always alone. Always alone.* Then the tears came.

The week before, Larry had showed me a recipe in the paper. "I think I'll make this for you on Mother's Day," he'd said. It was a coconut pie. That picture of the pie he planned to make for me on Mother's Day—it was like he understood. But I never would see that coconut pie. (Though later I did clip a recipe and considered baking one myself.)

On Mother's Day, while the sound of the television drifted into the bedroom, I didn't say all the things I was thinking. I thought he should just know. I just wanted to do something. Anything. For Mother's Day.

From outside I heard families, children. I knew I couldn't live with Larry anymore. I plugged my ears like I'd done since I was little. I didn't want him to hear me crying, but it's really that I didn't want me to hear me crying.

I was drowning in my gloom. Why didn't I go somewhere? Anywhere. I thought that maybe I'd go to the library to pick up books. My mantra chained me to my bed, though: *Always alone. Always alone.* Never truly suicidal, I simply wished to feel no more pain. Rather than die, different parts of my body malfunctioned just enough to keep me in constant discomfort. I had gone to more than 365 doctor appointments the year before, and I wasn't a hypochondriac. Somehow it all whirled together into a tornado of malaise: stomach pain, intestinal pain, rectal pain, and even car accidents, at least two of which had been avoidable—my fault, causing further pain. With each miscarriage, the intertwining medical issues seemed to increase, and it was not clear what had caused what or what had revealed what uncertain condition. Some time after the second miscarriage, one doctor told me that I might have lupus and that if I had a baby, the baby might need a pacemaker at birth. When we arrived home, Larry washed my feet in warm, scented water, massaged them, and lovingly tucked me into bed. Later, another doctor explained to me that I was perhaps "at risk for" but not diagnosed with lupus. Two of my doctors—the reproductive immunologist and the gastroenterologist—said they believed that giving birth to a baby would solve many of my problems, though they couldn't truly articulate the medical reasons. Or maybe I just couldn't understand them.

That day. Mother's Day. Me—pregnant six times. Six unborn children clamoring to have been brought to life. I felt of death instead.

My friend María Elena called. At first I didn't hear the phone ring because of my plugged ears and wailing. But she called back, and as my sobbing gained momentum, she said that she was coming to pick me up.

I had met María Elena Fernández when I first moved to Los Angeles and she was living with her parents. We worked together at the International Ladies' Garment Workers' Union, and La Familia Fernández became my adopted family.

María Elena's parents were an immigrant success story, having bought the apartment building where they had raised their kids. They stood in for me as the family that would love me unconditionally. After my first abortion, it was to them I went to be nurtured and be fed softly buttered toast with jam. (María Elena didn't tell her parents what I was recovering from.) She and I supposedly look alike—at least our most obvious features. Some people ask if we're sisters with our so-called ethnic features—"strong" noses (euphemism for "big"), pale skin, dark hair, prominent cheekbones. She was the friend who taught me the power of décolletage, having thrown off the vestiges of being an obedient Catholic, discovering sexy.

For years, María Elena had listened to all my tedious despair—my back-and-forth ruminations that went on for days, weeks, months; my unceasing need to turn back the clock on irrevocable decisions, abortions and failed relationships—until one day, years later, after seeing me through yet another crying jag of heartbreak, she would tell me, "¡Basta! It's simply too much to be witness to so much pain. I can't be that sponge." One time before she told me, "No más," she picked me up and drove me about while I cried and she held my hand. For a moment I wished that she was my girlfriend. I wanted someone as smart and beautiful as she, a soul mate. My dad asked me, after I'd come out as a lesbian, "Why not María Elena? That I could understand!"

"She's like my sister, Dad; that's incest," I said.

But on my motherless Mother's Day, she was still the one I turned to for consolation when I was inconsolable. Before María Elena and her parents picked me up to go out to eat, I went to a local nursery to look for a present for Señora Fernández, my surrogate mother. All the plants looked like they had been skipped over. I found a section of spindly little cactus plants with tendrils that reminded me of *The Little Engine That Could*. They were sorry-looking. But that whisper of a red flower was endearing.

So much of my experience of Los Angeles was like this—cracked sidewalks with a lone sprig of fragrant purple wildflower fighting its way to the surface. When I first moved to LA in 1988, native-born Angelenos adored hanging out with me because I saw the hidden beauty that many new arrivals didn't. They saw only the ugliness, the tackiness, the smog, the failed dreams. My friends who were born and raised in LA neighborhoods—Silver Lake, East LA, Hollywood, Pico-Union—they embody and see the beauty of the real Los Angeles, like the fuchsia bougainvillea and the purple jacarandas that arrive joyfully, inspired and reliable, every spring. Now, many years later, I live down the street from a jacaranda tree wrapped up by a brilliant scarlet bougainvillea. I still have that same comfort, that leap of joy—they will always return.

The florist took the best-looking of the straggly cacti and with a bright red ribbon made it into a gift. The best I could do; my eyes were red and swollen with days of tears. No baby this Mother's Day, but I was going to celebrate *mi mamá de* Los Angeles—La Señora Fernández.

"Oh, yes, this will bloom again," the florist told me. *But I won't,* I thought. The cactus might endure, and I knew Señora Fernández would. She'd love this cactus, just as she took in all the worn, the beat up, and the *acabado*—the wretched of the earth—knowing that someday they might perk up too after all, especially with her love, her cooking, and her *ponche* every Navidad.

Señora Fernández knew my struggle to become a mother. After the second abortion, when I'd broken up with my fiancé but he had seemed to want to reconcile, she had encouraged me to go along with the idea of being back with him and to "just get pregnant." I'm not sure she would have given her own daughter that same advice, but at that point, she knew my spirit was slipping away with longing. She understood my single-minded focus on having a child; she lived for her own children. But now I needed her to bless my decision to give up, to accept my failure to become a mom through giving birth.

Three years after starting the journey, I needed to be done with my indomitable attempts to make a baby with Larry. I needed to be done with all the strange treatments and the blood transfusions. Years later I would not remember the names of the treatments and diagnoses I had become so versed in. But I still remember the one that involved some kind of reconstituted red blood cells—blood taken from my older sister once and another time from Larry— that felt like a cigarette being burned on your arm and then having the flu for days. I remember the intravenous immunoglobulin (IVIG), being hooked up to get a blood supply pooled from more than one thousand strangers. I still remember the one doctor's warning that I might someday get some kind of disease from this theoretically screened donor blood.

On that Mother's Day in 1995, I let go into the nurturing arms of my adopted Mexican family, Los Fernández. I gave Señora Fernández the spindly little cactus, which she graciously accepted and has nurtured all these years. And I accepted that I could—and would—go on to build my own idea of family, even if it didn't look like the one I had tried to force into existence. At that point I didn't question why I wanted that so much. It was time to regroup and find a way to finance adopting a baby, by myself. I would somehow deal with the mountain of debt we had created in the process of trying to make a baby the biological way. No, it wouldn't be as easy as going to the store and picking up a baby. I knew that from the company I was keeping, the various support groups for people who couldn't have babies, who couldn't keep a pregnancy alive, or who gave birth to babies that died soon after.

I felt a huge relief in letting go—in realizing that I could not, by sheer will, make the world conform to my desires. But I could do something to create a family as a single parent, something I'd set about doing before I decided to try with Larry.

♦

During that post–Mother's Day week, I had to teach a career exploration workshop to the pregnant and parenting teen moms' classroom at John Muir High School in Pasadena. I considered canceling rather than facing all those big bellies while mine remained an empty tomb. The classroom walls were covered with pictures of very pregnant girls with captions like, "Will I always be pregnant?" My poster would have read, "Will I ever stay pregnant?" In this classroom, everything was about empowering these very young pregnant women to pursue their educations, consider career choices, all the while shoring up support, making sure they were eating and exercising and getting adequate medical care. It was all about nurturing the children having children.

As for me, I thought I was on the way to ending that chapter in my life, trying to give birth to a baby. But three days after Mother's Day, I still hadn't gotten my period, and because it was close to the time I could take a pregnancy test, again my thoughts revolved around the question "Am I pregnant?" And I was frightened, because I started to believe that perhaps I was, and I knew it would feel like speeding into a brick wall with no brakes if I weren't. With that came desolation; I could not imagine spending every day for the rest of my life anywhere. Doing anything. I figured once I stopped trying to get pregnant, it would be open season on looking to medicate myself: painkillers, antidepressants, sleeping pills, everything they gave to women who were in pain and depressed with what life had to offer. Everything I refused to take while I was trying to have a baby.

But it turned out I was pregnant with my son, Raphael, on that Mother's Day in 1995. And the sad little cactus I'd given Señora Fernández was named the Raphael Tree, after this baby with whom I fell undeniably, irrevocably in love.

The Raphael Tree is lanky, like its namesake, but not as tall, not as big as one might imagine it would be after twenty-one years. Its tendrils lean into the light, and these days Senora Fernández decorates it with loudly colored papier–mâché birds covered with little feathers. It's sparkly, the Raphael Tree.

Though I'm able to recall almost a dozen circumstances under which I learned of positive, negative, and failing pregnancies, I am absolutely stripped of any memory of how I found out I was pregnant with the one that would become Raphael. When did I first learn it was going well? That the numbers were going up the way they were supposed to go up? That I could maybe even be carrying twins? When did I find out that May 1995 in fact brought me a real Mother's Day? How soon did the famous reproductive immunologist Dr. Beer order the IVIG transfusion and assure me that the Chicago Medical School financial office was making arrangements—a special research grant—so we wouldn't have to pay the $30,000 a month to try to keep this pregnancy intact?

A couple of years ago, I e-mailed Larry to ask if he remembered when or how we first learned of that pregnancy.

"The one that took?" He e- mailed back: "Girl, I can barely remember when I took my last piss. LOL. I'll think on it."

I just remember that for a moment in time, soon after Mother's Day 1995, we too believed our dreams of family were possible.

We separated eight months after our son was born.

Singing Mommy

When Raphael was three, he overheard me telling a friend that I was a single mom and asked, "You're a singing mommy?"

"Yes, I am," I sang to him, "and you are a singing baby."

Raphael and I often sang together. Like me, he made up words to songs he couldn't remember or created entirely new songs about whatever his current passion was. For example, hot cocoa. Sometimes I joined Raphael in the "cocoa dance" to try to humor him out of a demand for immediate gratification. In Raphael's version, vocals were accompanied by foot stomping, heavy whining, and the potential for real complete baby blowup if he didn't get his actual cocoa:

> *I want my cocoa, and I want it now, yeah, yeah, yeah!*
> *I want my cocoa, and I want it now.*
> *If I don't get it, I'll have a cow, yeah, yeah, yeah!*
> *Give it, GIVE IT, GIVE IT TO ME NOOOW!!!!*

Stomp, stomp, yell, yell, fists in air, jump up, and go back to the refrain until the cocoa was ready and the crisis had passed.

I was a singing mommy. Finding a song to lift the weight pressing on my heart has often been a way to buoy my belief that I would be okay. When we can still hear music, we can also find some hope. I had been singing most of the time since Raphael's birth, except for a three-month period when his dad and I thrashed out a separation agreement, during which I took on the face of a war victim and could barely utter a word to Raphael, much less a song.

Sometimes I sang in only a whisper to myself, just to keep breathing. After Larry and I separated, I comforted my sleep-deprived self, singing Raffi songs while I nursed Raphael:

> *All I really need is a song in my heart*
> *Food in my belly and love in my family*
> *All I really need is a song in my heart*
> *And love in my family*
>
> *And I need the rain to fall*
> *And I need the sun to shine*
> *To give life to the seeds we sow*

To give the food we need to grow, grow

All I really need . . .

And I need some clean water for drinking
And I need some clean air for breathing
So that I can grow up strong
And take my place where I belong . . .

The air and water in the LA Basin weren't clean, and my fragile family was falling apart, but I kept singing.

◆

I like what Larry once told me: the Baptists believe that if you've got a voice, you ought to sing no matter the quality. I tried to take this to heart, and with Raphael I would sing as loudly as I could to our week's favorite song: "You'll sing a song, and I'll sing a song. / We'll sing a song together."

I had hoped that Raphael would get his father's voice. I was told that Larry's mother had the most beautiful voice in Louisiana, where she grew up, and she even won a talent show in 1953 for her singing. Larry used to sing with an African American Baptist choir, and his voice was one of the things that drew me: a soothing, smoky, slow radio voice that made you think you ought to listen. But I didn't like Larry's voice as much when he screamed, "You crazy bitch!" or spoke to me in muttered replies, if at all. A grunt instead of, "Hi, how are you?"

Our baby was the rich color of caffè latte, with probing, dark-brown eyes, lashes that seemed endless, curling around like baroque designs, and a "strong" nose that was round and long. His eyes were usually raccoon-like, underlined with dark circles, supposedly from asthma or allergies. He could have been mistaken for being from any number of different places in the world—Ethiopia, Veracruz, the Dominican Republic—but he was actually an Afro-Jew, African American and Jewish. He had inherited a love of music as well as a passionate temperament, quick to anger at times, from both sides of his family. I was astounded by the outrage he showed when his oatmeal was fixed the wrong way—the brown sugar mixed in, not left on top. But he had also inherited traits from two cultures in which food, humor, and strength in the face of hardship were at the core. And Raphael's soul seemed to house the spirits of the six unborn children I'd lost before his birth.

Raphael called me a singing mom, but one particular day, after I went to the mailbox, I wasn't singing. I had been hoping for a tax refund check and had opened up a letter from the IRS. They had kept my refund for taxes owed by Larry. How many times had I already mentally divided up and spent that long-awaited $685 refund—at least ten different ways? Like many single moms, I tried to make time and money serve a multitude of purposes, but both always ran out before I got to the end of my list. At night, while I lay awake, I would review my bills, the most crucial— medical, electrical, preschool tuition—and then consider the more frivolous. Wouldn't it be nice to have one pretty thing—the simple wood patio umbrella I was eyeing at Target—or to once, yes, just once, have a few dollars set aside for the next emergency? I shrieked at the IRS when I called them and they said, "Lady, you should've paid your taxes. We can do whatever we want." At that moment a crazed, not singing, mommy, I had yelled into the phone, "That's *my* money; my child will starve!"

I still wasn't singing after Larry stormed in, all 280 pounds of him. I braced myself and asked about the refund. He barked in his baritone, "Oh, give me a break. I don't need this right now! You can forget that money. I'll owe the IRS all my goddamn life!"

When I told a friend about Larry and the IRS, she said, "Now I remember why you could never get back together with him." I guess she forgot about the time he choked me and knocked me down on the same day I had had, for what seemed like the hundredth time, painful medical treatment for miscarriages. He was so angry with me for wanting him to check in with me if he was going to come home late that night. He called me a "fucking bitch," and I lunged at him. After he threw me down, I couldn't move for a long time. I lay on the floor in the living room.

A few hours after my encounter with Larry and the IRS, I took Raphael hiking on Eaton Canyon Trail in the San Gabriel Mountains. At a drive-through bagel place on the way to the trailhead, Raphael considered ten types of chips before deciding on one. A long line of cars waited behind us. My eyes pleaded with the clerk for patience. At Eaton Canyon, Raphael's feet got soaked crossing the river, and an unleashed dog galloped by and ate his bagel. Trying to find comfort, he changed his crying to singing as we pulled ourselves up the trail.

Today I cannot remember what we sang as we walked along the trail. I know it wasn't:

Gonna lay down my sword and shield
Down by the riverside, down by the river side. . . .
I ain't gonna study war no more,

I ain't gonna study war no more . . .
I ain't gonna study war nooo moooooore.

No, I was right smack in the middle of a war. Instead we probably went back to those same kinds of Jewish songs that have always soothed me:

It's the tree of life to them that hold fast to it
And all of its supporters are HAPPY [clap, clap]
Shalooom Shaaalooom . . .

Like me, Raphael loved those Shabbat songs. But he seemed to sing them with an inherited Baptist twist. You could practically see him jumping up and down, singing, "Yes, Lord, Shabbat Shaaaloooom!" In preschool Raphael sat up there with all those other little kids—Chinese, Brazilian, East Indian, Egyptian, Mexican, dark-olive-skinned Sephardim, and blondish Ashkenazi—all singing with their little yarmulkes perched on their heads.

It was at home and on our hikes that Raphael really belted it out. He danced around in circles to hip-hop, salsa, new age, Louisiana bayou, and his tape from music class. "More music, Mommy. Dance with me. I like that music!" He bellowed out his own versions:

Day-O Daaaaay-O
Daylight's coming and he want to go home.

If you're happy and you knooooow it, clap your hands . . .

Raphael Michael Avram Jones, that's my name.
So whenever I go out, the people always shout,
There goes Raphael Michael Avram Jones, na na na nananna naaaaaw!

"Well," my same friend had said to me of my marriage, "you got a great kid out of it." I couldn't have agreed more. I'd endured all those years before without singing, but with my son, back then I could always find a song.

Donor X

The first time I set out to have a baby solo was in 1992, before I got together with Larry. At the time I was thirty-two, single, and considered myself most likely a lesbian but open to being in a relationship with the right person of either gender. I attended two different groups for prospective moms. Single Mothers by Choice was made up primarily of professional, educated, mainly straight, single women in their forties. Maybe Baby was for lesbians, but I was the only one who wasn't part of a couple. I didn't fit entirely into either group.

Nine years later, when Raphael was five, I began to look into having another baby on my own, through a sperm donor. I had waited until I was forty-one to try for a second child, pushing the age limit but wanting to be financially responsible, to get Raphael's asthma under control, and to gather energy to handle another pregnancy. As a single mom with one child, I returned to Single Mothers by Choice. I also participated in a lesbian moms group, even though I hadn't yet met that special someone. One woman at the Single Mothers by Choice meeting was having an imaginary love affair with her anonymous donor. She loved his charming French accent, and along with his audiotape, she decided she'd love to have him for a boyfriend. I wasn't looking for a boyfriend, but I hoped to find an anonymous donor who would be a good match for Raphael and me.

I had learned the hard way that when someone you know contributes to the baby-making process, he will most likely be in your life forever, so picking a baby daddy, even if you are just asking for sperm, is a decision that needs to be made extremely carefully. In spite of agreements drawn up or promises someone might make to be or not to be involved in parenting, there are legal rules in place regarding the rights and responsibilities of fatherhood, covering everything from custody and visitation to child support. And you had better work well with that person, because he could become a bigger part of your life—and your child's—than you imagined.

I knew that with an anonymous donor there would be kinks to be worked out—having to explain to two siblings where each came from and why one had a known father and the other did not—but I didn't feel this was insurmountable. I strongly believed that the world was changing and that alternative methods of conception and different types of families would become increasingly commonplace. In my imaginary world, what made a family would be less rigid than in the past, and the "normal" nuclear family would be in the minority—like on the postcard on my refrigerator showing two people alone in a large auditorium, captioned, "Adult children of normal parents."

So I embarked on my original plan—pregnancy by insemination with an anonymous sperm donor—and started looking at donor profiles.

Searching through sperm donor descriptions bears some resemblance to perusing online dating profiles. I was kind of shooting in the dark. And these descriptions didn't include photos. In order to get much detail at all, you had to pay extra for the in-depth profiles.

I looked at a lot of two-line descriptions that basically gave age, profession, and ethnicity. I found one prospective Donor X who looked promising on the basis of ethnic breakdown, so I ordered the comprehensive profile, which included an audiotape. When I listened to the donor I'd picked out, I began to have some doubts. I wasn't crazy about his semi-whiny voice, and the only word he could think of to describe himself was "ambitious." His two favorite movies were *The Graduate* and *Pulp Fiction*.

Many years later Raphael's favorite movie would be *Pulp Fiction*, but at this time, I couldn't project a future relationship of bonding over *Pulp Fiction* based on my potential offspring's genetic propensity to like that movie. The choice of *The Graduate* just made me wonder if there was a Mrs. Robinson in my donor's life. And "ambitious"? Why didn't I find that appealing then? I might now.

While my potential donor's voice and self-description weren't all that compelling to me, his family history was—Jewish, Russian, African American, and Native American—and he spoke Spanish. Ethnically, his family description sounded like a fit for my family, as did the occupations: urban planners, judges, teachers, and social workers. The New York connection on his mother's side seemed close enough to my own mom's family tree that I thought, *Uh-oh, could he be a relative?* I was hesitant to ask my mom because I was embarking on this project secretly, as if I were a drug addict, which is what I looked like thanks to all the needle marks from having hormones injected into me and blood drawn out. I imagined my family might think that raising two kids on my own would be too much.

But I decided I liked this donor despite the deficiencies in his profile. I finally called my mom—without disclosing my motive—and made sure we didn't have any relatives from New York who matched the donor's description of his parents. Although I had hoped to find a donor who was "willing to be contacted" after the offspring turned eighteen, there seemed to be a shortage of biracial or African American donors, so Donor X seemed like my best option. I wondered if a child with him would resemble my son. I wondered if there was a whole generation of children with Native American blood cheated out of their rights to tribal registration due to sperm donor anonymity.

Months later, a big silver cylinder that reminded me of the monolith from *2001: A Space Odyssey* sat in the corner of my room. A special holding tank for my sperm, purchased from the California Cryobank, which would be thawed and injected into me. I wanted to point the cylinder out to Raphael. "See that? That could contain the beginning of your future little brother or sister."

I didn't go back to my expensive reproductive immunologist, Dr. Beer, who worked out of Chicago Medical School and had a private practice in Los Angeles. His treatment had resulted in my miracle of miracles: Raphael Michael Avram Jones. But I knew that returning to him would mean a new diagnosis, more talk of killer cells, and expensive treatment—a new medicine that all Dr. Beer's patients had been discussing online. The treatment might start out simple, but it would turn into the need for several additional injections and/or transfusions, each with different side effects.

So I decided to try my hand at what felt like the Kmart brand of infertility treatment at our HMO. It felt strange to be back there, going to the old lab in the basement near the hospital where Raphael was born. I remembered being there before I had him and taking yet another blood test, wondering if I would end up broke, childless, alone, and disabled from some weird disease caused by all the experimental treatments with Dr. Beer.

This time I got to experience a different side of the fertility battle, one that included several shots in the butt in preparation for insemination. The injections were part of the infertility treatment to maximize my chance of getting pregnant. Now I was in my early forties, which can mean declining fertility and increased miscarriages for many women.

The doctor I saw at our HMO was a high-tech type of practitioner, a private doctor who contracted with my HMO. He said, "Let's really crank you up," as if he was launching me like a rocket, projecting how many ovarian follicles I could produce. All I knew was that once I was filled with those follicles, I couldn't go more than a few minutes without feeling a tremendous need to pee.

"I have a good record on multiples," the doctor told me. "It's unlikely you'll have triplets or above." *And who said I could handle twins?* I wondered. Not me, the already often stressed-to-the-max single mom. I knew what twins meant; I'd seen parents go crazy in those early years.

I arrived at our HMO with my canister of donor sperm, but before he would inseminate me with it, the lead doctor demanded a permission slip from my ex-husband. Larry and I had never finalized a divorce, and technically we were only legally separated. The doctor insisted that a signature was required for insemination with sperm from someone other than the husband. "That is such bullshit!" I raged, taking full advantage of being pumped up with hormones. I roared and railed until the doctor let me sign something saying my (ex-)husband was nowhere to be found.

I spent my days in the craziness of running from work to doctor appointments, dropping off and picking up Raphael, arranging his classes and playdates and summer camp and school next year, building my new business, picking up sperm, and getting more shots in the butt—with little time left over to just sit and read to Raphael.

At the HMO's injection clinic they taught me how to mix various infertility drugs and inject myself. It seemed daunting; I had never been successful at chemistry experiments. Afterward, I drove to my son's school to bring him a chocolate croissant. I needed to remind myself that I did have one live son—the *milagro*. I was the lucky of the unlucky. I knew people who had tried and tried to have a baby and ended up with medical problems, bankruptcy, divorce . . . and no baby.

Back when I was trying to have my first child, I couldn't understand people who became obsessed with having a second baby. Why couldn't they be satisfied with the one? I prayed for just one chance, believed that one baby would be manna from heaven—*dayenu*, enough. But then it wasn't. And even if I couldn't have the three children I once dreamed of, I had begun to hunger for a second. I felt I could at least handle two. I had left the nonprofit world for tech PR so that I could improve my own economic mobility, and I thought that I had more or less figured out how I'd manage. I never got any rest anyway with one, so how would it be any different with two? I could basically say good-bye to any sleep, relationships, or writing career for another eighteen years or so. If I had to choose, I was choosing a second child. The rest could come later.

After the first insemination, when my pregnancy test came back saying, "Negative, less than five," I was stopped still. Those weren't the words I wanted to hear at all. I'd learned that early pregnancy is driven by numbers—the amount of human chorionic gonadotropin (HCG), which is produced during pregnancy. It was not the first time I'd heard, "Negative, less than five," but this time I really believed I should be pregnant. I was ramped up with lots of follicles, just waiting for my eggs to be united with Donor X's sperm. I was tired. My breasts were heavy. I was full of hormones.

Added to the steaming chemical cauldron for helping to get me and keep me pregnant was prednisone, a steroid that would later put me into early osteoporosis, but at the time made me feel and act like a cranky toddler, overtired yet unable to sleep. Though the combination of hormones and prednisone could have easily turned me into Psycho Mom, I was astonishingly calm. I knew the explosive potential I was carrying, so I greeted every onslaught of mood dynamite composedly, as just the work of raving hormones and steroids.

I started thinking of switching to a particular East Indian donor. He seemed to have different qualities from my chosen one. And, more to the point, a better pregnancy record. He combined high brain power—he was a physics professor—and a sort of Zen calmness, an easygoing personality, even some creativity, and a much more satisfactory self-description. The African American Native American Jewish donor seemed to have much more stress potential. I knew that he and I were made from peoples whose genetic mapping tended toward intensity and were generally not kicked-back folks. Maybe too many bad things had happened in our collective ethnic histories. Who could expect that a sperm with African American, Jewish, and Native American genetic content would combine with my egg and produce a relaxed child? And we needed someone like that in our household.

Or perhaps I should look for a Danish donor, I mused; I'd heard the Danes tended to be a very relaxed people. But I was trying to find a donor who would provide some color and ethnic similarity to Raphael and the rest of my family. Still, I knew so little about East Indian culture; how could I explain that heritage to my child? Everything felt fraught with complications, not to mention the problem of my relying on ethnic stereotypes. My search for a donor was beginning to sound like a bad Borscht Belt routine.

On top of my indecision about the donor, I had realized that I couldn't inject myself. The instructions overwhelmed me. I had a friend whose husband was a doctor of osteopathy, and I got him to give me the shot. But he didn't know how to mix and give injections, so we lost a good portion of precious Repronex, which meant fewer follicles releasing eggs to hook up with my donor's sperm. I also had a nurse friend inject me in the ER where she worked. When I went there, I frequently crossed paths with tragedies. One day two infant seats had been dropped off with security. In back, with my friend, I heard the buzz from the nurses: a car accident, parents dead. Someone would pick up the twin babies, remarkably unscathed, but never again to see their parents. I went home and held my five-year-old.

The second month I was inseminated, I fretted: Why didn't I feel the discomfort I'd felt before of having so many egg follicles inside me? Maybe nothing was happening. I had a dream in which couches were growing incorrectly due to medication, and a nurse was telling me to take my medication differently and ignore the doctor's orders so the couch could become bigger and wider more quickly. When I awoke I wondered if this was because, instead of buying a sofa, I was wasting my money on sperm that dripped out of me and swam away.

I went to the HMO clinic about ten times a month, which was still less than the number of visits I had made when trying to have Raphael, attempting to resolve the problems that had stacked up—rectal pain, bleeding, severe constipation, and the feeling of having an ongoing low-level virus. I don't know whether the doctor's predictions that these medical issues would go away with a successful pregnancy were true, but I did find that I was simply so happy after Raphael was born that my tortured look and all my aches and pains just vanished.

One day, after Raphael had spent another afternoon in an exam room filled with pictures of fetuses and vaginas, he asked me, "Mommy, are you too old to have another baby?"

I told him I wasn't entirely sure.

"Ask the doctor," he insisted. Then he asked the Question: "How do you get the baby in the stomach? Does the doctor do it?"

"Sometimes." I had explained this—kind of—before. And then he asked again, "How do you make a baby?"

Also kind of touched upon before. I answered, "An egg from a mommy and a seed from a daddy."

I had tried to explain that there are different ways of making or getting a baby. Sometimes the doctor mixes the seed with the egg and then, "Voilà!," puts it in the mommy's tummy.

A couple of years later, he would ask me, "Where are they getting all those cute Chinese babies? I want one!" We were at a family camp, and a lot of white families had come with their adopted Chinese girls.

And so I'd told him, "Perhaps we can adopt someday."

"You would have to work hard to earn money for that?" he asked.

"Yes, but then I won't have much time to play with you and the baby if I worked all the time. It's a tough situation," I told him—having time to be with your babies while working to earn money to care for them. "But having you is wonderful!" I gave him a hug.

"Having me is enough? You don't need another one?" he asked.

"Yes, it's more than enough, but it would be nice to have another baby."

Much later, I thought: *Was he too young for this information?* But even his pre-K teacher explained in vitro fertilization to her class, telling the parents, "I thought the kids should understand why I couldn't lift them up after the embryo transfer."

After two months and no pregnancy, I started wanting to convince myself to stop. That I could lead a good life with less stress with just Raphael and me. A study had come out suggesting that there was a negative impact on the kids when moms worked more than fifteen hours a week. Over the years I've seen a lot of those studies, often conflicting, and looking back, I have my own theories now. I believe that we'd all benefit from not having to work ourselves into the ground and raise children at the same time. And that the importance of "the village" to raise children and care for elders cannot be underestimated. Many of us are still searching for that.

Back then, my thinking was: Raphael wasn't too damaged from too many hours in day care. But then I wondered, was it just too much day care, as the recent study showed? The study backed up my feeling that Raphael would be a different person—maybe calmer, happier—if he were in preschool only a few hours a day.

Sometimes I'd wake up and question everything I was doing, from trying to have a baby to not always reading to my son before he went to bed. Why was it that I couldn't accomplish everything? Spending time with Raphael at school, playing, reading to him, going to work, getting new clients, trying to get pregnant, visiting our HMO, injecting at night, keeping my house clean and repaired, exercising, signing up Raphael for swim classes, basketball, summer camp, practicing tap dancing with him, working on a new business partnership, replacing the old, moldy shower curtain, allergy-proofing the house, putting away photos, planning my life, planning my finances, organizing, filing. What was it about me? Why was it so hard sometimes to do it all—the normal feeding, cleaning, taking care of one child?

I concluded that maybe I was doomed to failure as a mom, as a friend, as a professional, and as a lover—though there wasn't any activity in that arena. I didn't want to take the time to masturbate, let alone to try to meet someone. I couldn't even find my ideal sperm donor.

I was advised to do two inseminations the third month—around the time "we" (the medical folks and I) thought I'd ovulated. And I seemed to be bursting with follicles. So I did two doses of Donor X.

The most beautiful, hopeful, scary, almost orgasmic words I've ever heard are still "You are pregnant." It's a drug I thought I'd never stop craving—that feeling of unequivocal joy on hearing, "Well, you know, it is positive." Just like that, casual. I was so happy for those thirty seconds before she told me the number seemed low. I took another test the next day, and the number had gone up. But not as fast as "we" would have liked.

There are degrees of being pregnant and not pregnant. Sometimes, in the early days, you don't know for sure if you've lost the pregnancy. And there are all sorts of terms that mask the despair of a miscarriage: "blighted ovum . . . ," "spontaneous abortion . . ."

I was scheduled to fly to San Francisco to see my friend Debbie, who was dying of colon cancer and had fooled us into complacency for years by periodically getting better. We'd go out dancing. Or out for Chinese food. Being Chinese American, she would get us the real prices and good dishes. She would talk about the Chinese banquet she wanted if she stayed healthy. Not just at her funeral. Soon she wouldn't be able to eat at all, tubes and bags keeping her alive, moving nutrition in and waste out. So I wanted to visit Debbie and tell her my news.

I didn't call Dr. Beer, my crazy mad-scientist doctor-to-the-stars reproductive immunologist. I wanted to remain hopeful that maybe my luck or situation had changed, and I could stay pregnant without Dr. Beer. I couldn't imagine going through all the interventions I had done with Raphael.

The day I found out I was pregnant, I also made an offer on a bigger house. Now I was waiting for the seller's response. I was scared. If I stayed pregnant, I couldn't work as much, and it would be a stretch to afford this home.

"Girlfriend, you might get all you want now—another child, a new house," María Elena enthused. I also had several new business prospects pending.

At 1 a.m. the night before I was scheduled to leave for San Francisco, I was still awake. "Everyone" said rest was most important. I knew that, but I couldn't sleep. I didn't want to disappoint Raphael by not getting on the plane—he was going too—but I wasn't sure I could do it. Just too tired. I was still pregnant as far as I knew. And I was on prednisone again. Scared again.

I ruminated: *What to do—stay or go? Is there a reason not to fly? I hope not. I'm worried. I don't know. What if I still can't sleep?*

I prayed—though I'd never admit that's what I was doing: *Please, God, a thousand billion times over, let me stay pregnant. I'm not evil, careless, noncompliant. I'm merely doing the very best I can. Trying very hard to be a loving friend and mom, to balance my life. Please, please, please, please, please! It's a bit much, but I am trying so hard. I pray and hope I can stay pregnant with a healthy baby—such a long road to go.*

I prayed and prayed. *Let me be a good mother to Raphael, have this baby, sleep.* I rested until I couldn't anymore.

In San Francisco, Debbie told me, "I'm happy for you. You are a good mother. You really want this." No judgment. She had said that if she got better, she wanted to adopt a Chinese baby girl. But at that point, we knew that wasn't going to happen. I was glad I saw Debbie. I didn't know if it would be the last time, and I felt I had her blessing. Her love had seen me through so much before. I wished my love could help her.

In the Bay Area Raphael and I stayed with a close friend, Rose, and her husband and two kids. Her husband was unhappy with my choice. He said it was selfish of me to want a second child as a single mom. Rose had always supported me in my quest to have a baby. She was also the one who said, "The moment you start to even consider having a baby, you are vulnerable to the greatest loss."

Before we left, Rose's son gave Raphael a big toy water gun, and he carried it to the airport. We arrived rushed; I was feeling anxious to get back and check my pregnancy numbers. When we got to security, we were informed that he couldn't go through with the water gun. "It's just a kid's water gun," my voice rose precariously. "I don't even normally let him play with these, but it's a present!"

My usual calming mantra—"Carla, you know you are on hormones; be cool"—failed to kick in that time. Instead, I got that pounding feeling that made me appear not quite Unabomber but agitated enough for Raphael to sense—as little kids do—that things were escalating. "It's okay, Mom, we can leave it," he said. Bereft, I walked back and left the squirt gun on top of a garbage bin, hoping someone who wanted it would take it home. Raphael reassured me, "Mom, I can get another." Holding Raphael's hand, I walked dejectedly through security. I just wanted to get home and find out if I was still pregnant.

We Have Pets

When we returned from the Bay Area, I drove straight to our HMO from the airport to take another blood test. I wondered what Raphael made of this whole routine: going down to the hospital basement, making the same jokes with the lab technicians, giving my usual instructions to them to use the butterfly needle (usually reserved for kids) to make it easier to get blood from my sometimes-hard-to-find veins.

The next morning, I returned for a doctor's appointment and walked over to the nurse's station to find out my HCG level results. Was I still pregnant? The nurse looked on the computer while I anxiously watched over her shoulder. I saw a number. It was low. Lower than the number from two days ago. The nurse clicked and peered at the computer, "Oh, that's odd," she said. "Let me check."

But I knew what that number meant. I didn't need her to tell me it was bad. "You should discuss this with your doctor," she said.

I left sobbing.

As I drove through the Hollywood traffic toward the freeway, my doctor called me. "Carla, do you understand what this means? That you're having a—" He spoke like he wanted to slap me to get my attention.

I interrupted, heaving sobs. "Yes, I know." For a second I let my head rest on the steering wheel, almost at a stop. I hit the windshield wipers on, as if they might wipe the tears from my eyes and clear my vision. I resumed driving.

The doctor continued to talk. It was unlikely that I was anything but miscarrying. He did not tell me to go home and rest, only, "It's so early there shouldn't be much blood." Meaning losing the baby this early probably wouldn't cause me to bleed too heavily.

I hung up the phone and thought about Dr. Beer, the famous reproductive immunologist, and what he might advise me to do. He had often seemed like a mad scientist with his weird, painful, expensive treatments. Still, there were many "Dr. Beer babies." My son, Raphael, was one of them. Yet I couldn't really give myself over to the idea of going through those procedures all over again. And I didn't have the financial resources. After Raphael was born, a benevolent family member had paid off the house-size fertility debt. Now I was on my own.

I desperately wanted an easier solution, but I also wanted the assurance of Dr. Beer's superhuman belief in his ability to help women like me have a live baby. My HMO doctors only shook their heads. Their motto seemed to be, "Just keep trying, and you might get lucky." By the time I got home, I had decided to call Dr. Beer in Chicago. I hoped he would tell me something miraculous, that I wouldn't have to start over with the blood transfusions, the new medication, et cetera. And I wondered what he would say about why I hadn't spoken with him first.

When I telephoned his office, his nurse arranged for a conference call later that day. She noted that it was urgent; I was technically still pregnant. Dr. Beer told me in a stern voice, "You should have been in touch with me before you got pregnant," and said that to figure out the next steps, I'd need lots of tests. These included getting another blood pregnancy test right away, just in case I was pregnant with twins and one had died, causing a temporary dip in numbers, and immediately arranging for the costly intravenous immunoglobulin treatment I'd had with my previous pregnancy.

I felt sick in the pit in my stomach—it seemed ridiculous to spend thousands of dollars trying to preserve a lost pregnancy. My HMO doctors would think his "possible twins and still pregnant with one" theory was nuts.

I raced out of my house to pick up my son at school. Raphael was an actual living, breathing, sweet child, who curled up next to me at night.

The next day I didn't rush to the lab. I didn't call the home health service and order the IVIG treatment. Instead, I went on Raphael's school field trip to the zoo, as planned. Raphael wore a stuffed animal snake around his neck; the students had been instructed to bring a toy animal or a picture of a pet on the field trip.

"We have pets," Raphael told his classmates, not to be outdone by their boasts of birds, cats, and dogs. "We have ants, termites, a bird and her babies," he said, referring to one of our loud Pasadena birds who had built her nest in the hibiscus tree in the middle of our cluttered patio. I considered her skillful, a bohemian twig artist. "We also have fleas and skunks." Later that day I joined Raphael, his snake, and his classmates for lunch. "Hey, we didn't go to see the Lakers," he said. "Playoffs—'member, Mom?"

Going to the NBA playoffs was not anywhere on my list. Even with all the Lakers flags being sold on street corners and hanging from cars, I hadn't registered that LA was in the playoffs.

"Who's the bestest player?" Raphael asked.

I tried to think. "Shaquille O'Neal? He's more of a team player than Kobe, right?" That started a heated discussion among the kids—and the adults. I was surprised to find how much Raphael knew about each player.

I was glad I went on that field trip.

That day I told myself that if I could continue my life, my very precious life with my living son wearing the blue-green Converse sneakers and stuffed snake, I would be okay.

Late that afternoon, I got another blood test. My HMO doctor had ordered it, though he clearly thought Dr. Beer was wacky. He knew there was no baby; it was another miscarriage.

I called for the test results. "The number is down to sixteen," the nurse said.

No one sent me flowers or brought me chicken soup like they had with my earlier miscarriages. A colleague offered to bring me chicken when I explained why I couldn't work that day. I had been afraid to tell her because she was a fundamentalist Christian, and I wasn't sure she'd approve of my attempt to have a child solo. But she had responded with comfort food, the way my family might have had they known. I still wasn't ready to tell them.

A couple of days later, as I'd done so often in our lives, I finally did tell my older sister, Jane. She had supported me through all the miscarriages before Raphael. She had two children, but she didn't work outside the home, and she had a husband and a lot of help. She wisely steered clear of lecturing me on the insanity of having another child.

Jane invited me over to her house in Sierra Madre. I lay down in her hammock and napped, listening to birds. The orderly environment of her home was soothing, and she offered me tea and soup.

I called my mom in Seattle and told her about the miscarriage. "Would you consider adopting?" she asked.

After each previous miscarriage, that question had made me want to scream when posed so innocently by moms with their own 2.2 children they had carried to term. Coming now from my own mother—who, I knew, worried about each of her four children—that simple question felt loving. She didn't follow it with other questions about how I would manage with two children. For the moment I felt nurtured, not judged, by my mom, who seemed to want only to protect her daughter from enduring another baby lost. It had felt strange to be pursuing this pregnancy quest— something so very important to me—without telling my family. They had stood behind me so solidly when I tried to have a baby while married to Larry.

Soon after that last miscarriage, Raphael and I were cuddling after his bath and book. It was bedtime, and the Jewish lullaby tape with songs from around the world was playing. He looked at me and said, "Sometimes adults get scared when life is dark?"

I asked him to repeat his question. It was too deep for me. That was my five-year-old son, the one who insisted on sleeping next to me because his feet got cold. But I was the one who clung to him at night the week after I lost the last pregnancy. Each night I asked myself why I didn't go to sleep when he did, as he begged me to. Each night I tried to put him in his bed, me in mine. I didn't want to use his need to mop up my sorrow. But he always ended up next to me, spooning close.

"That's true," I answered my son. "I'm not afraid of the dark anymore, but sometimes . . . sometimes . . ." I trailed off.

I wanted to show bravery, rise to supermom status (albeit wounded), and not tell him just how alone an adult can feel. "Sometimes you feel a little scared, but then you get tough," I said.

In the wee hours of the morning when I awoke, things felt the most stark. Raphael was nestling up next to me, and I was reluctant to move, but his gentle kicks got me up.

In reality, I felt relief that I was still functioning almost a week after my eyes burned at the sight of the fallen HCG number telling me I wasn't going to have this baby, who likely would've had close to the same birthday as Raphael, another Aquarius: creative, already a dreamy intellectual. I was just relieved that I hadn't crawled under my covers for good. But sometimes I do still wonder: who might that child have been?

Responding to Raphael's needs pointed me in the direction of the resilience I carried with me most of my life. I fed, bathed, played with, and cared for Raphael, even while getting hit with heavy cramps the first days after the miscarriage. I had hot flashes from all the hormones I was taking. Lugging around a thick cloud of defeat, I put one foot in front of another.

I made an appointment with a therapist specializing in single parents, infertility, and adoption decisions. I knew enough about adoption to realize what a difficult journey that would be. It meant money, time, potential loss when an adoption fell through. But unlike my attempts to carry another baby, with adoption, if you persisted, you did end up with a child.

I knew that I couldn't thrash myself physically, emotionally, and financially to try again to get pregnant and risk going through more miscarriages. I had a five-year-old, and if I were to be put on bed rest during a pregnancy, that would be a good chunk out of his young life. Denial was no longer possible; I was finally ready to at least open the door a crack to adoption.

Early one morning, I wrote Raphael a letter. In it I apologized for my shortcomings as a mother, explaining what I was doing during that time in his life. "I want to tell you that when you were almost five and a half, I decided to try to have another baby. You were always asking me about a brother or sister, and I always wanted more. I used to want three when I envisioned a family that included two parents . . . and 'real' pets like the other kids."

I apologized for not having the energy to read to him every night, for sometimes falling asleep midsentence, for not always learning his tap routines to practice with him before his dance performances. And for not picking him up early at school every day, in time for "The Goodbye Song," when the stay-at-home moms arrived.

"Raphael—having you was and is my dream, and working is only a means to support us. If I have a secondary dream, it includes another child and the ability to focus on writing. And sometimes I can barely maintain the first, caring for you.

"Does it make a difference that I love you more than anything in the Universe, that I live to see your beautiful crinkly big eyes, touch your soft skin, and hear your loud, strong voice?"

Raphael woke up asking for oatmeal, and I put down my pen.

I wondered if he would ever see that letter. It has stayed in my journal.

♦

So much had seemed possible during that little window of time. At the end of the week after I lost the pregnancy, Raphael had smashed the roses in our garden with strong bursts of water. I was sad, but I figured, in time, the roses would grow back.

That summer after the miscarriage, we went out and bought a leopard gecko. Raphael named him Michael Jordan and fed him crickets. Flowers sprang up outside. Raphael said, "God provided them."

Pen Pals and
Prader-Willi of the Spirit

I was introduced to my cousin Janice as a pen pal when I was in fourth grade. We met in person about four years later, when her parents flew me out from Seattle to visit her in Silver Spring, Maryland. We became close—best friends, soul mates—and we sent letters and journals back and forth regularly for more than fifteen years.

When we were in our late fifties, I visited her again. She had saved my letters in meticulous order. As I read those early letters, I recognized my existential angst mingled with real-life family conflicts arising from my parents struggling to raise four kids on a small income, having known each other only a matter of months before getting married, and possessing limited relationship skills. At ten or eleven, I was already worried about money, and by junior high I was wondering why I felt so unhappy, anxious, and empty a great deal of the time. I had a beautiful older sister, a very cute and smart younger sister, and I . . . had a good sense of humor. I was also flat-chested. I had the lightest skin in the family and the biggest nose. I didn't make a huge hit when we moved out to suburbia (Bellevue, Washington), and somewhere along the line, bad-ass Sammy Boy from the inner city was misplaced.

But my earliest letters to my cousin show a spunky rebel. I was fearless, funny, and smart, and I had three boyfriends I hung out with in my fourth-grade class. I found the first letter:

April 21, 1969

Dear Janice,
Sorry about the sloppy postcard. I messed up (addressed and all). I got the card from my Hebrew teacher who is from Israel. You get a few words right or something and you get a stamp or postcard or something. Guess what? I found out a new way to bat. I look over my left shoulder. I use a wide grip because my wrists aren't strong enough to choke up. I swing up and start out low. In this way I can hit quite nicely and all I need is a lot of practice to hit grounders, I lower my swing and start out high. I can't anyhow but it's an improvement.

I like astronomy and law. I hate to write but I like to write letters, stories and poems and articles. I just have to tell you this even though it has to do with school. This kid Marvin is a big bully and I can't stand him. Well anyhow, the boys in our class and I decided to stand up to him. I had to stay after school. Norris Washington said he would wait for me but they still had the fight. Larry was scared but did a good job. Chris put in a few punches then ran. Stan Hummel (We call him Hummel) almost got killed. He fought Marvin for a while, then Marvin knocked him down the stairs on his head. The result . . . a sore head

a chipped tooth

Loose teeth

I luckly stayed out because Aubrey got in a few punches then got a few black eyes from Marvin. I was mad, I even began to swear a little. Next time Slauson (vice princible I think) said that some of those guys would be expelled. They were suspended until their parents came.

I like Aubrey. He's good in sports and a nice guy. I like Stan Hummel but he's the one who nicknamed me Sammy and I wish I could kill him. I like Chris. He sometimes seems to cheat in sports and he's always ranking me out but you have to learn to like a guy when he goes to reading and music and regular class with you. (We go to a special reading class that's harder.) I like Norris who is good in sports and strong, modest and scientific. He speaks in big words. One day after staying after school with a lot of other guys he said "I think Mrs. Kumata needs a lesson in child phsicoligy." I really like him. He's a nice kid. I like Larry Rock too. He's pretty nice.

The room has a section where the smart kids sit and the dumb kids sit. I'm with the smart (natch). We always get into trouble. Our teacher lectures us on how were good academicly but terrible citizenship wise.

Tired of looking at messy handwriting? Okay, I give up. I'll stop this stupid letter. Here's some neat handwriting

Love,
Carla Sameth

It's odd that I experience something akin to relief reading these letters. I see why, after fifth grade, I was always waking up feeling like shit or consumed with guilt, believing I didn't fit in. Something my son has talked about (not fitting in), something I thought I could fix for my children—that I could offer safety, a cocoon—and perhaps, in doing so, heal my own childhood memories.

A friend of mine was researching Prader-Willi syndrome, which is how I first heard about this horrifying disease. As I understand it, it is a genetic condition that starts in infancy and has many different components. However, what stands out for me is the insatiable appetite, which leads to extreme, compulsive, chronic overeating and multiple health issues with dire consequences, potentially death.

I began to think of this insatiable spiritual hole in many of us—the lack of self-worth—as something that we desperately seek to fill but cannot. We compulsively try to satisfy the emptiness with substances: drugs, alcohol, sex, food, worrying, relationships—you name it. I believe it can kill us too. In my case, I desperately sought self-value; I thought that I could fix the hole by creating a family to love and nurture. I believed I could raise children who wouldn't wonder about that hole inside of them but would instead feel loved and okay. They would get most of the classes and trips and shoes they wanted, go to the schools that were best suited to them, go to the universities of their choosing, and not have to worry about money. And they'd also have all the fun we did have in my youth: camping, raucous family gatherings with cousins and extended family, charades and Thanksgiving, more laughter, less tears. But this is easier said than done.

A House Is Not a Home

When Raphael was about eight years old, it seemed as if one of us would have to go on medication, so I decided it had better be me, and I did. He and I had been feeding off each other's stress for about a year, and when tensions rose, they accelerated at rocket speed. He and I were tied together by a bond tighter than any umbilical cord, which was liable to strangle us both if something didn't give. I'd finally abandoned the quest to have another biological baby. But we are social beings, and it seemed as if we were meant to be part of a bigger family: more kids, another adult, a couple of dogs (or at least a cat). Instead, it was just the two of us and Michael Jordan, our gecko.

And there was something else: I was lonely. While previously I had believed that it was more about the person than the gender, I had finally decided I was interested in women.

So I stopped shopping around for sperm and began searching dating sites for a girlfriend. After a few fits and starts, I was about to shut down my profile when I received a brief response—something like, "I don't know . . . I have a seven-year-old too." When I learned she had a girl, I became more interested, as I'd been imagining that it would be nice to adopt a girl. I had already met a *Brady Bunch* kind of lesbian couple in the lesbian moms group. Their blended family consisted of six kids between them! I felt a strong desire to have a partner and more children—happy chaos. Larry and I didn't coparent in any cohesive way. I was ready to be part of a team.

I met Lizette in the late spring of Raphael's second-grade year. We agreed to get together at Fatty's, a vegetarian place in Eagle Rock. She was attractive in an unadorned way, short brown hair, dark brown eyes, light skinned, and with lips full enough for me to like them. Though she was an artist, I would learn that she dressed for comfort, not fashion. She did not wear makeup or use much jewelry. I felt neutral—neither drawn nor repelled. I treated her to dinner and hoped she would offer to buy coffee, but she didn't. Was that an omen? It reminded me of my first date with Larry. He'd had a crush on me for years, but when we finally went out, he took me to an inexpensive Thai restaurant. The bill came, and he put down some money that didn't even equal half. So I did what I always did in those situations and said, "I'll take care of it; you get the next one." When I told a friend about this, she said, "Throw that one back in the sea." But I didn't.

Soon after meeting Lizette, I fell and broke my ribs. After a week of watching me move slowly, Raphael said, "Enough is enough." After all, I had eight other ribs. I stayed home to recuperate while Raphael went to family camp with another mom and her son. I was on painkillers, and part of the beginning of my relationship with Lizette was blurred by pain and meds. But also I wasn't driven by the extreme chemistry I'd felt in other relationships. Lizette didn't push it, and (other than holding hands on occasion) we seemed to be drifting away from dating and toward friendship. One day, however, on some impulse or curiosity or twinge of desire, we kissed. Then, as far as I remember, we fell easily into making love. I suppose we had an attitude of, "Why not give it a try?" It seemed to go well enough.

Soon after that, I met her daughter, Serena. Serena was short, brown skinned with black shoulder-length hair and a toothy smile. Lizette told me that Serena's birth family was from Mexico and New Mexico, and you could see the indigenous heritage in her looks. She was shy but warm in her greeting, and I felt her hand moving toward mine as soon as she gave me the first hug hello. When we introduced Serena and Raphael, they hit it off right away. From that point forward, I began to see the relationship a bit differently. At first we didn't tell the kids we were dating, but by the end of summer, just before school started, we had decided to inform them we were officially girlfriends.

Which is about how long it took me to decide I really wanted to be with Lizette. For me, the love affair began with the way the whole family seemed ripe for blending. I wanted a daughter. Raphael wanted a sibling. I had my vision of a bigger family that was closer to a village. It felt meant to be. *Beshert*, as we Jews like to say. I was already thinking about us adopting a third child together.

Raphael was delighted that I had a girlfriend. I hadn't been with anyone since his dad, which was before he could remember, and though I had told him I was a lesbian (explaining that two men or two women could fall in love), he said that I wasn't really gay until I had a girlfriend. He immediately wanted to announce it to the world. "Gaga," he asked my mother, "did you know my mom's a lesbian?"

"Yes, I heard something like that," she said. And Raphael proceeded to tell anyone and everyone that he was getting a new mom and a new sister. He started at a family gathering for an eightieth birthday party. The progressive Jewish old people in my family—artists, former Lincoln Brigade fighters, concentration camp survivors—were pretty accepting. In fact, they proved to be more tolerant than many of the young parents whose kids attended Raphael's "progressive" charter school.

Before long, Serena and I began to bond, and she asked, "Can I call you Mommy, Mom?" Her two moms, Lizette and Vilma, had been together for more than twenty years and had adopted Serena. They separated when she was about four, and Serena went back and forth between the two households. Serena told me that it had taken her much longer to bond with her other mom's partner, Mary, and I felt a sort of pride at being able to slip so quickly into a close relationship with her. Lizette and Raphael also seemed to connect immediately. Whereas I would get frustrated when my son was in a bad mood, Lizette could tease him out of it. And Raphael and I both enjoyed the luxury of having someone else to turn to when things got intense between us.

I had often envied large families, ones where the parents—because there were two—could each take a hand and swing the kids between them. I could see myself with Lizette, Serena, Raphael, and another child— a toddler I was sure we could adopt. When I initially visited Lizette's house, I could picture us someday fitting into it, adding artwork to the bare walls and the space evolving into a family home for us all.

Her home was bare of much decor; I imagined it to have a Zen kind of feel. Lizette seemed quiet, even introverted. Later I would see that she was withdrawn, isolated, disconnected from friends and family. But in these early months, I wrote the story in my mind that she was a hidden gem, quiet waters, something like what I'd said about Larry in the beginning, though I didn't remember this until many years later.

Lizette's family was from Cuba. They had left before the dictator Fulgencio Bautista took over, gone back at the beginning of Fidel Castro's Communist regime, and then struggled for many years to leave again. Her father had been put in a labor camp during that time, and her family seemed to retain a circling-the-wagons kind of mentality. When I met her parents, they showed me the clippings on their anti-Castro wall of shame, and I was careful not to mention that I'd gone to Cuba when studying Marxist political economy at the Universidad Autónoma de México.

Almost as soon as Lizette and I met each other's children, we noticed the similarities. And the differences. They were both born in Hollywood hospitals, only a few blocks apart, and though they looked nothing alike, they both had the same beautiful caffè latte skin color.

They also both nearly died before turning two. I was in Seattle with eighteen-month-old Raphael, visiting my mom. Raphael woke up and began to nurse; his lips burned my breast. I took his temperature: 105 degrees. We went in to see the doctor at Group Health in Seattle. Since the fever had gone down with Tylenol, she told me that I probably misread the thermometer, and that she was sure he just had a bad cold. But Raphael's fever continued to go up, and I kept calling. At the end of that day, I spoke with the consulting nurse and asked, "Could you just listen to him? Because he's breathing like he's asleep, but he's awake." She listened and told me that we had to go in right away. In the ER, they took a look at Raphael and rushed us back to the treatment area. The scene quickly escalated. Soon we were under a tent, medicine pumping into my baby, and I was nursing nonstop for three days—engorged like in the early days after his birth. He had croup, which is often characterized by a seal-like barking cough that's usually not dangerous; however, it can quickly take a fatal turn, since it causes swelling, closing up the portion of the airway just below the vocal cords. This can result in a child barely being able to breathe and not getting enough oxygen into his or her blood. Which is what happened to Raphael.

Serena's case also began with a high fever that kept going up, but it took several days to diagnose it as Kawasaki syndrome, a rare and potentially fatal autoimmune disease that can affect blood supply to the heart. As Lizette and I talked about how close we had come to losing our children, we found out that their hospitalizations had occurred at roughly the same ages and that we had both been told we had gotten them there just in time. The near-death experiences of our two children were eerily similar, I realized. I thought of the ER nurse telling me, as I lay under the oxygen tent nursing Raphael, that had I not kept calling back and brought him in, he would be dead.

One summer night in the early months of the relationship, Raphael and Lizette wanted to hang out and watch a movie at her house, while I wanted to go to an art museum opening. Serena, always eager to please at that point, offered to go with me, and Lizette and I agreed to trade kids for the evening. Serena got dressed up and was my "date" to the Norton Simon in Pasadena. We were giddy, in the beginning stages of being enamored with each other, new mother and daughter. We joined the crowd of adults sipping wine and nibbling fancy appetizers from passed trays. I selected a small sandwich for Serena and a glass of wine for myself. We held hands, and I watched the people watching us. This was a grown-up event, and I soaked up the smiles of adults as I strolled hand in hand with my well-behaved apparent daughter and looked at the art. I hadn't gone to any museum openings with Raphael, except in Paris, where the foreignness of it had allowed for some leeway on something that was now often out of his interest zone. *So this is what having a girl is like,* I thought, contrasting it with the strain of having my squirmy eight-year-old boy pulling on me and yelling, "Mom, I want to go!"

Serena and Raphael bonded over the Disney Channel and complaining about school. Serena drew me a diagram of the Disney stars so I would know who was who and each actor's significance: Zac Efron, Miley Cyrus, Corbin Bleu.

Effortlessly I fell for Serena and began to think of her as my daughter. She had grabbed hold of my heart and right away made room for me as another mom. Later she said, "I have a mommy collection, five: my two moms who adopted me, their partners, and my bio mom." (Whom she had never met.) She described it like a doll collection; she took out the ones she wanted to play with and put the others away when she was unhappy with us. I have always pictured this mommy collection in one of those Barbie cases that opens up, and when you realize that you are so done with them, you cut off all the dolls' hair or tear off their heads.

One afternoon, Serena and I got wild rock-star hair and makeup together at Club Libby Lu, a store in the mall where teenagers transformed young girls into mini–glam rockers—and their moms into ridiculous older versions—with sparkly eye shadow and teased hair. Lizette and Raphael had been in the video game store, and when we walked toward them, Raphael looked at Serena with a smile and then at me—in purple glitter lipstick and ratted-up hair—with disbelief and pure horror.

The kids were both about to start third grade. Serena attended Catholic school in Eagle Rock and was intent on being a good girl and pleasing everyone in her path. Her world revolved around being perfect. Since her two moms had split up, Serena went back and forth between their households, spending alternate weeks with each mother. Her moms didn't speak to each other, even when in the same room at a school function. They communicated only in written memos passed back and forth in Serena's backpack.

When Serena and Raphael discussed their visitation situations, Serena would complain bitterly about "the schedule," and Raphael would say, "At least they both want to see you. I don't see my dad much at all. He won't make a schedule."

Raphael had tried, when he was quite young, to get Larry to make a regular schedule. He presented his dad with a giveaway calendar, the kind with insurance or mortuary ads that comes in the mail, and pleaded, "Please, Dad, I need a schedule." But Larry insisted that his job wouldn't permit it. He was employed by a labor union, and I had tried to argue that if you're fighting for better quality of life for families, quality time with your son ought to be a priority. But he said it didn't work that way. And when Raphael got on his "last nerve," his dad stormed out, saying, "I don't have to deal with you. I have union members giving me shit."

Some nights we put on music at Lizette's house—Gorillaz or the Black Eyed Peas—and had a dance party. The kids and I danced together wildly while Lizette watched us, more of a bystander. The big problem was that when Serena went away, she was convinced that the party was continuing without her, which, in a way, it was. Whereas Serena traveled between two houses, Raphael was with me almost all the time. As Raphael and I started spending more and more time with Lizette and Serena's black Labrador, Max, I imagine that Serena felt as if this new faux sibling was encroaching not only on her mom but also on her dog. I later found a rescue dog, whom we named Slurpy II, after my childhood dog, and took her to Lizette's house to be Max's companion—part of our future blended household.

I'd already decided that this was what Raphael and I had been looking for and that I would ask Lizette to marry me. He and I had plans in December to meet my parents in Hawaii, and Lizette had determined that she and Serena would join us. It was then that I might pop the question. I imagined she was the woman I'd summoned up years before to comfort me when I thought I would never have a baby, when I lost pregnancy after pregnancy. I held in place a vision of a calm, loving companion. In my dreams, I had leaned back against her in a forest, our kids dancing around in front of us while she played with my hair.

I went to my good friend María Elena to ask for her blessing, believing this marriage would be different from my first. María Elena had suffered through so many of my dramas and catastrophes, had been on the receiving end of my relentless despair to the point of telling me she couldn't listen anymore. She gave me her blessing and said she would be part of our wedding and prewedding rituals. Later she would ask me, "Why didn't you tell me what was really going on?"

But around Thanksgiving, a month before our planned Hawaii trip, Lizette began to criticize Raphael's behavior. "He's rude to you. I know how that is; Serena used to do that with me when she came back from Vilma's. You have to nip that in the bud. I'll tell you how I did it with Serena."

At first I felt receptive, grateful. Perhaps she could be another adult who would influence Raphael for the better. When Larry got angry and yelled at me while visiting Raphael, sometimes Raphael would come over and hit me. I didn't know what to do to counteract this modeling. So initially I felt maybe this was what it was like to have a supportive partner.

Maybe she could help us. "He's not a bad kid," she told me. This seemed odd. Of course he wasn't bad.

Raphael struggled with anything involving small motor skills and focus. Origami gave him palpitations, but he was fascinated by sports, politics, and history. For him, it wasn't just what Ty Cobb's score was but also the fact that he was a racist.

Serena made a deal with him. She would show Raphael how to make lanyards, and he would teach her history. After a few rough starts, Raphael got through one lanyard. She then asked if he'd like to try an origami crane, but that was just too much for one day.

Raphael's history lesson to Serena began with ancient Greece, and when they got to the American Civil War, Raphael really hit his stride. "Now, when we think about President Lincoln, let's talk about why he really made the decision he did about slavery. What was his thinking? And do you know if he had slaves?" The lecture demanded interaction; Raphael was immersed in the Socratic method. After a couple of hours, Serena was exhausted.

The four of us went to Hawaii as planned and stayed in a condo next to my parents. Raphael and I flew in first. When Serena and Lizette arrived, I was relieved and happy to see them, but also distressed over a work issue: I had just found out I lost a major contract to a colleague whom I had had a falling out with, and financially, the loss would have a big impact. I woke to the roar of the ocean and a strong wind, a storm. The noise matched my fear about economic survival. But then I felt a warm breeze caress me with peacefulness as I realized I'd never again have to face life alone. I had gotten to enjoy the one-on-one intensity of being a single mom, but now I planned to have the big, happy, overflowing family. The *Yours, Mine, and Ours.*

The next night, we mixed exotic drinks with little umbrellas for my parents, and they watched Serena and Raphael while Lizette and I went out to dinner. As we were walking along the beach, I pulled her close and said, "Sit down here for a moment." I had spent lots of time trying to figure out the best scenario for proposing to Lizette and had hidden our rings in a little velvet bag in my pocket. We sat on a smooth rock by the water. "I've thought about it, and I love you and Serena. Will you be my wife, my life partner? I want to spend the second half of our lives together. To raise our children together."

"Yes, yes, I want all that." I took out the rings I had gotten for us from an Israeli jeweler, hammered silver stripes alternating with gold. She wasn't someone who spent a lot of time expressing her feelings out loud, but the "yes" was loud and clear, enunciated with a kiss and a hug.

The next day, as we set out for the Halaeakalā volcano, Serena cried hysterically, convinced that her "Mama Lizette" was being stolen from her, that she would be displaced by Raphael—even though we had decided to wait a bit to tell them we planned to marry. Lizette insisted to Serena that she had to accept we were together. A few days later, we were driving to pick up food. The kids were sitting in the back, and Raphael had begun to sing a happy-sounding song. Serena was annoyed and told him to stop. So he sang louder. It was as if a match lit the car on fire as Lizette turned abruptly around and yelled, "You heard her, Raphael! Stop it!" My first reaction was one of trauma. I rolled down the window, stuck my head out, and screamed. It was the beginning of a cycle of reactions that would repeat itself over and over again for the next few years: Lizette exploding at Raphael, me going into fight-or-flight mode, and the kids staring at us, or at each other, or joining in the crying and the yelling. Debris flying out in different directions. Road debris can kill you, and our family was always running into this foreign matter, more and more damage sustained.

Back home, the tension would build up whenever Serena got ready to go to her other mom's house and when she first returned to us. Serena always came back mad and frequently told Raphael, "My Mama Vilma said something about you."

"What?" Raphael demanded.

"You need therapy!" Serena's other mom and her partner were both therapists. Serena usually adjusted a few hours after returning, but she still felt left out of the group—Lizette, Raphael, and me, who were around one another all the time and seemed to be getting along great. If we all came to pick her up together, Serena's first feeling seemed to be one of panic, imagining herself replaced by my son. Though we were excited to see her, she was consumed with jealousy.

Raphael often still crawled into bed with me. After Lizette began to stay with us more regularly, I sensed her exasperation with Raphael's presence in the bedroom, but Raphael was adamant about sleeping in my room. Sometimes I made him remain in his own room, and then he would wet his bed. He wouldn't get up to go to the bathroom because he was afraid of the dark. His room had a door to the outside, and he even designed an elaborate alarm system with a hammer hanging over his dresser and a rubber band that would activate it if an intruder stepped just so, warning him.

One day Lizette became incensed that the dogs had escaped. "Who let the fucking dogs out?" she yelled at the children. Eventually we found them, and I took the kids to my house while she cooled down. Raphael and Serena walked around talking quietly, intimate co-conspirators. They decided they would prepare a meal for their moms that would bring us back together. "I know," Serena said. "Let's make a big salad for my mommy Lizette." (She was a vegetarian.)

"And let's cook chicken for my mom," Raphael said. (I often cooked chicken.) Even as our arguments continued to escalate, the kids were pushing us to move in together. On nights when things were going well, they never wanted to go back to their own houses, and sometimes we'd trade kids, at least until one or both wanted to go home in the middle of the night. Other times, we just had one big slumber party.

In a collage art class I took with my older sister, a vision of a blended family began to emerge. Never having been able to draw concrete objects or anything other than stick people, I couldn't sketch a blender. But armed with images from magazines, I found that wasn't an issue—I could create a visual of the complexity of my dream. What I depicted were body parts, bits and pieces of our kids' psyches, a crushed-up dream and a chopped-up nightmare, a grating grinding together of unlikely ingredients all but breaking the blender and resulting in an undefined, muddled, mud-like color, like what Raphael and I created in our art projects by mixing too many colors. But in my imagination and in my collage, I saw beauty in the messiness of our family.

When the kids were around ten, about two years into our relationship and shortly before our wedding, we all began living together in my 900-square-foot house. The first night Raphael wanted to sleep on the floor in the long master bedroom, which also contained a space for Serena. He didn't want to be banished to his own room. "You see," I said to Lizette, "we could all live easily in less than 900 square feet on one side of the house."

"Just wait," she told me.

Serena was sprouting small breasts that soon became big enough to warrant a training bra. She was exuding large amounts of body odor, and Lizette was constantly reminding her to use deodorant.

Serena's Catholic school had a comprehensive sex education program, perhaps in response to the church's sex abuse scandals. Sex education was not taught at Raphael's charter school. By ten, he was in need of more information than what I'd provided thus far. So one day I read to him from a primer on boys' development, which I hadn't prescreened, and—boom—it went right into sexual intercourse, almost in the first paragraph.

Raphael asked, "Mommy, why does it do that?" I looked down at what he was pointing to: he had an erection.

"Hmm, sweetie, let's read on . . . 'The blood rushes to the . . .'" I read, stumbling for the right explanation in the next paragraph.

The following day we picked up Serena from her other mom's house, and I heard Raphael and her discussing their mutual experiences with sex education. "Did you hear? So gross!" Serena said.

"I thought people were really just sleeping together when they said that." Raphael sounded disgusted.

Lizette continued to erupt with anger, and I continued to either panic and run or stay and go nuts. Once I even threatened to jump off the balcony. Or I would just wail, hanging onto her or her car, begging for understanding, for compassion, for her to see the amazingness of Raphael, how lucky we all were to be together. As her anger upped, so did my "crazy" — my MO when faced with predictably unpredictable rage. Other times, I was calm, like a Stepford Wife, explaining how I thought we could live happily ever after — if her rage would stop. A repeat performance from my last marriage.

That wasn't the only thing that Raphael's dad and stepmom-to-be had in common. I used to tease Raphael that he had a full set of working eyes between the two of them, since his father and Lizette each had vision in only one eye. As a teenager Larry had suffered a detached retina, which possibly could have been saved if he hadn't been contending with the poor quality of the LA County hospital into which he was admitted. Raphael often would speak wistfully, sorrowfully, about his dad's pain: a lost mom and a lost eye. (Later Larry got an artificial eye that he could take out, and Raphael would ask him to demonstrate for his classmates.) Lizette had a congenital eye problem. The first time I met her I had to circle back and ask her about her eye, because it gave her an odd affect — kind of like she was looking away or the eye was fading out. So his dad and stepmom had only one full set of working eyes between them. And a lot of bitterness and anger ready to fly out. That similarity didn't escape Raphael when Lizette blew up one time in Las Vegas, where we'd gone to visit her parents. He looked at her, really taking in the explosion, and said, with a not-so-amused smile frozen on his face, "Now you sound just like my dad."

At age eleven Serena's hormones seemed to really kick in. She started getting pubic hair and stopped running naked into our room. She also threw off her mantle of obedient Catholic girl. "I don't know which Serena to expect when I come in," Raphael said. But her overt mood swings were easier for him to deal with than her silent treatments.

Serena was not the only one being attacked by hormones. With two moms moving into our upper forties, the Bermuda Triangle of perimenopause, Raphael was trapped in the House of Hormones.

Plus it turned out that Lizette had a deep-seated anger toward her brother—and, therefore, boys in general—not to mention a host of other issues fueling her uncontrollable rage, all translating into her using Raphael as her scapegoat.

One night Serena said, "I don't know, maybe the problem is that you guys are Jewish, and he's Black, and I'm just not used to that kind of thing." That was simply too much for Raphael. He cried out, "What is it with you guys? Because I'm Black? Because I'm a boy? What is it? Why don't you like me?"

Around that time Raphael's liberal charter school was turning a blind eye to the homophobic taunting that mirrored the country's culture wars over same-sex marriage. The white administrators were convinced that they were being tolerant of a small group of Black families who were evangelical Christian and antigay, as if homophobia was an inherent part of African American culture—an idea that other Black and mixed-race families found offensive. Regardless, Raphael got a clear message that his family was not "normal." The antigay messages came at him through the other children: "That's okay if you come to school, but just don't be talking about the two-mom thing here." And Raphael found no sanctuary from the bullying when he came home, where a different type of war was being waged as his stepmom raged intermittently against his boy-ness. I fought at school and I fought at home to protect Raphael. Desperately. But unsuccessfully.

We hired a contractor to remodel Lizette's house—we called it "the big house"—and she and I spent a lot of time dragging the kids around while we painstakingly picked out Spanish tiles and soapstone counters. We were fortunate enough to have accumulated equity in both our homes, and the real estate market was booming, as was my business. A friend volunteered to be our interior designer, and I began to feel as if I might have my chance to remodel a kitchen, picking out custom colors and hand-painted floor tiles, a role I never got to play as a low-income single mom. Then the contractor began to show fault lines in his ability to handle a job that size. The money kept flowing out, the house was all torn up, and things in our family, along with the remodel, were going south—as Lizette also began to fall apart. When she wasn't silent, withdrawn, and in a dense state of depression, she was sullen, angry, explosive. After one episode she tried to explain the flying off the handle and dark moods to the kids, saying, "I have a disease. It's called depression. I'm trying to get help. I'm talking to a therapist, taking medicine. The remodel is so stressful."

In my desire to fix whatever I could, I offered to take out all of my equity (we'd already used some of hers) to finish the remodel on her house. I saw it as one big kibbutz: "Take what you need; give what you can." When money worries surface, I tend to be as generous as possible. Between my Russian revolutionary grandfather, my socialist Jewish summer camp, and my own family's tendency to band together in times of crisis, I come from a quasi-socialist ideology. And I figured that we would be fortunate to have one big home, even if we had to get rid of mine. We were planning a wedding in Canada, where same-sex marriage was legal (it was not yet in the United States), and I was still convinced that adopting a toddler was a great idea. Both Raphael and I had wished for another baby in our family. Serena came back from her other house reporting that Vilma and Mary were planning to have a baby, and Raphael questioned her: "How old is Mary? She might have a lot of miscarriages like my mom."

Raphael was navigating the strange period of preadolescence to adolescence—that sweet balance between child and teenager—on his way to manhood. At thirteen you are supposed to become a man—bar mitzvah time. I had told Raphael he wouldn't be a man until he did his own laundry (which he started doing before thirteen, after I accidentally washed his iPod).

Right before we got married, we learned that Lizette—a vegetarian for many years—was dangerously anemic, and she began to eat meat. Supposedly, this anemia could cause wild mood swings. I hung onto this diagnosis, wanting to believe that my desire for happy chaos, family harmony, and a safe haven was not just a cruel parody of the frightening reality in which we actually lived.

In a pre-Cosby-scandal world, Raphael wished for nothing more than to live in a family like the Huxtables, with full bio siblings and two middle-class African American parents who were happily married to each other. He struggled in school and in sports and wanted to be "normal" like his Black classmates, who played football, got good grades, and lived in intact heterosexual families. Being a disorganized, dreamy, awkward Afro-Jew with poor handwriting, a stepsister, and a lesbian mother and stepmom did not win him any points. About five years later, as reflected in the Supreme Court's decision on June 26, 2013, the majority of Americans would shift toward support of same-sex marriage. In that time, Raphael grew from a self-conscious preteen to a seventeen-year-old who proudly called himself an Afro-Jew and was at ease with having a lesbian mother.

At seventeen, Raphael posted as his Facebook status, "Don't hide behind the Constitution or the Bible. If you're against gay marriage, just be honest. Put a scarlet 'H' on your shirt and say, 'I'm a homophobe!'"

A short debate would follow among his friends, with the majority liking his post. But when he was younger, the message Raphael heard in his school was that having a queer mom was worse than being sold for crack by a straight mom. And society's disapproval was echoed in the laws that discriminated against gay marriage. It would also have been illegal for me to marry Raphael's father prior to 1967, when the US Supreme Court unanimously ruled that state bans on interracial marriage violated the Constitution.

Our wedding took place on Salt Spring Island in British Columbia. A videographer followed us around and recorded the beautiful things our family and friends had to say. (Mine, anyway—none of Lizette's attended.) The rituals, the food, the music, the vows, Raphael running out in the middle of the ceremony saying, "I have to pee!" and coming back to stand under the rainbow chuppah with us. We spoke of the importance of community and family. Guests said it was the most meaningful ceremony they'd attended and left feeling that the world was a better place. But when I look back, I see that I was headed into another marriage in which I sought to build a precious holy shelter for our family while living in a secret tunnel of hell.

Nine months later we took a cruise for LGBT families put on by Rosie O'Donnell, her wife, and their kids—our family honeymoon. And we began living in our long-awaited remodeled family home.

The kids had spent a long time thinking about how they would decorate their rooms when we moved into the big house. From ages eight to twelve, boys' interests shift from puppy dogs to war video games to Beyoncé. That transition was a collage of sorts, what you saw decorating their walls. Raphael's room was sweet and loving, angry and remote. For his walls he chose dark blue, gray, and maroon stripes, on which he hung his pictures of huskies, Jackie Robinson, and Halo Wars. His bed and curtains were New Orleans Saints decor, black and gold. Serena chose bright tropical colors—to which Lizette had originally objected—that clashed but blended. There were pictures everywhere of teen stars, puppies, and a Happy Bunny sign on her door that said, "Trespassers will be butchered." A hammock full of stuffed animals hung over her bookcase. Everything was exactly in its place. No matter where we went or for how long, Serena always set up her spot, putting out her little objects and putting away her neatly folded clothes. Sometimes when we went on trips, she tried to show Raphael how to do this. He would get interested in her organizing methods for a while, but it never lasted. Or he'd try to get her to do it for him.

The day before Raphael was to have a slumber party, he wrote out a sign slowly, so it was legible, despite his awkward writing: "Welcome, Come In, 50 cents to enter, Girls are Free." Lizette was working downstairs, silent. Hot fumes seemed to emanate from her, as they often did when she receded into a dark place. She was bolting the bookcases to the wall and ceiling so they wouldn't crush Raphael's friends in the event of an earthquake. Ten adolescent boys were coming over, and for weeks I had wanted to get the furniture bolted in the room where they would be sleeping. Lizette had insisted she'd do it, and now that she'd finally gotten started, she was making great efforts to show how pressured and resentful she was. Seething, she came upstairs, anger flowing from her pores like smoke from a volcano. On her way down she saw the writing on Raphael's door. Lizette seemed to fly into the air like the Wicked Witch of the West, ripping the paper with Raphael's crooked lettering off his door and screaming. We weren't sure what she was saying. She seemed to be accusing my eleven-year-old son of being an "exploitative misogynist." Raphael was whimpering, "I didn't mean anything wrong . . . please, please!" Later Lizette apologized, but the damage was done. The cyclone followed by the apology had become a pattern. Once, after watching a film on the Holocaust, Raphael told me, "They said, 'Never again,' but now we have Darfur. Lizette is like that. She says, 'Sorry, it won't happen again,' but it just keeps happening."

♦

After dragging the kids along for more than a year to purchase those tiles and select those paint colors, after they'd witnessed our anger and desperation as the remodeling costs escalated into what would become obscene amounts of money, we were now living there. We woke each morning to the soothing tea-green color of the bedroom with the Spanish-tiled Jacuzzi bath and the Mexican brightly painted hers-and-hers washbasins, the sun coming up over the hills beneath the otherworldly tropical view from our deck. I had imagined preparing our meals on the soapstone counters we'd picked out in San Diego in the kitchen with the violet-blue faux finish Lizette had painted and the tiled Mexican pueblo scene with the big lake. It was hard for me to understand how Lizette could persevere in such depression, such darkness. Sure, our kids could be exhausting, but I was so grateful to have them both in our lives. For a while, I had convinced myself that things looked so promising. My business was booming. A company I helped start got funded a second round, making me the darling of the venture capitalist community. Lizette held a stable job with an entertainment company, which came with the fancy Motion Picture Industry Health Plan. But less than four months after we moved into the big remodeled house, it all fell apart.

One evening, Lizette got angry at Raphael for something. Then angry at me for playing my comfort song too loud: "Ooh-oo child, / Things are gonna get easier." Then even angrier at me for cooking my comfort food: chicken and pork adobo, one of the first meals I prepared in the remodeled kitchen. She grabbed my neck and pushed me against a hot rice cooker. Raphael walked in and saw her choking me, my back arched against the cooker.

She let go and stormed out of the kitchen. I snatched my purse and keys to flee somewhere with my son. But before we could leave, Lizette came back and chased us around the house shouting, "Your mom just wants to be with a man. She wants to be back with Henry."

"No," Raphael insisted, "she just wants to be a single mom again." He faced her and shouted, "Look, just leave my mom alone!" And he threw his Pokémon cards at her.

"Pick those up," Lizette ordered.

I wanted to yell, "Don't you touch him! Raphael, you don't have to do anything." But instead I stayed frozen, mute.

Later I felt ashamed because I'd said nothing. I had just wanted to get out of there before there was more violence. I had tried to make everything okay, tried to keep our family from breaking up, tried not to fail again. But I couldn't keep this flailing family together anymore.

Raphael and I fled for the weekend but returned to stay in the house while I paid for Lizette to live in expensive temporary housing. She agreed to this initially as I imagined she felt remorse and hoped that we might reconcile. Foolishly, Raphael and I believed we could keep the rest of the family together, that if he and I remained temporarily in the big house, Serena would come stay with us. And I wasn't yet sure where we would go instead; our old house was rented out, and I'd taken out the equity to remodel the house we were in, drastically raising the mortgage.

It took at least a few weeks for Raphael to understand that he wouldn't get to "keep his stepsister" and still lose the angry stepmom. The one who raged at him and couldn't seem to be content with our blended family. Furious with the decisions the adults brought into his life, Raphael threw our wedding pictures off the deck. "See this? All broken. Like my heart," he declared. "You made two huge mistakes: first my dad, then Lizette." His dad he loved regardless of the rage, but he'd felt for some time that his stepmom was crazy. His stepsister, though, Raphael missed desperately.

When Raphael's dad came to visit, I told Larry that I felt like a failure. "Am I really so bad that I caused this to happen to both of my marriages?"

"No," he said. "The problem isn't about you being so bad, it's about you being too good." He was so kind that day, my son's dad.

The real estate crash, the recession, attorney's fees, and our disintegrated family—all left me floundering, bereft of money and dreams.

The reserve I'd saved for emergencies, my retirement, and Raphael's college, the equity in our "little house," all gone. So were my plans to live out my life in our newly created family of two moms, Jewish and Cuban; our faux twins, Afro-Jewish and Mexican-American; and the third child I had hoped we'd adopt. When my attorney showed me that Lizette had forged checks in an attempt to show that I did not pay for the rest of the remodel, I was confounded as to how to mourn someone whom I no longer recognized.

Raphael and I lived in a ghost house. In what appeared to be a morbid post-stepdaughter exhibit, we preserved everything in Serena's room, exactly as she had left it: the door with the Happy Bunny "Trespassers will be butchered" sign, walls covered with pictures of puppies and Disney Channel movie stars. We knew we'd have to go soon too. Raphael said that he was digging a hole in the closet of the house that would cause it all to collapse.

At first we were still able to arrange for Serena to come visit. She sometimes sobbed, begging to stay with us. Once she lashed out at Raphael, yelling, "You fuckin' stole my house!" Soon Lizette began to prevent Serena from seeing us. But Serena's other mom, Vilma, reached out to me and asked if I intended to stay in her daughter's life. "Serena is close to you," she said, "and she's already had so many losses." I told her that Serena was like a daughter to me. Over the years my relationship with Vilma would evolve into a coparenting of sorts, though I was clearly the noncustodial parent. When Lizette would keep Serena from speaking with me, Vilma would let me know how she was doing. But things would never be the same. Serena no longer lived with us, and our relationship became tenuous.

Though I continued to call her my daughter and she called me her mom, I was never far from feeling her absence. I covered that void with resentment and the bravery of surviving—but over time I was forced to acknowledge the reality of losing Serena, my second child.

♦

After over a year in limbo and no sign of ever getting back any of the equity I'd put into the big house, it was time to make a move. Raphael came back from visiting relatives in Palmdale, an inland city in the Antelope Valley, raving about the size of the homes there and the square footage you could get for a low price. Other times he liked the idea of living in urban Echo Park in the hilltops with views, but when I brought home a flyer for a condo, he railed against the high cost of square footage there. Sometimes he just wanted to go back to the little house we still owned in Pasadena, but it was still occupied by tenants and held the memory of failure. He was twelve years old. He was looking for home.

Love in the Time of Foreclosures

"Did I tell you I'm in love with your soul?"

It was a text from our leasing agent, Jessica. Picture pretty, Cubana Mexicana, always made-up and buttoned-up. Over the phone she used a bright and bouncy realtor voice that I soon learned hid both her sadness and her passion. She was thirty-six; I was almost fifty. She was a homecoming queen; I was a hippie girl.

Without thinking, I texted back immediately: "I don't know what that means, but I can't stop thinking about you."

When I met her with my almost-thirteen-year-old son, he begged her, "Please rent us this place; my mom and I *really* need to know where we're gonna live."

The Pasadena condo she showed us felt safe and spacious—soothing sage tones, empty but full of promise, a fresh start. Maybe we'd buy the condo and never have to move again. It was located within walking distance of everything we needed, including my office, the Metro, three movie theaters, and one of the city's last standing and most inviting independent bookstores, Vroman's. It felt like a change, somehow more urban than Lizette's neighborhood. We were gradually moving south, first from northwest Pasadena, then from northeast Los Angeles.

We were leaving the family home in the hills of Glassell Park—near Glendale, Eagle Rock, and Highland Park, parts of town that would burst forth in gentrified hipster glory about eight years after we decamped from the embattled big house. Back then, it was time to find a place to land after more than a year of paying for Lizette to stay somewhere else, with no resolution in sight.

♦

When Jessica revealed that the last occupant of the condo had been engaged, then had gone away for a weekend and committed suicide, I vowed to change the condo's karma. *This place could be our safe refuge*, I thought. As we healed from my failed marriage, we'd put the ghost of the owners' unhappy daughter to rest. I had just been torn apart from my own daughter, Serena—the scorched-earth effect of our unblended family. Without her, I felt as if my arm had been cut off. And Raphael still missed his sister.

Jessica called with good news: "It's yours!" I sent her flowers.

Although a spark of flirtation seemed to have infused our texts, the flowers were strictly a gesture of gratitude; I thought I was dealing with a straight girl. I was stunned when I got her text back about my soul.

She invited me to lunch at a nearby restaurant along with her visiting grandmother and great-aunt. I was very self-conscious with them since I was wearing a shirt that revealed lot of cleavage, something I seemed to have acquired more of during perimenopause. When we headed for the dessert bar, she asked me if I liked to go to gay bars and said that she went there with her gay guy friends.

Before I moved into the condo, Jessica and I decided to go out. I left my son with his babysitter and her toddler son. She was the nineteen-year-old mother who Raphael complained was taking over the motherly duties that I should have been carrying out. Her family dramas had started to become his, but I figured perhaps that was a good distraction from ours. I arranged for him to spend the night, just in case I was late coming back. Jessica and I met in the empty condo in the early evening. She suggested that we stay there so neither of us had to drink and drive. It felt odd to be there; I was thinking that a first date—if that was what it was— should be somewhere romantic. We both seemed to know we wanted something. I believed alcohol might loosen us up, but we didn't drink anything. She had a blanket from her car. In the nighttime the space felt less like a refuge and more just chilly, vacant, even lonely. Not like a future family home for Raphael and me, so I decided not to think about that.

She turned on the gas fireplace and sat beside me.

"So what do you want to know about me?" Jessica said, before proceeding in a steady, monotone stream: "Relationships aren't easy for me. I was sexually abused by my grandfather from age seven to twelve. My first relationship was with a woman when I was eighteen. I was crazy about her, but when I returned from a trip to Spain, my feelings were gone. My boyfriend is an older man from Zimbabwe. I've been living with him since I was nineteen."

Maybe she is almost done with him, I thought. Then she added, "I'll never leave him."

I wanted to touch her. Badly. I reached out, almost stroking her face.

Jessica said, "I think we could be friends for a long time, so maybe we shouldn't do anything."

"But don't you want to?" I asked. She looked at me. Surprising myself, I leaned over and kissed her. We caressed faces . . . grabbed hair . . . I loved her curves, the compactness of her body on top of me, and her dark, curly hair falling all over my face.

Jessica had opened the door to a pit, and I jumped right in—falling into the craziness of doomed relationships again, convinced she would make up for all that I'd lost.

"Let's just have fun," she said. "No one can know." That hurt, but I didn't want my son to know either. I'd promised it would be just the two of us until he was eighteen. I added only that we might need another person to help out with the rent at some point, but there would be no more stepmothers. Or stepfathers.

Jessica's office was across from the condo. It was a small office, which would later close, on a little street close to the grander Lake Avenue, which I still pass frequently. Years later, I would see the gated condo and remember sitting there on the stoop with her, grabbing a few minutes before Raphael came out to see what was taking so long. When we first moved in, the condo complex looked inviting with its little courtyard, outward-facing doorways, and Spanish-tiled central fountain, which lulled Raphael to sleep at night. I imagined a co-op of sorts, but it turned out to be nothing like that. The day we moved in, we set out our little Mexican patio table in front, just as the neighbor had set hers out, but she contacted the realtor to tell her we weren't allowed; only hers, which was "grandfathered in," could be there. From that day forward, the neighbor seemed to want us out. She began to complain of noise when we went up and down our stairs. I worried about having to move . . . again. Jessica said that she had told her Zimbabwe boyfriend about Raphael and me. "I asked him if you and Raphael might live with us in our house if things got worse with the neighbor, and he seemed open to that." I was speechless.

Every night after our first time together, Jessica texted, "*Te quiero. Te amo. Te necesito. No me dejes.*"

I assured her I loved her and needed her, too. "*Duerme con los angelitos.* Sweet dreams." At night, it was the last thing we told each other.

We sent each other romantic songs. She wrote me love notes; she begged me to rip off her shirt and push her against the bathroom wall in her realty office. We were on fire. Magnetic. Inseparable. Even when we couldn't be together, when I was with Raphael or Jessica had some kind of commitment, we were in constant contact by text. Raphael informed me that I was appropriating his generation with my continual texting. I didn't tell Raphael that I was tumbling into a relationship, but he acted fidgety and suspicious around Jessica. When she noticed his dark looks at her as he glanced back and forth between us, she said that she wanted to run away. Fast. I sat down at night with Raphael and again assured him that it would be just the two of us. I couldn't guarantee I wouldn't ever be in a relationship, but she wouldn't live with us. "How about with a man?" he asked.

I said, "No, no one will live with us. No more stepparents."

One day I poked around in a part of the bathroom medicine cabinet I hadn't seen before and found a hair, black and long. I knew it had to be from the owner's daughter, the one who had killed herself. And that's when I began to wonder. What had caused her so much pain that she saw no other way out? Could I ever feel that way? It was creepy, but I was determined to make this place one of refuge and heal the grief—mine and theirs. Many months later, when I went to the bathroom to sob away from Raphael, I felt like I was letting them down—the spirit of the daughter and her grieving parents.

Just as I had always fantasized, though it was only December and we'd only just moved in, I was already making plans for the summer to attend Outfest, the LGBTQ film festival, with arm candy—a hot girlfriend who was hot for me. Jessica was more beautiful than any woman I'd ever been with. She was my fantasy: tough as nails but with *tacones*, high heels, feminine to the max but not afraid to get dirty. When I almost burned down the condo by leaving a candle lit, she jumped up onto the counter in her heels and offered reassurance while she scrubbed the scorched wall.

Jessica signed her love notes, "*Tu chiquita.*" I sometimes signed, "*Tu vieja.*" One time, she looked at the wrinkles between my eyes. "Is this what people look like when they're fifty?" she had said as she applied my eye shadow. I'd started wearing makeup again; she seemed to like it. She pampered me, bathed me, washed my hair.

Even Japanese tourists stopped to gawk at us, snapping a picture outside a shopping mall where we were sitting one day. Jessica held my face with one hand, intently applying new makeup she was trying out on me. What were they saying about us in Japanese, I wondered? Maybe, "Aren't they sweet? Look—two California lesbians."

Jessica adored me, showered me with *besitos*—little kisses—but said we couldn't be together because of my son. She'd want me all to herself but wouldn't let me neglect him the way her mom had neglected her. I didn't plan to do that, but I had been relegating more of Raphael's care to a series of young women who substituted for me when I was not available. The latest one was skeptical of my new relationship, but she was a tutor, a mentor, a buddy of sorts for Raphael when I couldn't be.

As Raphael prepared for his bar mitzvah in May, we discussed what trust and vulnerability meant to us. I said to Raphael, "Well, perhaps you and I open our hearts too easily. We get hurt."

He responded, "Mom, you should open your heart again. If you don't, you'll miss out on a lot in the world." And I did open my heart up. Sometimes Raphael heard me sobbing; I locked myself in my bathroom. That small condo had three bathrooms! He banged on the door; the less present I was, the more fearful and demanding he was.

♦

I told Jessica, "If you're really in love with my soul, you should know that it's the soul of a mother." She claimed the soul she loved was me alone. Jessica's Zimbabwean boyfriend had a teenage daughter, but she was not interested in being a stepmom to her. Her boyfriend had not told her about his daughter until several years into their relationship. I couldn't stop thinking about my own stepdaughter; Serena was still a phantom limb. I missed her presence. I could still feel her hand in mine from years ago, the fierceness of our bond.

When you love someone like that, a visceral memory is imprinted upon your soul. You recall everything about her: the particular glowing tint of her skin, the concentrated line in her brow, the warm, sleepy look when she first woke up. Years later, I can't remember the color of toothbrush I'm using some mornings, but I still recollect the soft, downy hair on Serena's neck and how she curled up at night next to me, gently hugging me, the light and steady sweet breath on my neck as she lay beside me. How soundly she slept, difficult to wake once she fell into that deep sleep.

I learned from Serena's other mother, Vilma, that Serena had started to cut and was admitted on a seventy-two-hour psych hold because of suicidal thoughts. Jessica urged me to let Serena go. "You don't need any more problems," she said.

♦

You might wonder why I didn't run away from this doomed love. And yet there were times when I was so desperate for Jessica's love that I wished my son was already grown and gone—something I never thought I'd feel. When my son made plans to attend President Barack Obama's inauguration with his dad, Jessica said she would take me to Hawaii. Before we left, I accidentally met her live-in boyfriend, and reality intruded. He shook my hand and said, "Hey, I've heard a lot about you and your son, Raphael."

That night, I told Jessica that we couldn't be in a relationship anymore.

It seemed only right to tell her before she took me to Hawaii. But we went anyway.

On Kauai, we danced in our hotel room while watching the new first couple at the inaugural ball. Jessica decided to get drunk. After half a glass of wine, she looked less buttoned-up. She emptied the bottle and looked positively reckless—wild, snarling, yet bereft, like she was ready to wail and make passionate love to me at the same time.

We came back home, and Jessica insisted that it was impossible to be "just friends." I felt adored . . . yet desperately alone. She returned to her big house with her boyfriend, and I felt like we had discovered something precious out of the wreckage of my life, but it slipped through my fingers as we went back to our real lives.

I explained to Jessica that when we met, I had thought I was at bottom—alone, broke, almost fifty. When I was going out of my mind with legal documents for loan modification, dissolution of domestic partnership, and—the ultimate defeat—bankruptcy, Jessica was there to comfort me.

Jessica was having financial struggles too. Although she helped others get loan modifications, she couldn't help herself. "It's just bad timing for us," she said. She often spoke to me about why "it" might not work out for us. Finances, my teenage son, her fear that our love might vanish at any moment. My age.

Safe and cherished but in danger and desperately alone is how I felt with Jessica—a potent and addictive combination. "I'll be there for you always. We'll be together. Just be patient," she had soothed me. And later, "I just don't know why love goes away."

In Jessica I saw a miracle that I had hoped would save me from the depths of despair and make all the losses okay. She told me that she'd felt dead for years. "I'd always fantasized about someone like you, rescuing me from my life. You came along, and, dammit, now I can't quit you."

I still held out hope that we would each go off and fix our lives, then come back together. But, like the California real estate market, I hadn't hit bottom yet.

My friend from the Bay Area visited; her teenage son was impressed. "Wow, Carla has a *hot* girlfriend!" He also observed, "Carla's too skinny now." I just kept losing weight. Food made me nauseous.

When Jessica did fall asleep briefly while with me, she liked to sleep on top of me. One night, apart, we dreamed the same dream . . . about sleeping together, her on top. We had only been able to spend all night together during the time we were in Hawaii. Back home, she'd always insist that she had to return to her house with her boyfriend before the end of the night.

Finally, she told me what I'd longed to hear: "Ok, I'm going to stay with you. All night." She said she'd go back in the morning and tell her boyfriend that she was gay and didn't want to be with him anymore. I felt like I was saved. I also felt nervous—it was a lot of responsibility. And what about my son?

In the morning Jessica went home and told the boyfriend. When I finally spoke with her, she said things were tense at home. "He read scriptures to me and said that if I chose you, he'd take the house." She had put the house in his name a long time ago, although it had been bought with her down payment. He said that he would kick her out along with her mom, her grandma, and her three dogs. That same day she came out to her mom. Jessica also told her about the incest. It turns out that her mom had known about the incest but didn't want to talk about it.

Later she wrote to the boyfriend, "Ever since I was little and my grandfather told me to be a good girl while he raped me, I've tried to please my family. I am in love with Carla. But I will probably stay with you forever since I don't want to disappoint them."

Jessica had tried to break up with him before they even moved in together, over fifteen years earlier. "He threatened to kill himself, " she remembered. "Sometimes, I'd just lie there and count while he pounded away on top of me, just go somewhere else." But she couldn't bring herself to leave. Being a good girl meant staying. She was used to him, she said. He took care of her mother and grandmother and sometimes her sister and nephew. He washed their cars, bought their groceries, and cooked their meals. And now that they finally had gotten over her living with an African man who was so much older than her, they were crazy about him, she said.

Where is the rage? I wondered. Now, I have realized that rage can find all sorts of routes to take, deforming itself into entirely different shapes.

Jessica couldn't bring herself to move out but informed me she had moved downstairs. One day when I was at her house, I found her blow-up mattress gone from the room where she claimed she was sleeping. Later, she said that she was not sure why she had moved back upstairs. "Please don't leave me," she begged. But she wouldn't leave him. "I'm stuck," she said.

Another time, we visited a condo in the same complex where I lived, one that had been foreclosed. It looked like the last inhabitants just ran out, leaving the toilet paper unraveled, a single sock, a wrinkled dress shirt on the doorknob, unwashed dishes—all the flotsam and jetsam of a life in desperation. *But what happened?* I wondered. Like our condo owners' daughter who had committed suicide, like my own unblended family, how did their lives change so drastically?

Later that summer I went with Jessica, María Elena, and Raphael to see Al Green at the LA County Fairgrounds in Pomona. "Let's Stay Together" seemed meant for Jessica and me. On the way home, we dropped her off at her big house in Sierra Madre. "Who does she live with here?" asked Raphael, dumbfounded. When I said that she lived with her grandma (when she visited from Mexico), her mom, and her "ex-" boyfriend, he just said, "That's so lame." I knew that I didn't want him to have our relationship as an example.

"Girlfriend, I'm worried about you and what's happening to you in this relationship," María Elena told me later.

I decided that I didn't want my son to see me so unhappy again. I sent him to his dad's for a week while I stayed in bed crying, unable to eat. I believed that this depth of sorrow was from Jessica, but it really came from loss piled upon loss, starting long before she came into my life. She was just the catalyst. I'd heard of mothers who couldn't get out of bed, but I never had imagined being one of them. Now that Raphael was away, I could stop functioning as a mother, temporarily.

Jessica used her rental agent's key to let herself in. She came upstairs and pulled me up out of bed. "You have to let me go; I'm not healthy," she said while simultaneously begging me not to leave her.

Finally, I pushed her away. "I'm sorry, I just can't do tragic love." I had to get out of bed, and I couldn't depend on her to drag me out. I was dazed and heartsick, but I was realizing that she was not the way up.

My son came back home and started doing the cooking. He served me a hot banana-nut muffin with cinnamon, butter, and brown sugar melted inside, and my appetite began to come back. I did the dishes listening to "Here Comes the Sun," and I began to see a glimmer of hope. *While this wasn't the life I had planned, it could work*, I thought.

My family and close friends helped me to pull myself up, and little by little I realized I was going to survive.

A year after we'd rented the condo, when Raphael was ready to start high school, we moved into a smaller apartment in South Pasadena. The beautiful manager brought me homemade brownies. She fit my fantasy: sexy but maternal, wore high heels as she cut the banana trees around the complex with a machete. My son looked at us and said, "Mom, don't even go there."

The Year of Eating Banana Splits

Food Makes Me Sick

Between the ages of thirty and fifty, I couldn't eat when I was unhappy. Anything but fruit and yogurt smoothies and chocolate malts would turn my stomach and make me feel as if I was cramming Cancun cockroaches down my throat. Those smoothies were the only thing I could shuttle down my digestive system during periods of cranked-up stress and anxiety.

Food, eating, and cooking were things I associated solely with happiness. For the most part, hunger for me meant that I felt happy. I'd lose my appetite and then lose weight, sometimes a lot, when I was unhappy. Or at least that is how things used to be. Before I hit those changeling fifties—moving into menopause. I found out just how intractable that middle bulge can be, when it is no longer vanquished by an infusion of stress.

But It Wasn't Always So

My eighty-nine-year-old grandma once said this: "I'm almost blind. I can't walk. I can't hear. But I just made a plate of raspberry blintzes, and I'm feeling pretty good. Come on over!"

She loved to feed us, though she did sometimes try to feed my sister Sheli while at the same time telling her she was gaining weight.

Being nurtured by cooking for someone and by being fed are things I learned from my own mom and from Henry, my longtime Filipino boyfriend. My mom has raised me to always start cooking when someone is sick or has died. First thing to do. Interesting thing is, in Filipino culture, you cook for the guests; in my Jewish tradition, the guests come to nurture the bereaved. You bring food immediately to the funeral, to the seven days of sitting shiva and for however long it is needed.

My mom also taught me that when someone is ill, you immediately make chicken soup. I've learned to cook all kinds of chicken soup, and I've been nurtured by a number of them. The Filipino chicken soup that Henry showed me how to make has side pork, bok choy, jalapeño, cilantro, and chayote squash. Mexican chicken soup, like the one María Elena brought me after my first or second miscarriage, has lovely pieces of avocado floating around, and each ingredient is added carefully so as to not overcook it. But Jewish chicken soup is the one where you dump everything in—even a whole chicken, all the vegetables remaining in your refrigerator or that your neighbor gives you—and you cook the shit out of it. To this day my son says he doesn't like chicken soup, but I still can't stop myself from wanting to cook it for him when he is sick. Maybe it only makes me feel better.

Smells Like Home

Early in our relationship, Henry was cautious about how he told me he loved me. "I'd like to grow old with you," he'd said. I was twenty-three. He was almost thirty. After I left Henry, I'd chase that golden line forever.

The first time I cooked for him, I made a Spanish chicken dish I found in *Joy of Cooking*, and it was pretty good, but thereafter he cooked for me, my friends, my family. Every kind of Filipino dish that he'd been taught by his Aunt Emily, the family matriarch in Seattle, where they lived near Garfield High School.

One day many years ago, when I still lived in Seattle, I smelled home from down the street in the form of adobo, Filipino chicken soup, and at least five other pungent dishes. I was living with Henry on Beacon Hill, working at the Seattle Indian Health Board, and going to school, exhausted and demoralized as my first real adult job was going sour. I was tasked with starting a family violence program for the largest urban Indian clinic in the country. Bob was a close friend of my manager. Closeted but outwardly homophobic, a batterer, he held a powerful place in the Indian community.

During one of the regular drunken Friday-after-work bar nights, Bob found out I was Jewish and not Chicana, as he had assumed. He declared, "Jews are the worst kind of white people!" Assuming we are all white. He made my life hell. I'd heard that his wife was writing her dissertation on battering in the Indian community while he beat her. Eventually, I needed to leave that job.

That day, though, I walked into the home Henry and I had been sharing for several years, looked around, and burst into tears at the smells, the comfort, the folded clothes. Henry's mom, Masing, his sister Janette, and her son, Darwin, who knew me only as "Auntie Carla," all stared at me.

"Hi, honey!" Masing said, coming over to greet me. Masing always felt like my only real mother-in-law. "Why are you crying? Honey, you don't like? We won't do . . ."

"No, it's just that . . . no one does that for me. My mom hasn't even washed clothes for me since I was young . . . ironing? Never," I said, still sniffling.

They ran over, my Filipino family, and hugged me, concerned. "Honey, you are tired. You eat now." Masing led me to the table, pulled my chair out, and heaped food in front of me.

"Don't cry. You are my daughter; he is my son. Eat now." This was her only demand.

That last year at the Seattle Indian Health Board, I just worked harder and harder and stopped eating and sleeping. This was the start of my having jobs and then relationships that I persevered at no matter how abusive and unhealthy, convinced that if I just did the right thing or said the right words, people would understand, and I could fix the situation.

This was also when the first seeds of having children in a calm, nurturing family (with lots of food) took root. With Henry. I was working with teen parents, and frequently one would hand me a baby and say, "Here, hold this," and that did get me thinking. Having had a pretty chaotic childhood (and not always happy chaos), I had not been absolutely convinced that I would even have children. But with Henry, when we first began to talk about having kids, he told me not to worry, have the babies. He would raise them and tell them that mommy had to go off to do important things, whatever those things were. But I knew in my heart that if I did have a child with Henry, I'd never leave Seattle, which felt like way too small and sleepy of a town for me, with too much rain.

Love, a Full Refrigerator, and a Dirty Martini

At twenty-nine I left my native Seattle, my family, Henry, and his family, and I moved alone to California. The comfort and safety of having those large Filipino and Jewish families around us was also becoming stifling, and I felt strong enough to want to go out again and explore the world.

The close-to-unconditional love that Henry gave had allowed me to experience the freedom to spread my wings, feeling both secure and encouraged. Settling down and having kids was something I thought would be attainable in the future, no problem, when the time was right. I set the conditions: we weren't really broken up, but we could see other people. When I went back to Seattle to visit, I always left with a package from Masing, fragrant with aromas of a Filipino kitchen. When Henry came to visit me, he brought fresh ice-packed fish he'd caught. Soon after he'd arrive at my apartment, he'd have to go shopping. He'd fill my refrigerator, unable to bear the idea of me living with an empty one.

I called Henry's family "in-laws," though he and I had never married. Still, we had been more involved with each other's families than anyone I've known since. Years later, Manuelita, Henry's wife, told me, "You are family. Our kids—they know that they are cousins." One day, over a dirty martini, she had told me that she had always hoped I'd raise her boys if something happened to her. When Henry's mom died many years later, Henry and Manuelita asked me to welcome the guests and to speak at the rosary the night before the funeral.

One Hundred Years of Solitude?

After Henry, when relationships involving more magical realism than comfort blew to smithereens, I often gave the impression I'd waste away to nothing. And in the times in between, I denied and begged and wailed and drank and cried and raised hell, wanting the truth not to be the truth.

But in the moments when it all seemed to be boleros and breath-stopping kisses, *camarones con chile y limón y aguacate en la playa, jarocho* trios serenading us and semi-drunk, knock-down, unprotected sex with the crazy Nicaraguan with the six kids (I had thought he had two and lived alone or with his mom, not six and living with one of the moms of his kids), I'd suddenly be ravenous—entitled to all the richness of the food he cut up and fed to me, greedy to devour everything I could. When he left, he took his things and left only a bottle of Nicaraguan Flor de Caña rum and Gabriel García's Márquez's *One Hundred Years of Solitude*. I couldn't sleep, and I lost all the weight again . . . and those meals were in the blurred, nostalgic past.

My steadfast Henry had fed and nourished me in real time, not in magical reality. I felt I needed to starve myself when I threw him away, along with our dream of having children together, in exchange for men who could think only of themselves while they told me how much they adored me. And I found a woman or two who were like that as well. It's the women who would really kill me in the end.

Gestational Diabetes, Beets, and Baskin Robbins

When I finally became pregnant with Raphael after so many miscarriages, I decided that I would thoroughly enjoy my pregnancy. I started ordering banana splits delivered from Baskin Robbins until gestational diabetes (a side effect of treating recurrent miscarriages with prednisone) put a stop to all that. After that, the only time I cheated during pregnancy was in error—when I ate a bowl of borscht. Who knew that beets were super high in glucose?

When I started to go into labor, Raphael's dad asked me for Henry's recipe for Filipino chicken soup. "I need it to get through this labor and delivery," Larry said. It was the last thing I ate before full-on labor, so at least I had that to vomit.

I had vowed that after giving birth, I would eat a pie a week. I would pronounce my son five pies old instead of five weeks. After Raphael was born, Larry went to Kream Krop Bakery in Inglewood and brought home two pecan pies. At first I couldn't touch them—I was too wired on post-C-section painkillers and too focused on getting used to nursing—but after a few days, we demolished them.

Pecan Pie and Peach Cobbler

My second marriage, to Lizette, was going down the tubes. My appetite vanished, as it always did back then—the stress diet.

Smells of home coming down the street before you even get there, telling you what awaits—that's what love used to feel like to me. In my Jewish culture, food is integral to the celebrating of life and the mourning of death. And I was starving for love but never hungry for food.

One day Raphael and I stepped into a Southern bakery complete with 7UP cake, sock-it-to-me cake, peach cobbler, sweet potato pie, and my favorite, pecan pie. I must have looked scrawny and sad, because the good-looking baker told my twelve-year-old son, "Take care of your mom."

Raphael went to his dad's apartment for that evening, and the pies came home with me. It was Saturday night, and I had decided to experiment with a friend's suggestion that instead of wallowing in self-flagellation, obsessive regret, and longing to redo my life, I'd eat a whole pie, as was her custom. I put on Susana Baca and danced around the Mexican-tiled bright-blue kitchen, eating through a good portion of that pecan pie. I knew that soon Raphael and I would be gone from that house that I had dreamed up for our blended family. After the pecan pie, I ate half of the peach cobbler. I danced in between bites; I didn't feel sick. I went to sleep with sweet, warm dreams.

I got up early on Sunday and called the handsome baker to tell him that his pecan pie had changed my life, but his elderly father answered and just listened in confusion to the crazy lady raving about pie. Later, my friend told me, "I didn't really mean for you to eat the whole thing."

Adobo, Ribs, and Warm Banana Muffins

My son and I had moved out of the big house in the hills of Glassell Park and into the condo we rented with the gurgling fountain outside, which we hoped would soothe us to sleep at night. There Raphael discovered two ways to channel his angst, his creativity, and his surging hormones: cooking and photography. A good combination, as he cooked and then photographed his creations. I was willing to clean up the mess he left, provided I had *música* and the delicious food.

He became our chef. Raphael particularly loved the ubiquitous Filipino dish chicken and pork adobo, and he learned how to make it, winning popular acclaim in his high school cooking contest. His father's family is African American, and I imagine that I may have paved the way for future generations of adobo-eating Afro- Jews.

I chose to ignore the warning signs that my thirteen-year-old son could be falling behind in school and settled into the delight of rediscovering the nurturing power of food. I learned that even when I felt depressed or defeated, the smell of intense flavors and spices would revive me. Smells that stood out like our strong noses, *comida con calor* — chile, *ajo* (garlic), ginger, Chinese five spice. Our kitchen would have dirty pots and pans, knives and cutting boards flung about, perhaps left over from his tilapia adventure. (His friends had learned that I was the mom who let the kids cook, provided they would cook for me.) They'd get up early in the morning and make tilapia and eggs before their mothers came to reclaim them. The BBQ would still be on from their midnight foray into making ribs. Raphael had researched the ideal recipe from a YouTube video and gleaned the secret for removing the membrane.

Raphael began baking banana muffins. He looked up a recipe that called for an inner mixture of cinnamon and brown sugar and decided to add an additional tributary through the muffin made up of butter, sour cream, brown sugar, and cinnamon, drizzling the same outside. He perfected his hot banana muffins into a soul-soothing antidote for all evil and despair. I accepted that maybe this wasn't the happy chaos I thought I'd be living—several children, animals, moms. It was just Raphael and me. And that seemed to be okay.

Full Stomach, Full Heart

Raphael and I went to see Masing, Henry's mom, just before she died. She told Henry in Ilocano, "Feed them—they are too skinny."

Henry's mom was still beautiful—glowing, regal, sitting tall as she always did, stubborn, commanding my attention. "No, honey, I am not beautiful; I am so old and ugly," she insisted, while surrounded by her large grandsons—Henry's boys—and the smallest boy, my Raphael.

Masing and the boys began looking at old pictures. There were even some photos of my family, my Grandpa Sam and Grandma Stella (my mom's dad and my dad's mom), now long dead. They had been at a picnic in the backyard of the house where Henry and I had lived. In another picture, I was dancing the cha-cha-cha with my ninety-five-year-old grandpa, my wrong foot forward. My Grandma Stella was animated, talking to Henry's dad, José, and holding a plate of BBQ pork butt. That's what Henry and I used to do—feed people, the spicier and fattier the food, the better. Both our families' traditions are to fill our loved ones with food, hoping that by filling their stomachs, their hearts, too, will be full. In Filipino culture, men are often cooks. Henry's Uncle Jonnie was a big, fat merchant marine, a cook—but only when he was drunk. When he would stop drinking, he would stop cooking.

A short while after Raphael and I returned home, Henry called to tell me his mother had died. Then he observed, "Your son has a good heart. I know because he loves to cook and likes to feed people." Henry ought to know—that's what he always has done.

"An hour before she died, my mom asked if we were hungry," Henry told me. "The night before, we brought her warm boiled eggs, as she had requested. I started to feed her, but she reached out and insisted, 'Let me feed myself.'"

The Year of Eating Banana Splits

Back home, I fought with my son when he lost his generosity with me and decided to give all his BBQ ribs to his friends at school.

My Year of Eating Banana Splits started around this time. At the store, I bought all the fixings: hot fudge, strawberry topping, pineapple topping, nuts, whipped cream. I let the banana splits give me the sweet love I needed.

I embraced the idea of comfort food, nurturing my body and soul when no one else would or could. When I wanted to avoid calling the hot ex-girlfriend, instead I had a banana split. When I couldn't settle anything, didn't have a clue how to make things go away, it was time for a banana split with strawberry sauce. A mom, so tired, cut off from her stepdaughter? Time for Raphael to make ribs! I'd put on *Grey's Anatomy* and accept the explanation that his homework was all done.

At that time, I couldn't wait for the challenges Raphael faced in school to go away. My dreamy intellectual: attention, homework, budding hormones, organization—or the lack thereof—all made a swirling mass not conducive to studying. I was ready to ease up on the pressure and for us just to be mom and son again. Eating ribs, tilapia, and banana splits and watching *Ugly Betty*.

Late at night I would sit alone, watching *Nurse Jackie, Weeds, Mad Men*. Eating banana splits.

I have been blessed with a son who really appreciates women with meat on their bodies, who frequently told me, "Mom, you don't have curves; you're a stick." But during my Year of Eating Banana Splits, he walked in when I was partially clothed, and his eyes happened on my stomach. Very big. Ballooning over my—rest of the body. His mouth fell open.

"Uh, wow . . . I guess you did gain weight . . ." He tried to recover: "But Mom, yeah, you look great. Yes, you have curves now."

I wasn't sure if, technically, an extra mountain coming from just below my breasts (intersecting, given the sag) and falling over what was once a waist (though never a pronounced one) counted as curves, but I guessed there was a round element.

His Aunt Leslie, Larry's sister, looked at me and said, "Woo-whee, Carla, you got yourself some hips!" And there was no doubt that she saw this as a compliment. She is a big woman, comfortable in her body.

I was proud, finally. When I ran into the hot ex-girlfriend for the first time in a year, I told her, "Look, I'm fat!" Maybe I wasn't *really* fat, but I was on the heavy side for a skinny person. And I knew that she approved. She had told me that her mother, who was angry at her for "becoming a lesbian" on my watch, said I looked ghoulish. Luckily, on that day I was wearing a shirt that showed cleavage and not so much stomach.

In the past, at my most diminished, I wore baggy clothes and was so thin and hollowed-out scary looking that people would stop me in the elevator (the one place where it seemed you could either do pleasant weather talk or say one thing you really meant). They'd tell me, "You are *really* losing weight!" followed by, "Are you okay?" That all changed during my Year of Eating Banana Splits. I began to hear, "You are looking healthier. You have gained a few pounds. Your face looks fuller."

I'd joke about my Year of Eating Banana Splits daily, and they'd respond, "Ah, it can't hurt you." Eventually, though, it became polite silence or, "Oh, well, you'll lose it in no time."

Finally, I realized I had to slow down. My teenage son and I went to the Dominican Republic to be part of a global volunteer work project. We celebrated the New Year, 2011, in a country that depended on ample hips for good merengue dancing. I ate Helados Bon, the pride of the DR— *vainilla con nueces y chocolate orgánico*, my first ice cream in almost two weeks. I know that losing weight and reinventing oneself is hard. It may have been true that there in the Dominican Republic, I was not too heavy at all, nor did anyone stare at my ample *panzón*. My face at fifty-one had definitely benefited from the extra pounds, which is what they say about women.

But they also say that a large stomach and extra weight can lead to health problems and an earlier death. They certainly led to a change in jeans size and to the inability to wear tight clothes without looking like an obscene caricature of a pregnant fifty-one-year-old.

Tacos al Pastor, Caldos de Borrego y Tortas Cubanas

Over the years, I have made an impression on some people when they saw just how much food I could put away when I was feeling happy and well loved. It was more than they might have imagined for someone my size. Perhaps that is what happened in Mexico City that year when I was about twenty and gained so much weight. I was too full in my life, and I went around the *mercados*, eating *tacos al pastor, caldo de borrego, tortas,* and *elote* with plenty of *crema, queso, chile y limón*. I danced all night and ate *caldo de camarones* in Veracruz, where I also discovered *mole, tamales de elote, pastel de las tres leches*, and a million other delicacies.

After a year or two of living in Mexico, I came back thirty pounds overweight. In Mexico being called *gordita* (little fatty) is affectionate; I vastly preferred it to the pejorative *gabacha* (foreigner).

I had seen myself as perfectly healthy, happy, gordita. Being called "little fatty" in the United States is a different story. It was a shock to come back home to a country that saw me as fat, and I discovered that I had reverse anorexia of sorts. I looked in the mirror and still saw a skinny person. Only when I went clothes shopping with my older cousin was I surprised to find that I was hard-pressed to fit into a size 13 junior or a 12 to 14 regular. She quickly gave me the diet talk.

Years later, if I had gone to Mexico in my emaciated state, what I would have heard was concern, not cruelty:

"*¿Estas enfermita? ¡¡Tan flaquita?!*"

(Are you sickish? So skinny?!)

Ice Cream and Hot Tub for Mother's Day

Age fifty-one. No spouse, no house, but on Mother's Day, my daughter of the heart, Serena, came back in our lives. Raphael, Serena, and I spent the weekend at my sister's beach house. In the evening we sat in the Jacuzzi, arms outside the hot massaging bubbles, eating cookie dough ice cream.

Gordita Again

Having curves—real hips—and showing off "the girls" are all aspects of womanhood I've grown into. My body has traversed the range of shapes, as if I were made of Play-Doh. From completely titless when I was fourteen to me now? *Con curvas* and love handles. And a substantial stomach.

At fifty-six, my curves—well, I enjoy them. And I enjoy women with curves—the hips, the cleavage. But my *panza* (stomach bulge), that I could do without. I don't like men at all who are *panzones,* but I'm fine with women other than me who have a bit of stomach.

I am very full and very happy, and when the heat stands still, thickening the air around me, I actually waddle. Maybe I experience some sort of a faux or hysterical pregnancy (though I am not hysterical, I'm lethargic). But it's tropical . . . it's humid . . . it's from another world, this weather, this waddle. I was only pregnant once for full term, but I think that my body says otherwise. I've been pregnant at least eight times that I am aware of, and it seems I should have the right to this pregnant waddle much longer. But at fifty-six, that ship has sailed.

My Year of Eating Banana Splits is over but not forgotten. I have the panza to prove that it has never gone away. And at fifty-six, I'll still say, "Fuck it," and sometimes kick back and eat artisan ice cream, like lavender, salted caramel, or orange chocolate, as I binge-watch *Orange Is the New Black.*

One Day on the Gold Line

I crouched, handcuffed and in a pool of my own blood, on the Highland Park Metro Station platform, begging, "Help, someone, pleeease!" and crying out, "Mommy." Passengers were walking in and out of trains but making a wide berth, staring, not stopping.

I was a fifty-year-old Jewish woman, a single mother of a thirteen-year-old Afro-Jewish son, a writer, and the owner of a PR firm in Pasadena. I frequently rode the Metro to appointments in the downtown LA area. On that day, December 28, 2009, I just wanted to go home, have a glass of Chardonnay, and watch *Weeds*. I was glad the year was almost over, a rough one that included the unblending of our blended family and the crushing impact of the recession on my previously thriving business.

I had left Union Station, boarded the Gold Line, and was gazing out the window when an LA County Sheriff's Department deputy asked me for my ticket. I had not paid attention to the fact that they patrolled the Metro, which, as I would learn later, was the responsibility of new deputies who had just finished their stints at the LA County jails. I dug for my Metro Day Pass in the usual chaos of my bag. He barked at me to "keep looking," then said, "Give me your driver's license," which I did right away, though I was surprised by the aggressive tone. I found the receipt for the pass that indicated the date and time I had bought it, though not the pass itself. I showed it to the deputy, who gestured impatiently for me to follow him off the train. "That's not good enough; you can show it in court."

I was not eager to go to court or pay a fine. "Wait, please don't cite me; I can find the pass; I know I have it."

"You'll have a much worse day if you don't get off right now!" he shouted, and I got right off. As I exited, I heard the crackle of a two-way radio.

I knelt to look for my pass, but a female deputy ordered: "Get up. Put your hands there." Sheriff's department deputies immediately surrounded me—brown uniforms looming over me, blocking the view of the 4 p.m. rush of passengers swirling around the station.

"What, you are going to search me?" The words flew out before I could think, but I immediately put my arms on the pillar. I was on automatic; everything happened quickly and felt surreal.

She searched me, shoving her hands roughly around my body, over my breasts, around my waist, and down beneath my underwear. I had never been patted down before, other than at the airport, and never this aggressively. Instinctively, I reacted to her hands jerking around my body, poking, grabbing. "Stop—you're hurting me," I said and pulled to the side.

Within a second she bounced my head—SLAM, SLAM, SLAM—against the pillar, simultaneously snapping handcuffs behind my back.

I both heard and felt a loud crunch—the impact of bone hitting a hard surface. For a moment, I genuinely thought I was just having a bad dream.

One of the deputies whistled and said, "Oh, dear, looks like she broke one."

I saw bright red blood spurting out everywhere. My nose, mouth, ears—I wasn't really sure where all the pain and blood were coming from. I thought of myself as a strong woman, but at this point, I was broken. My earring had fallen to the ground and was floating in my blood.

The deputies stood around chatting, ignoring me even when I begged, "Please help; let me call someone" and "I hurt so bad; everything hurts."

I squatted, dripping blood and mucous. I could not fathom how I had ended up where I was and felt as if I was in some kind of alternative universe, one that I cried out to be released from. Another asked, "Did you call?" And the response: "Must be a busy day for the paramedics."

"We told you to keep your head back! You can't use a phone until the supervisor gets here!" they shouted at me, annoyed at my cries for help. I tried to lean back but choked on the blood. I fell backward, twisted up with the handcuffs. The tight metal dug into my wrists. The female deputy remained impassive, silent, even when I asked her, "Why did you hurt me?" None of the deputies moved to help me; they continued to talk among themselves. I heard one belch. I began to feel an odd sense of disassociation. Trains rattled by in both directions. People walked by me, staring ahead and avoiding my eyes.

There was a general din around me and a thick, clogged feeling in my nose and ears. I tasted metal. I felt dizzy.

A "supervisor" arrived with a video camera. For a moment I hoped he was someone who would make sense of the nightmare. But as he interrogated me, it was clear he was not the one.

He started out asking me, "Ma'am, are you hurt?"

"Yes, I hurt all over," I said as I sat on a gurney provided by the paramedics, who had also arrived. Blood covered my nose and upper lip, as well as the Metro platform where I'd crouched. He proceeded to ask where I hurt.

When I began to respond, he cut me off with, "Can you tell me what happened?"

In front of the woman who broke my nose, he questioned me—"So then what did *you* do?" — while two paramedics checked me out. I was handcuffed the entire time. Both impatient and dismissive of me, his attitude suggested that I had clearly done something to cause this.

Months later, when my attorneys showed me that video, I was both horrified and reassured that my memory was accurate. I felt so sorry for that woman calling for her mommy. There really was a large pool of blood in front of me.

That day, I was put in an ambulance, and the supervisor continued to interrogate me. One of the strangest parts of my experience was receiving medical "care" while being held captive, handcuffed.

In the ambulance I asked the supervisor, "Why did this happen? Am I in custody?" I asked again to use a phone.

He switched the video off. Practically spitting out the words: "These questions you are asking is why. Now *I'm* telling *you* what's going to happen. Be quiet. Lie down. You're going to County."

Arriving at LA County Hospital, I was embarrassed by the handcuffs and tried unsuccessfully to hide them under my coat. I'd never been handcuffed or in custody before. Also, I used to work for a union representing many of the workers there, the Service Employees International Union. I was hoping I'd find a friendly face. The male intake nurse with an SEIU button looked me over and politely asked, "What did your nose look like . . . before?" I didn't actually know what it looked like right then, but it was throbbing and painful, and I was having a hard time breathing. It felt enormous and stuffed.

Another deputy pushed my gurney down the hallway into the locked facility.

With a deputy present I was directed to take off my clothes and jewelry and put on a gown. My handcuffs were taken off for a moment. Feeling as if I might faint, I struggled with the gown. I tried to pee but couldn't. I saw myself in the mirror for the first time: my face was covered with snot and blood, and my nose was definitely bigger, swollen. The gown was falling off.

I was left in a corridor of a larger room, alone, crying, in intense pain. The wall was bare except for a sign that said, "You have the right to ask for pain medication."

For hours I intermittently called out, "Excuse me, excuse me," asking for help — ice, medication, to make a phone call. A few people paused and told me they would get me something, but I didn't see them again. I was told to be quiet or no one would help me, told I'd be moved to a "fine room with a phone and television," and later told that I'd never make a call there. A nurse shook her finger at me. "Ain't no patients using the phone here; might call their families, other gang members."

I asked less for help as I realized that my survival depended on being quiet and compliant. My arms and legs tingled. The pain in my right ear and side of my face became more intense and felt strange, alternately numb and then throbbing.

Someone gave me an ice pack. Another person brought me pain medication and a small glass of water, but I was nauseous from swallowing blood.

I wondered where my son was right then. I didn't want to think of him being in this position. If this could happen to me, a middle-aged Jewish woman, what might they do to my Black teenage son? I'd read the statistics—an estimated one in three African American males would go to jail in their lifetimes. I had already become fearful of my son being racially profiled. He was thirteen and Afro-Jewish, had just had his bar mitzvah, and still didn't have hair under his arms, but as he got taller and we moved further south (to a more affluent, whiter area) from northwest Pasadena, he began to be treated differently. Though I was familiar with the term "police misconduct," I had always operated on fear for my son, not for me. It was terrifying and absurd that anyone might have seen him as threatening. And yet here *I* was. I'd never been on the prisoner side before except to give writing workshops in juvenile detention facilities. That day I became, and I remain, acutely aware of the difference between prisoner and visitor.

A doctor came to examine me. He was youngish and greeted me with an open, concerned expression. He seemed to see me as a human, not merely an inmate. He told me that he thought my nose was fractured and ordered a CT scan.

I really had to go to the bathroom. The deputy who originally took me off the Metro was nearby again, ready to take me to get the CT scan. "I think she's going to need help getting up," he said to the nurse. I appreciated that. It was like trying to walk after my C-section. I was brought a bedpan.

The deputy wheeled me on a stretcher. Now talkative, he complained that he'd worked more than nineteen hours straight and couldn't leave until I did. When we were almost hit by a swinging door, he said, "With my luck that would injure me; my day has been bad enough."

"*Your* day?" I said. But the deputy just continued to talk without responding.

Eventually the doctor came back. "I'm going to discharge you," he said.

"You'll need to see an ENT specialist—your nose is fractured. The septum was pushed to one side. They'll have to see it when the swelling goes down. Put ice on it and sit up sleeping so you can breathe. I'll make you an appointment. You'll probably need surgery."

I begged him, "Please don't release me to the officers." I was really scared that I would be made to "disappear." The doctor looked at me hopelessly. "What can I do? I can't keep you."

I asked him about admitting me, hoping for that room with the phone. "If I admit you, they'll put you in the prison hospital. You won't be able to make any calls or talk to anyone. You don't want that," he said.

He left. I lay there.

Two deputies arrived, and I was told to put one item of clothing on and I'd be taken to jail. I still don't know what they meant by that; they had taken away my clothes earlier. I was terrified and confused as to why I would be taken to jail, but I'd also become resigned, a sense that my survival depended on shutting down and following orders.

I asked about reaching my son. One said, "You haven't spoken with him yet—right? So why should it matter now?" I was not sure that I would make it out of there and desperately needed to make contact. My son was staying overnight with his dad. No one knew where I was. As I look back at this moment, when I was a prisoner, I remember how little value my life and role as a mother had to that deputy.

◆

Suddenly, the deputy who first took me off the Metro appeared and told me to sign a citation and I was free to go.

"Why are they releasing her?" the others asked.

"I don't know," he said and shrugged. "They just told me cite and release."

"All I have to do is sign this and I can go?" I asked in disbelief, afraid to move. While I was getting dressed, a deputy grabbed my envelope with the follow-up appointment and doctor's instructions, citing it as "evidence."

Around midnight—eight hours after having my nose broken for not showing my Metro pass—I stumbled out of the hospital jail facility, clutching a few of my items: one earring in a bloody plastic glove, my blood-soaked rebozo, which I later threw out, and my bag, which I didn't use again for over a year.

I didn't know exactly where I was or how I'd get home. My phone was dead. I walked, then almost ran out of the locked hospital unit, putting distance between me and the bars. I stopped in front of a security guard in the hospital hallway and couldn't hold back the sobbing. I asked to use his phone.

I tried all the numbers I had memorized; no one was home. Finally I reached my son's dad. "What happened, sweetie, what did they do to you?" Larry said, alarmed, but so present, soothing, as I sobbed into the phone.

I grabbed for Larry's deep familiar voice, at that moment a lifeline, a voice that had once been a comfort when he'd sung to me, "Ooh-oo child, / Things'll get brighter."

"They've messed with the wrong person. I'm on my way," he said. This, too, was Larry. I remembered.

I couldn't stop weeping, "You have to tell Raphael right now: never, ever question an officer; do exactly as told."

Larry picked me up after one in the morning. Our son was with him. Of all the places I thought he'd see me, this was not one. And not in this condition. I hugged them both, holding Raphael tightly. He listened to my story and said little.

When we got to my house, Larry told him that he needed to stay with me. To me he said, "Look in your bag for the Metro Day Pass," and I found it where it had slipped behind my wallet.

The price of misplacing a Metro ticket. My ears stayed full of blood for a day or two. At first the doctors thought my skull was fractured, since my nose and half my face were bruised and swollen and I had a black eye. The dentist told me that my tooth was cracked and marked from the pillar. "Perhaps you were being profiled because of your Middle Eastern looks," the dentist said, staring closely at me.

My nose was broken, with little chips of bone or cartilage floating around. An ENT specialist later cautioned me, "If you have surgery, we'll have to rebreak your nose. Be ready to be retraumatized."

About a week after the assault, my brother took me to speak with civil rights lawyers. They explained that the LA County Sheriff Department's deputies were trained in a culture of brutality in the jails, then let out on the street. Their first job was patrolling the Metro. They were taught that "these people" (in jail) were animals and needed to be controlled. They became accustomed to dealing in an aggressive and violent way with anyone (civilians) whom they assumed had broken the law in some way.

A friend warned me that when they break something on your body, they usually will charge you. I discovered that my citation indicated "resisting arrest," though I was never told I was under arrest, nor read my rights, nor allowed a phone call while "in custody." In fact, charges were never actually filed.

My brother-in-law was convinced that the deputy who broke my nose, a woman young enough to be my daughter and about eight months out of jail duty, was simply showing off "for the boys."

Civil rights lawyers filed a lawsuit against the LA County Sheriff's Department on my behalf. I later read the deposition of the supervisor who took the video. He claimed that he couldn't remember much. He couldn't recall whether or not I was injured or if he questioned me in the presence of the deputy who broke my nose. He didn't give a clear answer when asked if it was standard practice to interview victims in front of their assailants.

The deposed deputies were all unclear as to whether it was standard practice to search passengers who couldn't immediately find their tickets. Their answers were all over the place—yes, no, maybe so.

In the months after my experience on the Metro Gold Line, I became aware of the many stories of sheriff's department misconduct published in the *Los Angeles Times* and *Pasadena Weekly*. With story after story of deputies beating unconscious inmates while shouting, "Stop resisting," I couldn't believe that my case wasn't settled sooner.

More than two years later, we accepted an offer of $199,000. I had little desire to go to trial. Having worked for the Seattle City Attorney's Office in the Family Violence Project many years earlier, I had firsthand knowledge of the experience of victims without power in the criminal justice system. Usually, the juries tended to decide if the woman "deserved" to be beaten or not—despite instructions that assault was a crime, even if it was done by a relative. I wasn't confident enough a jury would conclude that people in uniform, sworn to "protect and serve," could be that brutal. The sheriff's department's defense seemed to suggest that I somehow injured myself, eerily similar to the batterers' stories of women knocking their own heads against the wall.

I wrote a cover story on the assault for the *Pasadena Weekly*. For years after the story was published, my son and I were amazed by the number of people who approached me about it. People from a variety of racial and ethnic groups told me about disturbing and violent experiences they had with the LA County Sheriff's Department deputies and thanked me for my courage in telling my story. I wrote another story for the *Pasadena Weekly*, "Bashing the Bashed," about revictimizing (blaming) the victim.

Though I'm glad I didn't have to go to trial, I didn't feel like enough happened as a result of the lawsuit. The deputy who had broken my nose, the deputy who had taken me off the Metro, the "supervisor" who had interrogated me in front of my assailant—no one ever admitted wrongdoing or apologized. I was not aware of any reprimands or training ordered as a result of my case. For a period of time not a week went by without another news story about violence committed by the Los Angeles County Sheriff's Department. Years later the violence and civil rights violations came to a head. Criminal charges were filed related to the violence in the jails; Sheriff Lee Baca, then the top elected official in the department, was pressured to resign and was later prosecuted on criminal charges. Former Sheriff Baca, former Undersheriff Paul Tanaka, and other deputies were convicted of felony charges in federal court.

Looking at what happened to me and at what happens inside the jails, I continue to ask: *How many more stories like mine are out there?*

I have survived, but I will never forget this experience, nor will my son, who saw me immediately after the assault.

We didn't talk about it a lot, and he's never seen the video, but he told me that he still has nightmares of "them doing that to you." And when a student intern came to stay with us, my son warned him, "Be careful on the Metro. Hang onto your ticket."

Several years after I was assaulted, we went to see *Fruitvale Station*, based on a true story of a young Black man, Oscar Grant, who was killed by a Bay Area Rapid Transit police officer in Oakland. Raphael took my hand halfway through and held it tightly.

Afterward he told me, "Mom, it reminded me of you." And I said to him, "Now do you understand why I worry about you and the police?"

When Hormones Collide:
Part I

Does it count for or against me that I tried to make the bacon—fat, juicy, unhealthy—that my son always sneaked into our grocery cart? I tried to make the bacon, but I burned it to a rapid crisp, which I hoped didn't result in creating a carcinogen, in addition to all the other risks in the world. I'm not talking about the sort-of-charred, just-scrape-it-off kind of burned, but the crumbling, hardly edible kind. I did like my bacon cooked crispy. So did my mom. My mom told me that her Russian-revolutionary-turned-failed-capitalist immigrant dad used to sneak out from their kosher household with her and her siblings to get them BLTs.

I was not just failing in my ability to consistently bring home the bacon, I was also managing to burn it. But who had time to monitor the cooking when doing fifty things at once? By 7 a.m., I'd already worked several hours, done the laundry, and argued, wailed, and whined for about thirty minutes with several officious Bank of America loan modification assholes (until they hung up on me). Then I tried to rouse my son multiple times out of a deep sleep in an attempt to get him to eighth grade on time. As a finale, I spilled the oatmeal, partially on myself and partially on the table and floor. But that did not stop me from having a bowl of that oatmeal down on the table with plenty of brown sugar on it long before Raphael got there. Never mind the fact that at best he'd take three bites.

Once upon a time, I had brought home the oatmeal *and* the bacon. Left my nonprofit, social-change type of work to be a PR star. (For some reason, they always say, "You are a rock star" in the exaggeratedly peppy PR world I inhabited. It was as if this is what we all aspired to, when, in fact, being a publicist was the opposite of being a rock star; you were strictly behind the scenes most of the time.) I started my own business so I could have the frenetic flexibility to take care of my often sick, often school-challenged son and still earn the income to keep us in a reasonably decent style of living. Money for travel, food, "enrichment activities" (from tap dancing to piano lessons to tutors to summer camps he might endure so I could get more work done), and all the necessary electronic accoutrements that boys his age "needed." Then, that all went south: my ability to be the single mom who could pay for all the lessons, go on all the field trips, volunteer in the classroom, bring home that bacon, and throw damn good birthday parties. I was treading water. Barely. So burned bacon and unattractive oatmeal was all I could manage those days.

On this particular morning, I grabbed for things in the refrigerator that might constitute a lunch. Sometimes it felt like I fixed my son's lunch mainly to make me feel better that I had sent him to school with something to eat (especially since he usually ate so little of it). This time it was made of food that he had bought the night before while I was at a get-in-shape "boot camp" for moms, mostly younger than me, whose sons and daughters were part of a kids' basketball camp run by the same coach. Raphael had told me that while I was out, he had watched the Lakers game with our neighbor and then gone out for Chinese food, vague as to the source of the money. ("Some you gave me a while ago, but I didn't spend.") Why hadn't that come up last time he asked for money, I wondered? Money disappeared so rapidly in our household. Anyway, I couldn't complain too much, since I had gulped down a good part of that Chinese food for dinner.

Then, just when I expected to read myself into a quick stupor, Raphael recruited me to transcribe his "Romeo's Diary," which, of course, was due the next day: "Should I give up or should I keep trying? Her love for me won't change, but mine for her might. Good men have trained me not to think of Rosaline, 'but to examine other beauties.' But how can I when I am so love struck on one girl and one girl only?" They were studying *Romeo and Juliet*, and in addition to being assigned to write mock journals, they were working on a performance of the play, complete with a hip-hop ballroom scene. We started at 10 p.m. and stopped close to 12 a.m. He still had more to do, and I didn't know if he had finished when I found him in the morning, sprawled asleep in his clothes, the rest of his wardrobe of the past week strewn across the floor. As for me, I felt the *Romeo and Juliet* diary provided a nice bit of mother-son bonding.

Raphael and the other eighth graders could completely relate to Romeo and Juliet. They were the same age and ready to jump the bones of the woman of their dreams. Relationships were life-or-death for them. And short-lived. Also, they were often tragic, at least judging by the way they played out on Facebook. Great divisions were wrought, and not even a kindly priest or nurse could save them.

Kids didn't seem to write in journals anymore, though. They had Facebook. When they first went on Facebook, in about the sixth grade, Raphael and all his friends "friended" their parents' friends. There weren't a lot of secrets yet. One day, I went to my son's computer looking for evidence of how he kept charging iTunes on a card from a long-gone account, one lost in my bankruptcy saga. It was bad enough, I thought, that

I, who always had perfect credit before, had to resort to what I called "committing bankruptcy." What now would I be accused of—credit card fraud? I didn't keep track of these charges; I had way too many items clogging up my brain, and the fluctuating hormones from the journey into menopause kept me guessing about whether or not I was going nuts. Fortunately, my bookkeeper watched my charges, both for business and home, and since I was on an austerity budget, she noticed when there was unusual activity.

Raphael's hormones seemed to be making a steady ascent too. The testosterone took his intensity to a whole different level, bringing to mind perhaps a whirling dervish—or himself at age two on steroids for croup and his wild dancing after he was discharged from the hospital.

Then again, perhaps I was the whirling dervish, especially when perimenopausal surges of hormones caused whiplashes of insanity. Like the environment in my childhood home (which I had never intended to duplicate): one minute we would have intense conflict escalating to high-pitched screams and slammed doors, splintered from repeated kicks, and the next minute we would have unstoppable laughter.

I warned Raphael about the explosive mixture of hormones brewing in our home. We needed to be cautious. I wanted to post a big sign: "Danger! Extreme Caution! Hormones at Work!"

A phone call interrupted my uneasy surveillance of Raphael's Facebook activity; I let it go to voicemail. I also monitored his homework activity. Raphael conducted both simultaneously, as much as I tried to control that. In my case, I found that my own frenetic switching of roles had brought me steadily down, the so-called multitasking overload where I never seemed to be enough as a mother, writer, publicist, daughter, or worker. And I was also a reluctant landlord.

"*Hola, Carla, ¿como estas?*" A message from my tenant. "*Es que el árbol grande en frente de la casa, nada más, creo que hay algo que debes de saber acerca de eso . . .*" My tenant ended the call here, trailing off.

He was talking about the big tree in front of the house I owned, the first and only home I'd purchased as a single mom, squeezing out every dollar available from first-time homebuyer programs to buy the cheapest house in the best neighborhood, out of sheer luck amassing equity that could have been my secret safety net for old age and college for Raphael or even for an emergency or for adopting a child. I'd lost the equity, floundered down the rabbit hole of financial hell, and then tried to get a loan modification and, later, to file for bankruptcy using an attorney who closely resembled the Mad Hatter.

Now my house was underwater with the housing crash, and the tenants had just stopped paying rent. That big tree in the front yard would have destroyed the house and its inhabitants if it had fallen. Including and especially their little kids, who played in front of it. It was the tree with the swing hanging down that had figured big in my dreams about the house with the swing. The swing, which sometimes inadvertently bonked some kids on the head (or was it pushed purposefully, one kid to another?), meant something to me. The tree had probably been there longer than the house, which was built in 1923. It was part of the house and provided shelter, all the shade you needed in the summer, and a sense of home in the years we lived there. We had pictures taken in front of the tree that documented my son's early birthday parties and sleepovers. Now that tree was apparently menacing the lives of the tenants.

I didn't immediately return the tenant's call. Instead I went back to my son's computer. When I saw his Facebook page up and some chatting fraught with teenage angst around breaking up, I decided to take a closer look. After all, it was only a few weeks earlier that I had received the call from a fellow mom alerting me to Raphael's "tight pussy" posting (apparently a cartoon of a sexy cat with breasts hanging out). Another friend, a single mom of a sixteen-year-old, was less appalled, just said that her impulse was to post, "God, I wish mine still looked like that," referring to the perky breasts in the picture. I felt like posting for all his friends to see, "Fifty-one-year-old mom here, and there ain't no tight pussy," but that wasn't the point.

Raphael was Facebook friends with my ex-girlfriend, Jessica, and with Serena. Just before I got the call about his tight pussy post, he had brought me to the computer to see Serena's posts about her love of smoking marijuana. "Mom, I told her that I thought, as her former stepbrother, I should warn her that she shouldn't do that so much." He forgot to tell me about his own stellar social media behavior. With his pussy post, he temporarily became the pariah of his friends' moms and his friends who were girls. Though most of the time, he was "the nice guy friend" whom all the girls asked to the prom. I knew I'd deal with his Facebook antic later, when he got home.

◆

Earlier that morning, since burning the bacon (which I could no longer afford to bring home) was not enough, I flung open the refrigerator in a mad scramble to augment Raphael's lunch. He had requested the Chinese leftovers, though I had cautioned him many times—none of which was heeded—about the risk of death from eating leftover crispy salted Chinese shrimp that was left out in the hot sun. And soon, he'd be on free school lunches. The wine bottle I had opened the night before (how did all those bottles pile up, anyway?) popped out, or rather fell out, and wine spilled on the floor. I only briefly contemplated licking it up. Way too dirty.

I did quickly clean up my spill. It wouldn't do to have someone drop by and find a house reeking of burned bacon *and* wine. Hardening oatmeal remained on the table and floor. A path of underwear and other boy clothing cast onto the floor each day snaked around from the living room desk and into Raphael's bedroom.

But that was a good morning. No arguments, no yelling. Raphael left for school. I only admonished myself silently that the charred bacon should have been the first sign and the spilled oatmeal the second—time to slow down. Breathe. We had finally landed in a town, South Pasadena, where my son would be able to walk to school and back. He had started going on frequent walks, and I was glad that he was getting exercise. Though in time I would start to wonder where exactly he went and with whom he hung out after school.

I briefly contemplated walking to the South Pasadena Children's Memorial and Healing Garden in nearby Garfield Park before leaving for work. It had been built in memory of children who died, and it reminded me of all I should be grateful for. "Nothing can shade the light of your beautiful miracle" was one of the phrases engraved on a bench—a place for grieving parents to sit, reflect, and remember.

But there was no time; I was off and running again. Hoping that big tree didn't fall on the house before I dealt with it.

Feed Me, Fund Me, Leave Me Alone

It was my son's first day of high school, and I wanted to crawl back under my covers. I was not ready! How had we arrived there from the moment of my first knowledge that he might be here to stay, might be the one that took? It was only months before that he'd started getting body odor. We were in his room, and I noticed a strange but familiar smell. I leaped up and shouted, "My little boy's grown up!" I thought of adding it to his baby book, but there was no spot for that. He still didn't have any facial or other body hair that I was aware of. Fortunately, like his friends, he used body wash and cologne and showered regularly. I had tried to accustom him to finer scents like Armani, but his friends had been known to unleash an entire spray can of TAG in his bedroom.

My son's walls displayed Tupac, Bob Marley, and Martin Luther King. When Raphael was twelve, we went to Israel for a wedding and a pre–bar mitzvah trip. Jerusalem was oppressive with its overarching trifecta of religious intrusiveness. But leaving for Tel Aviv, Raphael spied the olive-skinned sabras wearing bikinis and sporting Uzis and said, "Now, we're talking!"

At fourteen, Raphael still had a few stuffed animals close by. Besides the classic soft, comforting puppy, he had Brian, the perverted dog from *Family Guy*, a show he watched nonstop if allowed. His voice had finally deepened.

We had moved to South Pasadena so Raphael could attend high school there. We were starting fresh again in a new place, but we'd done that repeatedly over the last three years. The night before school started, I lay next to him for the one second he'd let me. "Mom, I'm tired; please let me go to sleep," he implored. But I hugged him and kissed him for a minute longer, then teased him, threatening to sing a lullaby, until he gently demanded I leave. "Mom, come on, I have to sleep."

As oppressive as a mother's love, worry, nagging, admiration, and even the sound of her breath can be, I knew for a fact that my fourteen-year-old son and his peers still craved and demanded the hugs, the caresses, the permission to throw their arms, their bodies close to their moms. But only on their terms. When the affection was initiated by me, I was sure to get anything from a polite rebuff and a pull-away to a snarl. Yet he loved telling me about something that was weird and exciting and funny, maybe even crude. He fought with himself on whether to confide in me about a girl he'd known since fourth grade. A girl he had started "liking." I didn't mind the idea; I was friends with her mom. But once I got interested, it was all over; the secret went away and was filed off-limits until he might throw me a scrap of information. I was, after all, his mother. Not a sibling, not a friend, not his dad, who fell somewhere in between. I was the one who could be predictably unpredictable, sometimes just flying off the handle, but with a word from him, either making me laugh or warning me I had gone too far, I often snapped right out of it.

Ahhhh, those damned hormones. Those ages—mine and his. These changes didn't happen overnight. And I wasn't adept at teasing him out of his rage or irritation or just simply exasperation with me, my existence. My presence. The sound of my being.

Perhaps the reason I had felt so melancholy for so many days, apart from my empty bank account, was also this transition. He was constantly disgusted with me, rejecting me. I knew this was normal teenage behavior, but it had the effect of creating an illogical outrage in me. (I know now the extent to which that outrage was also caused by my hormones during perimenopause.)

I would rant, "How can you not want to ever be around me? Not want to be part of this household?" (And by that I meant cleaning, cooking, taking out the garbage . . .) "How can you this? And how can you that?" And it all only brought us back to Shel Silverstein's poem. The first one Raphael ever memorized. Our mantra, "A Cat, a Kid, and a Mom." The poem tells us not to be shocked when the cat, the kid, and the mom behave just as they should: cats and kids off adventuring, not always wanting to snuggle up, the mom not always being tranquil and patient. Take that poem plus a heap of hormones minus one cat, and you would understand us.

One day my older sister took a cartoon from her refrigerator and gave it to me. "Here, maybe this will help you. I don't need it anymore," she said. The cartoon, captioned "Teen Translator," featured a disinterested, hunched-over teen with an empty voice bubble and his tired-looking, hunched-over mom with saggy breasts, and it instructed us to push a button for a translation. The translation was "Feed me, fund me, leave me alone."

The night before Raphael started high school, he didn't try to crawl into bed with me as he had done so often before and would continue to do, on occasion, in the future.

In the morning I got out of bed and made Raphael breakfast. I grabbed one last hug and snapped a picture. He walked out the door to his first day of high school without a backward glance. On that day, he was impatient to get to school on time; he wouldn't allow me to take any more photos.

When Hormones Collide:
Part II

I started up my computer and began checking e-mail, looking for the Magical Message. *You have just won one billion dollars or the equivalent. We are offering you, we need you, we want to pay you to do whatever you do best when you want to with whomever you want to. And we know that you are good, so you tell us what you think is best. Oh, and BTW, be sure to leave time available for writing. We know you have an important voice to be heard in the world, and we need for you to leave time. You are almost fifty-two, and it's about time you got back to writing. Less crying. More writing. If you need to cry a bit, that's okay too. You now have enough money to go see a therapist, that trauma therapist, the little Jewish man with the purple shoes whom you love so much. Just going into his room, you can breathe again. And then you want to cry. Sometimes you do.*

Also, we'll pay you up front for the year. We don't want you to have to spend your valuable time chasing down payments or worrying about whether you are ever going to get paid at all.

We have assigned a mentor, sort of a big brother, for your son. He just happens to be an Afro-Jew as well. He has made a few hip-hop recordings and is probably going to be the next big thing. Right now, though, his thing is to spend time with youth like your son, Raphael, and support them in finding their passion, feeling good about themselves, and succeeding in school. Also to relieve their exhausted single moms. He knows that family relationships are key and wants to help take the pressure off yours. So you can have more of that quality time you had when Raphael was about four or five months old.

And here's a preview of what that day would have looked like, also contained in this Magical Message: My day starts off with a freshly made latte brought to my bedside by my son, who crawls in next to me, cuddly and sweet smelling, before he cheerfully gets dressed and ready for school. I make his oatmeal, and he's off with a hug and kiss. Then it's time for reading and meditation, some writing, and a dip in the hot tub that has been installed nearby. After that it's breakfast al fresco, which is prepared for me (don't ask by whom): coconut French toast with blueberries or huckleberries, fresh whipped cream, homemade sausage, and one egg, poached medium (perfect, not too hard, just a bit soft, not runny). I'm not picky.

I go back for more writing after my breakfast and then break for some exercise, a hike in the local San Gabriel Valley hills. When I return, I meet a friend for coffee and some more writing. Raphael comes home and tells me about his day, which contains no undone assignments, no complaining teachers, and no trips to the school counselor. We have afternoon tea, perhaps, with some homemade scones that Raphael and I bake together. Afterward, we take a long walk and talk about his day, his hopes and dreams, and his plans to work for peace on earth. I tell him my book is . . . coming along. In the evening, we play some music. I've taken up trumpet again, and he accompanies me on the different instruments he plays— saxophone, piano, drums, cello—or we just sing in harmony together.

Later, we both work quietly, me writing, Raphael on a project that he stops now and then to discuss with me. Then it's time for a bath. And though he's older now, in ninth grade, we still read a bit together before it's time for each of us to go to sleep.

The night before I had this fantasy of the Magical Message, I dreamed that I was working in some retail environment, low pressure. I found that there wasn't much to it. The cash register was easy. There were no irate customers. It was fun. I was helping people, though I don't recall what we were selling. I worked with Ellen DeGeneres, who turned out to be a very down-to-earth person for the most part. At the end of the evening, her wife, Portia de Rossi, came by. Even dressed casually, with her hair shorter, she was still beautiful. And you could really see why they worked so well together. I was getting to know Ellen a bit, and I thought about the end of my evening, wanting to tell my former hot young girlfriend about it and how I was actually working with Ellen. I could see how Ellen might get a little intense just before she went on camera, but I was quite sure she wasn't the tyrant that Rosie appeared to be. (Apparently, when we went on Rosie's cruise, she was just unglued, seasick, and without Kelli, who'd stayed home from this particular trip.) In my dream, there was also a birthday cake involved, but I can't remember whose birthday it was. And some kind of Costa Rican drink that made everyone a little sick. That part of the dream might have morphed off my real-life experience of a wine tasting with the Jewish lesbian *chavurah* group I had gone to in hopes of finally meeting a Jewish woman. In my dream, I thought about how it would be good to do more hours at this store with Ellen. After all, I'd even talked about getting a retail job, and this one seemed very pleasant and not stressful. But it was awfully far to drive daily to the Westside somewhere.

And then, just as I was beginning to ponder all this, still dreaming, I was jolted awake. Adrenaline racing, late. It was time to get Raphael up and ready for school.

"What don't you understand? I have to go!" Raphael said after I urged him to eat a few bites of the oatmeal I'd quickly prepared for him. I started to respond halfheartedly as he headed to the door: "Don't yell at me . . ."

I trailed off because . . . how many times had I yelled at him? I, too, was bellowing the night before. Maybe not in the manner that Raphael's dad did, or even Raphael had that morning, but in my own shrill way.

Just as I was warming up for a real rant, he interrupted my yelling with what felt like a ten-minute hug, and he saved me and himself. He knew just how to stay alive. And to keep me alive.

♦

I was miserable, I admit, after the day before spending almost two hours on the phone for a grueling job interview that convinced me I could never get a decent-paying, fascinating job that was perfect for me. That job was so—*not* perfect. The recruiter couldn't understand anything I was saying. I couldn't seem to follow the directions a CEO former client gave me: that I should be concise so people like the recruiter (who, it so happened, might have had some leftover negative feelings toward that CEO, as she was, at some point, caught in some crossfire) don't get impatient. I was getting impatient just trying to spit out this sentence. The bottom line was that it was dismal. And after she told me more about the job and how I'd have no other life but THE JOB and how the last person who held that job was so incredible and could do everything and had to be "*heavily* recruited," I could see—as she had already decided in the first five minutes—that job was not for me. She finished and left me with the same admonishment the CEO former client had given me: I'd better be concise if I should get a phone interview with the senior VP, which, she implied, was still a possibility since my CEO former client carried a lot of weight with her. That senior VP would cut me off quickly, though, if I didn't "up my game," she said, since clearly I couldn't complete a project on time if I couldn't answer a question in time.

But don't think I didn't do my part in this family to keep us afloat! Prior to my telephone interview, I was at another two-hour meeting, Raphael's 504 evaluation for special services at school, with most of his teachers (though, in their defense, it was long because, as Raphael loved to tell me, I talked too much). He had just started high school, ninth grade; he was fourteen years old. Seeing the grades for the first time, I was a little stuck as to why I could get an e-mail saying how great Raphael was doing one day and then see an F on his report card a day later. They told me how it can just change from one day to the next. *So then what,* I wondered? *Should I e-mail every day?* Actually, they said, "Grades can turn on a moment," like the last moment of the period when Raphael had admitted he didn't do whatever fifty-point assignment was due, since that was really the only assignment that carried any point value for the whole grading period. And apparently at the moment the teacher went to put down the grade, she saw that he hadn't turned that assignment in. So I wondered, *Should I call and e-mail every moment? Every second? No, because this might be based on a previous second.* I wanted to return to the copacetic flow of my life in my dream with Ellen.

I got it: it was augmented reality. I had been trying to work on that concept for a client. There was a conference coming up entirely devoted to augmented reality.

{Mashable definition: Augmented reality (AR) is a live—direct or indirect—view of a physical, real-world environment whose elements are augmented by computer-generated sensory input such as sound, video, graphics, or GPS data.}

I really didn't know what was going on in my son's school, despite the fact that I e-mailed the teachers every Friday as instructed. He still came home, got on his computer (if he hadn't loaned it out) or mine, and cruised the Internet, telling me it was for a school assignment. But the Word doc for the assignment would be blank after his name. One night he was using my computer and erased two hours' worth of work I'd done and hadn't saved, and the night before that, a strange sex chat came up: "Diverse choices, for Sex Chat, now." "Pop-ups," Raphael said, "not me." Well, perhaps a pop-up sex chat might do me some good, but I was greatly annoyed—bordering on enraged—that it was on my computer, which Raphael had clearly borrowed. (All without permission. I couldn't afford to have another work computer mysteriously die on me because of water on the brain—the computer's, not mine.) I wondered, briefly, if this sex chat could be a moneymaking opportunity that I could take advantage of after Raphael went to sleep. But the likelihood of him crawling into bed with me when I was in the middle of servicing my customers was disturbing. He still sometimes told me that his feet were cold or gave me some other reason he needed to come into my room and sleep next to me.

What didn't I understand? Why the dishes piled up day after day? And why I tried so hard, and it all felt completely futile on mornings like that? Why I felt like calling the hot ex-girlfriend, Jessica, even knowing that she didn't have a clue or the slightest desire to learn about difficulties related to child-rearing, or maybe she didn't even want to know about me?

What didn't I understand? Why I could look at myself one minute and feel so beautiful and then look at myself again and feel so worthless and ugly after my grueling telephone interview and after running into the ex-girlfriend for the first time in a year? And being just plain exhausted. Oh, and having that roll of stomach fat after my Year of Eating Banana Splits.

So much I didn't understand. I would never try to answer that question completely, since Raphael didn't need to hear the extent of what I didn't understand.

◆

My Magical Message didn't appear in my e-mail that day. Perhaps it was trapped in my spam filter. Perhaps it was contained in my son's hug before he went off to school. Or embedded in my dream with Ellen the night before, the dream that still makes me laugh when I remember.

What to Expect When You're Expecting: The Teenage Years, When "Molly" Is Not a Schoolgirl

When your child was little, you worried about all sorts of things. (See earlier chapter 2 on lead paint, acid reflux, playdates, et cetera.) Prepare yourself now for new stay-awake-at-night moments during the transition from tween to teen. When your son or daughter is ready to enter middle school, you will want to start buying real cream and whipping your own. (See "Whippets" in the glossary.) You will learn that aerosol whipped cream is just one of many common household items with which your budding young drug addict may begin to experiment.

Back when your child moved into toddlerhood, you learned how to baby proof, but now you must *teen* proof. We're talking about looking for drugs that can be found in almost any home. Here are some tips to get you started.

The liquor cabinet: This is a favorite place for your young scientist to look for his or her first mind-altering experience. Start with your own stash. You probably have bottles in there that you don't even remember from all the traveling you did back before you had kids. From the Israeli Sabra liquor to the Nicaraguan Flor de Caña rum—even the old two-buck Chuck from Trader Joe's—they all have to go.

Prescription drugs: Mother's little helper has now become your teenager's. Stressed out by the English assignment you never started or the upcoming math quiz? Try mom's Ativan. Bummed out about the girl who was ready to give you your first hand job last week and now won't talk to you? Maybe Vicodin will take away the pain.

Cold medications: You may think your son is just trying to deal with his sniffles, but kids have been trying this one for a long time. Now teens take Robitussin or almost any other cold medication to get high. There is even a name for it: "Robocop." Or "Robohead." Or something.

Everything but the kitchen sink: A true addict will try anything available—cleaning products, felt tip markers, even vanilla extract and powdered nutmeg. (Don't let your little chef tell you he's baking a cake.) Showtime featured a story on a desperate eighty-year-old alcoholic who died drinking hand sanitizer.

Cow pastures: To all you parents who want to live out in the country so that your kid can have fresh air and good rural fun, do you know how well those magic mushrooms grow in cow shit? (At least, they did when we were kids. Perhaps you are fortunate enough to live in a more urban area where there may be chickens but no cows.) And anyway, most of these specialty products can be locally sourced on the teen market.

Bath salts: Has your teenager told you that she needs to take long baths . . . with bath salts? Think twice! Bath salts are sold over the counter at places like little grocery stores in Chinatown. And though it says, "Not for human consumption" on the package, you can be quite sure that your teenager is smoking it. Synthetic marijuana! It's been known to make a person want to chew off someone's ear! Of course, it is remotely possible that your kid just wants some privacy to look at porn and masturbate. But don't bank on that. The best porn is found online (see chapter 3), and kids know better than to bring electronics into the bathtub with them.

◆

As your child goes into the early teen years, you might be excited that he is taking longer and more frequent walks. Perhaps the hikes you enjoyed as a family in the younger years will return. How nice it is to get daily exercise! How lovely it is that you live somewhere (if you do) where it is safe for your child to walk around. How age appropriate that he is feeling more independent!

Soon you'll notice some indications of trouble in paradise. It might start with a little discovery as you attempt to tame the growing odor emanating from your teen's room, picking up moldy, unidentifiable-food-encrusted dishes. You decide to do a little deeper cleaning and straightening, and upon opening up her bedside drawer, you find the telltale signs of foul play: little green blossoms (marijuana) and a gun. Okay—back up! The gun is not a real gun, despite its appearance. It is just an old BB gun. Your daughter says she got it from the ice cream man! I guess those kids aren't just chasing after the music for a Fudgsicle. On further research, you discover that some of these trucks do sell real guns too.

There will be more surprises, and one of them might be part of a treasure hunt, as you look through your teen's Facebook account when he turns up missing. He told you he was studying at the library, but you realize it's a national holiday. Facebook shows you his real activity: a string of his messages searching for items you'll have to look up. A bar? (Don't we have soap at home?) Turns out this is a form that Xanax comes in.

{Urban Dictionary: A 2 mg Xanax that is shaped like a bar I ==== I. Can be divided into 1/4s. Abused by many.}

I just snorted a xanax bar, now i fill like rockin. You'll find him later, but it won't be pretty. That barely recognizable person staggering around over by the Metro station really is your son. Tip: better to be safe than sorry. Rush him to the ER when he doesn't identify what drugs he was taking and just wants to go to sleep.

When your teen is about fifteen, you can expect to look into potential outpatient drug programs. Your kid may even have a rehab playlist for the two of you to enjoy on the way. It will have songs like Rick James's "Mary Jane," Eric Clapton's "Cocaine," and Wax's song—you know, that one that says he's in love with the "Dispensary Girl."

Relax. This is a rare opportunity to bond with your teenager. Your nights of watching *Breaking Bad* together may be numbered, but you can learn important information during this time. For example, "Molly" is not the name of someone's girlfriend.

But buyer beware. Some programs, such as the outpatient one that your local HMO offers, might have some requirements for you parents, too, such as attending your own twelve-step group (Al-Anon or any other you might need) several nights a week. And most importantly, they might ask the parents to refrain from using any nonprescription drugs or alcohol during the period when you and your teen are attending their program. They will tell you this is a *family* disease.

For those of you spending a decade trying out different inpatient and outpatient programs, please refer to appendix 1, "Choosing the Best Treatment Program for You and Your Family: Top Ten Factors to Consider." The first one you might want to think about is money. Addiction is a huge business, and many programs will cost you the equivalent of a private college education or a good-sized house in a prime market. Cheer up! Many of your children will never make it to college, and this may be a better investment. For those of you without resources, this could be a great time to let your teen find her own "bottom." When she is ready, there are free rehab programs, like the Salvation Army's. But the truth is, most of us parents will do almost anything to keep our kids from hitting bottom when that might mean incarceration, homelessness, or death.

When your teenager is about seventeen, you can expect to take him to the local vape bar. He will most likely want to pick one with a high rating on Yelp. Buy him an e-cigarette kit and some special flavored e-juice in mint chocolate or watermelon. Everyone says that smoking is a necessary evil when going through a twelve-step program. Vaping may help him quit actual cigarettes—at least, that is what he says, now that he has confessed that he's been smoking for years, and no amount of hand-wringing or raging on your part is helping him quit. You can tell him what a disgusting habit it is, and you can remind him of the many times when he was little that you had to rush him to the ER for the asthma and respiratory problems that almost killed him. (And now he's smoking cigarettes?!) You may even want to force him to take a shower each time he comes home smelling like smoke. Don't try it. You will look ridiculous. You may both laugh about it later, but you'll have a big fight at the time.

Case study: Your seventeen-year-old daughter steals a few bottles of Robitussin from the local Ralph's. The paramedics take her to the ER at 10:30 p.m. You stay in the hospital with her until 7:30 the next morning. The release paper work reads, "Intentional overdose, nontoxic." To get this diagnosis, they used a Foley catheter to retrieve the urine at around 5:30 a.m., since she has been unable to pee all night. Then the doctor had to research what you already know (since you are now reading *What to Expect When You're Expecting: The Teenage Years*).

Don't panic if the test indicates that your teenager is taking PCP. Many common cold medicines mimic the effects of crystal meth or PCP. But don't breathe a sigh of relief either. Instead, read our chapter 4 on "Roboheads" and permanent brain damage. Be sure to access your support system when you spend those long nights in the ER. A great way to connect with other MOTA (Mothers of Teenage Addicts) is through Facebook. (*Mota* also means "pot" in Spanish—just thought you should know.) And don't forget to check in on all your social media accounts when you arrive at the hospital! Hashtag: #another5150. If you aren't already aware, 5150 is the mandatory seventy-two-hour psych hold used when your child is found to be a risk to herself or others. Usually, taking eighty to one hundred Robitussin caplets will qualify her for this.

Here's an important tip: if you are broke and struggling to pay the rent or mortgage while still attempting to finance your teen's treatment, consider fixing yourself first. Though that's near impossible; you'd lie across the train tracks if it would save her life.

If you are one of the lucky ones, you will find your own recovery from the insanity of codependence and addiction. You will learn, when the miracle happens, that you "detach with love" (a completely counter-intuitive measure for any mom). The first time you hear someone use that phrase is after your kid is caught smoking pot with friends and you get a call from the police. When the cops come and pull out their guns, the other (all white) boys run away, but your own (Black) son stops with his hands up. You call the mom of one of your kid's pot-smoking friends, and she says, "I'm working my program; I'm detaching with love." You hang up and think, *That mom is so irresponsible!* (See appendix 2, "More about Recovery.")

Expect to spend large chunks of time in therapy, banging your head or another object against the wall and wailing, "What did I do?" If you are honest with yourself as you look back at your son's history, you will realize that you could have predicted his struggles with addiction when, at two and a half years of age, he was still attempting to nurse around the clock. Yes, his gateway drug was breast milk! You had to put him into NA (Nursing Anonymous) because there was no way you were going to have one of those boys who stands up and demands, "Wanna nurse, wanna nurse!" Or have him hitting the teenage years and asking, "Mom, can I borrow the car? And how about a quick suck of the tit?" on the way out. You told him he had to get off that shit now.

Please keep your eyes out for the next edition in our series: *What to Expect When You're Expecting: Rehab Mom.* **Here's a sneak preview.**

Sometime after your daughter's third intensive drug-treatment program (two inpatient, one outpatient), you will run out of a meeting with her rehab counselor sobbing uncontrollably, with snot splayed out over your face. You are undone over your complete failure (and everyone else's) to stop your teen from her committed descent into a state of eyes-rolled-back-to-the-head, dead, desolate darkness. You, too, will feel misunderstood and underappreciated, and you may decide that perhaps your only alternative is for you yourself to start using. Become an addict too.

"You could do that," one sagacious young counselor (a twenty-five-year-old addict with a two-year-old son) told one parent. You will learn that some of the addiction counselors who are in recovery and young enough to be your children have the wisdom of Obi-Wan Kenobi. So, buck up—that is what recovery could do for your teen. Becoming an addict yourself will only create new demands on your time. Although you might be able to get thirty days off from your daily life. But if you are a rehab mom, please read on!

"If This Is So, Why Am I?"

In three years, how did I get from standing on the bimah for my son's bar mitzvah to visiting him in the adolescent wing of a psych ward? Raphael was there on a seventy-two-hour hold, which is when a social worker from the psychiatric emergency team evaluates a person under eighteen to see if they are a risk to themselves or to others. This was the first time my son had been put on such a hold related to his escalating drug use.

I drove somewhere down the 605 toward Santa Ana to a hospital with an adolescent psych ward. I was buzzed into a locked unit. I entered and signed in, looking eagerly around for Raphael. The large room where the visits took place had posters on the wall. Some were informational, listing rules, and others were friendly, with pleasant scenes and inspirational quotes, but they didn't take away from the stark, institutional look. This was not to be one of Raphael's favorite places for a psych hold. Subsequent adolescent wards and treatment centers we went through might have had bright murals, and I do not even remember exactly where this one was, but it was only a way station to the next step that I hoped would arrest the downward slide. The physicality, the geographic location, of his first seventy-two-hour hold is mostly a giant blank in my memory. I've been told that trauma can do this, above and beyond the normal menopausal memory drain.

I decided to mentally retrace the days leading up to that Sunday night. I began with Raphael's return from his high school trip to Ireland and Scotland eight days before. He had seemed happy and showed me pictures: a lot of time sitting in cafés. Very green, lush vistas. I noticed what looked like a beer here and there, but he moved fast over those images. He was supposed to be sober. We had spent about a year going to an outpatient substance-abuse program, one that also required me, the custodial parent, to abstain from using alcohol and nonprescription drugs—something I wasn't altogether happy about, having become accustomed to the nightly glass of wine to create the happy hour illusion of a buffer between the demands of work and the demands of home. "Come on, honey, we're out of here; we don't need this," I had wanted to say when they first told us that rule. Hell, my dad had just died less than a week earlier, the day before Father's Day, and for us it's almost a custom to drink wine or liquor, the so-called post-funeral schnapps, sipping with the old Jewish men who are still alive. We were practically still sitting shiva. But I had complied with the rule, even when Raphael said, "Go on,

I won't tell."

Raphael had had several relapses over the last year-and-a-half and had moved from using marijuana to trying various pills and synthetic marijuana, labeled as "bath salts" and/or "incense" and sold in Chinatown. We had looked at internet accounts of psychotic reactions to synthetic marijuana and read about someone biting someone's ear off after using. I remembered the night I saw the foil package in the bathroom, which I first thought was a condom wrapper. I would have been relieved at that point. Instead, it was labeled "not for human consumption," and the crazy redness and movement of Raphael's eyes showed that the wrapper contained something else.

By the time the HMO therapist suggested that he wasn't really getting much out of the outpatient substance-abuse treatment program anymore (after about a year in), we were both ready to stop going to weekly family group sessions. I was looking forward to being able to have a glass of wine when I got home. The high school had known about his drug-treatment program, and it hadn't occurred to me to remind them not to allow him to drink alcohol or use drugs on the trip overseas. Looking back, I am outraged; that seemed a no-brainer. But I had never been a sixteen-year-old in Ireland or Scotland, where there seemed to be a lot of leeway for teens drinking.

Sunday, the day after he returned from his overseas school trip, he was up early. "Make me breakfast, Mom!" he demanded at 6:30 a.m., and I did. I thought that ten days apart had been good for both of us. He promised to study for a makeup test he had missed last quarter, said that he was going to go to the library, and walked out of the house with his backpack a couple of hours later.

I was straightening up the dining room table and noticed that his computer was on. Something looked suspect on his screen, and on an impulse, I began to look at his searches: "What's the best way to take Xanax—snort or shoot up?" I'd never wanted to be a private investigator or drug tester or probation officer type of parent to my son. But I could no longer assume that what I didn't know wouldn't hurt him, and my role had changed over the past year. I opened up his Facebook page and saw a path of drug-related messages. Question: "Hey, can I get bars?" Answer: "I've got ten . . ." And so on. All this had been taking place before he went to Ireland and then again on the night of his return and into that morning.

I decided to go find him at the local library, but I suddenly felt stupid when I realized that it was a national holiday. It was unlikely he'd be there, but for some reason I went anyway. Of course, the library was closed. I walked back, calling and texting him, and when I got home, I also sent a message to one friend via his Facebook. I began to cry. I phoned my older sister, and she said, "I'll call him and tell him that if he doesn't call you right away, you'll call the police." I called my girlfriend, who told me, "Stay there. I'm coming over." She arrived about an hour later.

And then the phone rang. I demanded, "Where are you?" I couldn't understand what he was saying, and at that moment I didn't feel like I was really talking to my son. I'd never yet heard him slur his words or sound so unlike himself. "Acchhh, donn't know, didn't like that libbbrary."

"Raphael, where are you? What are you doing? What have you taken?"

"No, no drugs, naah." Somewhere in his mushy speech I caught the name of a park.

"Wait, we're coming for you, don't leave." The phone clicked. Disconnected. My girlfriend drove me to the park while I sobbed and tried to call him again. He answered after the second call, but his speech was no longer even translatable. "You are at the Memorial Park Metro station? Wait, we're coming over," I said. Again, the phone call ended. But by then, we were almost there.

When we arrived, it was afternoon, already getting dark early, as it was November. Raphael was stumbling around, his backpack missing, like one of the junkies who inhabited the large, tree-lined, graffiti-streaked park. I couldn't believe that I was looking at my sixteen-year-old. He had appeared so tall, handsome, and sophisticated the day before, when he got off the plane from Ireland. When he was explaining the decades-old conflict in Ireland and why he liked Scotland the best of the places they visited.

On the way home from the park, I called the HMO consulting nurse from the car while my girlfriend drove. They told me that I should probably bring him into the ER, but I didn't. I remembered my son's pediatrician warning me about the poor conditions of our HMO's ER: "Only go there if you are really dying." So I decided to wait until the next morning, thinking I could take him straight to the outpatient youth addiction program when they opened. I was certain that they would take action—refer him to something more intensive, inpatient, something that corresponded with the desperation that I felt.

We arrived home, and Raphael said that he was starved. My girlfriend made him some steak. It was impossible for him to cut his own meat. He could barely keep his head up, and he didn't want to listen to my questions while I cut up his steak for him. He took a couple of bites and then stumbled into his bedroom. Within a few minutes he was in a deep sleep, passed out but still alive. So I decided to take my sister's suggestion and rummaged through his pants pockets.

I felt something right away and found a bag with pills of varying sizes—round white ones and blue cylinders. Plus little clumps of very ripe-smelling weed in a plastic cylinder. It didn't look or smell like the marijuana I remembered from my youth. I wondered what he had taken and realized that the blue cylinders were the bars of Xanax we had seen in the picture I'd looked up.

I listened to his breath again and shoved him a bit. He didn't wake up. "Raphael," I whispered. I wasn't sure how much jet lag contributed to his comatose state. But my girlfriend confirmed that he was breathing, and I let him sleep.

In the morning, he got up and climbed into my bed and under the covers. I was prepared to drive us to the outpatient rehab program. When he began to protest, I said: "Don't—please don't start lying to me. You owe me that respect."

I had it all—the pills, the pot, the computer search for "inject or snort Xanax," and the Facebook messages, all thoroughly documenting his madcap search for drugs to take with him on his school trip to Ireland, to consume when he got back, and to use throughout his so-called sober year of rehab. He stopped arguing and curled up against me.

"You should watch the DVD of your bar mitzvah. Remember who you are, the poetry you wrote, what you are capable of," I told him in a tone halfway between demanding and desperate pleading. Together with the rabbi, he had distilled his bizarre Torah portion—"What to do if your wife is unfaithful?"—down to issues of trust and vulnerability, peppering his sermon with vignettes about teen prostitutes and Bernie Madoff. Later, he read his poetry. Watching him up on the podium, I had believed that he would be more than okay.

"I was smoking crack cocaine then . . . with Joey," he announced.

I got a chill and asked, "When you were thirteen? Where would you buy it? You're kidding me." I begged him to cop to the unfunny joke.

He looked utterly serious, not the deadpan "fooled you, hahaha" look. "No, really, I was. We got it from the old Black man in the wheelchair on Fair Oaks and Woodbury," he said.

I froze. I asked him again. "Nah, not really, we just snort cocaine," he said.

My chest was tight and painful as he leaned into me, his dark, tight curls brushing against my face. He was warm with musty boy smell, cuddly like when he was sick as a baby. But he was not one or two or even eight. He was sixteen, and the night before he had been stumbling around the Memorial Park Metro station, slurring his speech into incoherent sound bites.

Then, as I felt him snuggling up against me, I wanted to weep, remembering the times we had sat cuddled up like this when he was a warm, sweaty baby boy, hot with fever, nursing or just sitting close. Back then, I existed in "mommy time," forced to slow down by a high fever, severe croup turned to asthma, or week-long stomach flu.

I had saved his life once, long ago, by taking him to the ER after calling over and over again, saying his breathing just wasn't right, his fever kept spiking. I wondered now if I could save him. Back then it was easier. I could help a two-year-old with few words, no poetry, just barely able to say, "*¿Mamá, ese, ese?*," asking about all the hospital machinery, lines going in and out of him, the beeping yellow monitor. We'd been living with his babysitter from El Salvador and her son, and his main language was still Spanish at that point.

Now he was sixteen, and his language was a cross-section of teenage boy, an early code-switching ability (without calling it that), hip-hop lines, and mannish utterances of bravado, denial, denial, and denial until I shut him down with my successful drug scavenger hunt. Even marijuana seemed different from when I was younger, though I didn't know because I hadn't tried the new breed. And at his age, I'd already slowed down with the pot smoking and had never really had anything too strong. We had picked psilocybin mushrooms in the cow pastures across from my high school. But I was already on my way to graduating early, taking extra credits at the school for dropouts in addition to my regular high school classes.

And the other drugs—the bars of Xanax and the round ones I couldn't identify? When I was a kid we turned our noses up at stealing our mom's prescription drugs—"mother's little helpers." That seemed so . . . *Stepford Wives* to us. We were cooler than that, trying illicit LSD or mushrooms. Prescription-drug usage is an epidemic among kids now—Vicodin, Ativan, Xanax, and all the drugs for ADD. But I hadn't yet acknowledged my own tendency to turn to a pill or alcohol when I was feeling severely anxious or stressed out.

There was a Martin Luther King, Jr. picture on my son's bedroom door saying, "MLK lifted us all up," showing Dr. King lifting up a child, advocating nonviolence. I took Raphael to the HMO's addiction medicine department, where we met with an outpatient therapist. I went there intending to leave without Raphael, sure that he'd go straight into some kind of inpatient care that would speak to the urgency of his condition. He'd nearly overdosed, and he was still high and bleary-eyed from the night before. But Raphael wasn't ready to go into inpatient, and instead they proposed a program of counseling and AA meetings. He came home with me and immediately went into his room and fell asleep.

Later that day, his dad arrived. I had called Larry to tell him what had happened. Though Raphael had lived with me full-time up until then and didn't have a consistent visitation schedule with his dad, Larry had talked about "trying him out"—having Raphael live with him and his girlfriend for a few weeks.

Larry showed up seemingly seething with anger. He sat at a desk in my living room, his girlfriend on the fainting couch. Raphael was still in his room. Larry looked at his e-mails on his phone and saw one he didn't like; he erupted. The e-mail was from my sister, urging Larry and his girlfriend to work together with us on supporting Raphael. In several family meetings I'd called over the last year with Raphael's aunts and uncles, his dad and his girlfriend, I had tried to get us all to operate as a united family. But we weren't that. Larry and his girlfriend—who happened to be trained as a social worker—often talked about what I could have and should have done differently to "manage" Raphael. This was no longer sitting well with my siblings or me; I was doing the best I could.

Furious with my sister's e-mail, Larry burst into Raphael's room with the MLK poster on the outside urging nonviolence. He screamed, "I'm going to beat your ass!" I heard scuffling, crashing noises. Larry's girlfriend looked at me and said, "Just wait." I didn't. In a split second I was banging on Raphael's bedroom door and yelling, "Stop, let me in!" (Later I asked her, "Would you have waited while someone threatened to kick your daughter's ass?" And she admitted that this did give her pause; she probably wouldn't have waited.)

Raphael was tall and normally more fit than his dad, but his dad was a big man. When he raged, Larry appeared even more enormous to me. That day, after his near overdose, Raphael didn't seem in any shape to fight back, and when I pushed the door open, he was looking at his dad with a strange, quizzical expression. I'd seen him with this look before, and I had leaped between them before. Sometimes Raphael had told me— as he did later about this time—that he deserved to get his butt kicked. But even if you believed in the occasional spanking, which I didn't, this was not what was happening with his dad. Larry was coming from a place of uncontrolled and unrestrained rage—an adrenaline rush he seemed to embrace whenever it came over him.

As I pushed my way into the room, Larry shoved me out of it, knocked me down, and slammed the door shut against me. It was not an accidental fall, as his girlfriend, the police, and our son later seemed to want me to believe. He was out of control. I picked myself up, ran past Larry's girlfriend (who still sat passively, helplessly, it seemed, on the fainting couch), and went downstairs and into my neighbor's apartment crying, "Call the police!"

A little while later, Larry's girlfriend walked downstairs where I was with my neighbor and told me what had happened. Larry had said to Raphael, "I'm done with you," that he never wanted to see him again, and run out of our apartment. Raphael had chased after him. She pleaded with me: "Please, it's all a terrible mistake. Raphael is with his dad now. It just got out of control. No one is hurt." She didn't ask me if I was hurt or how I felt.

Two policemen showed up and asked me to go upstairs to our apartment; Raphael was now upstairs too. They asked what had happened, and as I tried to explain, they began to holler at Raphael, "You see what you've done? You made your parents angry, caused fighting between them . . ."

I interrupted the policemen to tell them that the anger, the arguments, the violence had started before Raphael was even born. They turned to me and asked me over and over again, "What happened? Did he push you down on purpose or maybe accidentally to just try to get out of the way?"

I didn't know how to answer. I used to work in domestic violence many years ago, when I was in a healthy relationship with Henry. This line of questioning, trying to explain away the violence, made me think that perhaps some twenty years later, the handling of "these kinds of cases" hadn't progressed.

Then they asked, "Do you want to press charges?"

I said no, I didn't. So they got Larry and asked him to sit down at the dining room table and asked Raphael to sit down. "Look, man, we've been through this," they said to Larry. "We get it. We were raised like you. But these days you can't hit your wife when you get mad; you can't hit your kid when he acts out. It's against the law. You gotta work together on this."

Larry looked up. "Well, we just think this happens every time she lets him go on a trip. She . . . ," as he pointed at me, the mother.

Before I could say anything, Raphael spoke up. "No," he said quietly. "No, Dad. It's not because she let me go on the school trip. It would've happened anyway. I take drugs. I'm an addict."

Larry stared, his anger temporarily abated by shock. I, too, was stunned by Raphael's honesty, his willingness to say this. Later, I would see this as the first moment where Raphael might have considered or acknowledged that his drug and alcohol use was more than normal teenage experimentation. The first time his dad was really forced to see the significance of the problem. When I had put Raphael in his first outpatient program, I got the distinct feeling that Larry, his girlfriend, perhaps even my family initially thought I was overreacting to some casual drug use. My experience with Raphael was that he was struggling with organization, focus, and school already, without drugs. Like so many of the young men in the program, he too had already begun to have the school interventions and problems related to attention, disorganization, and other challenges. The drug use sometimes—often—seemed like a coping mechanism for these boys to get through an inhospitable environment: school. A form of self-medication. And even when some of them (including Raphael) might try out the ADD medication, that too became something they would abuse, not improving the school situation.

I turned to his dad and said, "Please, please, can we work together?" as I had pleaded so many times before. The police looked at him. "Hey, man. So can you work together to help your son?"

Suddenly they had become impromptu social workers—imperfect, but I was ready to credit them for effort. Today, so many years later, I can't remember what Larry responded or if there was a barely perceptible nod of agreement.

Raphael and I bumbled our way through the next day, as if in a sloweddown, sluggish kind of nightmare. The inverse, the paradoxical, of the dreamy sensation of joyful "mommy time" with a newborn, when everything slows down. Where I had felt utterly in the present, no place I'd rather be, now I was inhabiting territory I'd never wanted to visit. A stranger called, a young woman who said she found Raphael's backpack somewhere. I drove to pick it up, and the girl answered the door and handed me the backpack. I imagined that she looked at me with a mixture of pity, curiosity, and relief that she could get rid of this toxic relic of teenage free fall. In it was more drug paraphernalia that even I could recognize—a pipe, lighters, a few loose unidentified pills—as well as his notepad, phone, random crushed school papers.

A day later Raphael was with his aunt, my sister. I was working late, and she called to suggest that he stay overnight. They had just returned from a temple event. "He's been so great tonight; everyone at temple stopped to say how handsome and respectful he is. He wanted to cook fish for me, and it was delicious." She described shopping and cooking with him and told me that he was in the bath at the moment. Then I heard, "Wait, I have to go . . . I smell pot!"

My sister called back. Raphael was already asleep and denied smoking marijuana, but the bathroom clearly smelled of weed and sulfur from the matches, she said. Then I knew he'd gone over the edge—he would never have been so brazen at his aunt's house if he hadn't.

Before Raphael was conceived, my sister gave blood to me, even though she hated having blood taken. I'd had more than four miscarriages already, and they were trying a treatment that involved taking her red blood cells and mixing them with mine, inserting into my body subcutaneously, a burning, painful experience that left me feeling sick for days. "You've got a piece of me in you," she always told Raphael. She felt close to her nephew. But that night she felt betrayed.

On Saturday my sister agreed to attend an Al-Anon meeting with me. I dropped Raphael off at his therapist's office. My sister was trying to understand what was happening to Raphael, and the concept of "detach with love" sounded a lot like giving up to her. "Detach with love" means not doing for someone else what they can do for themselves, as that allows them the dignity to take responsibility for themselves. The first instinct when a teenager is this out of control—almost dies from an overdose—is to lock them up with you and hold on tight twenty-four hours a day. There were parents in the rehab program who did just that, never allowing their children ever to do overnights anywhere, and their kids still managed to get hold of drugs and use them frequently. And there were parents out there whose children had died even as they tried to hold on tight and save them.

When we left the Al-Anon meeting, I saw a message from Raphael's therapist. He had gotten Raphael to agree to go to the ER for an evaluation so he could be considered for a psych hold. Raphael had left his office and was supposedly on his way home.

I got in the car and drove over to my house, where I found Raphael, and we headed over to the ER at our HMO. Later, the social worker spoke to us both and decided that Raphael should be put on a 5150 hold, as he was a potential danger to himself. A police officer was then stationed outside the room Raphael was in. Standard practice, as I would learn.

Two days later, I drove up to the hospital psych ward. The adolescent psych ward was not a part of the HMO where Raphael regularly went for care; it was about forty-five minutes away, and I walked in cautiously, not knowing what to expect. I left my phone and valuables in the car, as requested, and signed in. It seemed that he was not intentionally suicidal, but his actions were "spiraling out of control" and could result in death.

I was late arriving for the ninety-minute visiting hour, but Raphael was done before it was over. "I'm tired; I want to sleep," he announced.

"Wait," I said. I wanted to hang onto him.

Other families sat huddled together, talking softly, and a few teens sat alone, without their parents. I saw a mom braiding her daughter's hair, another parent comforting a weeping child. Who comforted the parents? I remember my sister telling me when I was pregnant, "It turns out that they are so much safer in the womb."

And yet, when the pregnancy with Raphael stayed put, and he first came into the world, I felt happier than I ever had in my life. *Im kein, lamah zeh anochi?* "If this is so, why am I?"

I had been handed these Hebrew words early that morning at the Jewish meditation group I sometimes attended. If "this" was my son landing in an adolescent psych ward because his drug use could kill him, then the "why am I?" was a question I could not answer. I only knew that Raphael was safe for two more days.

Road Trip

Every moment I was not visiting my son in the adolescent psych ward during another one of his 5150 holds, I was rallying to get him into the best inpatient rehab center that our HMO insurance would authorize. This would be the fourth time around for inpatient treatment, and I was still caught in the crazy-mom hamster-wheel routine of trying to find the exact fix for my son. One mom in an Al-Anon meeting approached me and said, "Hey, if my son was under eighteen, I'd do my damnedest to get the HMO to pay for the Center for Inspiration."

I didn't care about the organic vegan chef or daily trips to the gym, yoga or tai chi, but I prayed the level of nurturing the Center for Inspiration had, including the daily therapy sessions, would be the magic bullet of drug treatment. I urged the HMO addiction counselors to refer him there.

On the day that Raphael was getting released from his psych hold, following our HMO's protocol, I was instructed to pick him up and take him back to their substance-abuse team counselor, who would evaluate him and decide the next steps. The team would not promise me the holistic summer-camp-like treatment center, but it was one of their possible referrals. I didn't trust my current driving ability, having just recovered my vehicle from the latest mash-up, another casualty of driving with Freaking Out about Son Syndrome. So, I had enlisted my sixteen-year-old stepdaughter, Serena, to drive. She had recently gotten her driver's license and already showed stronger driving skills than mine.

"It's not going to work," she told me adamantly regarding Raphael getting sober. "I've seen it before; my sister and brother did the same thing." (Her bio siblings.) But Serena was game to drive and see Raphael, and by the time she jumped into the driver's seat of my newly repaired car, she had a better attitude: "Maybe this time will be different." She'd been through her own thing with a seventy-two-hour psych hold four years earlier, during her cutting phase, when she casually dropped the idea to one of her moms that she might like to die.

So we started out on a sort of road trip to save Raphael. I'd always imagined a different kind of road trip with my kids, and they had too. We'd gone only on short trips to the beach. Raphael, María Elena, and I had taken one road trip to Tijuana, on the border with Mexico, to check out a writing residency that was held in an arts center converted from a former drug smuggling house/tunnel. (Raphael wanted to make sure I wouldn't be murdered by narco-traffickers.)

Our first stop was to pick up Raphael at the adolescent psych ward on the far end of the San Fernando Valley. The route was familiar; it might have been his third or fourth stay there—I'd lost count. That went without a hitch. I cast one last longing glance at the teens lounging in their fuzzy PJs, watching *To Sir, with Love*. What a nice break it would be just to kick back with some Ativan in front of a good movie, not worry about cooking or paying the bills. Seventy-two hours would be enough; I'd hate to be stuck there a longer time. On the way out, I gave a big hug to one seventeen-year-old young woman I'd grown fond of during my visits, a mixed martial arts champion. I told her, "Maybe I'll see you out there sometime, when you're famous. I can say I knew you back in the day!"

She laughed raucously. "Yeah, perfect, you can say you knew me from the psych ward."

We piled into the car, Serena at the wheel. Raphael said, "I call shotgun" and sat in front, eager to get hold of an iPhone or at least control the music selection. I sat in the back and encouraged Serena not to follow the cars so closely. We hit the 110 Harbor Freeway and made it over to our next stop, our HMO in Hollywood, where a team of substance-abuse treatment professionals—all white (unlike my family), none parents (unlike me)—would decide my son's fate.

This particular psych-ward-and-HMO-referral triathlon had grown complicated. In order to get into inpatient treatment, he usually had to go through the seventy-two-hour psych hold. As always, they required that the patient be agreeable to the inpatient treatment. If not, they would deny authorization. On this occasion, Raphael was on board, which took care of the first hurdle. Perhaps with the allure of a potential rehab romance— the treatment center we were pushing for was co-ed—Raphael was willing to give it another shot. Other inpatient treatment places kept the guys strictly separate from the girls.

The counselor left us waiting about an hour after meeting with Raphael and then returned. "Okay, we authorized an inpatient treatment center." The one we were hoping for. That would be our third stop. The counselor said, "They are holding you a spot. You need to go right now."

It was now going on five hours since I had left my place and picked up Serena in Eagle Rock to start our journey. I was operating on five months of little sleep and had been pining for a long rest, or at least a shit, shower, and shave in peace, without coming home to my son's bleary, red-eyed look that led to 911 calls. "We'll take it," I told the counselor as if I were grabbing the last hotel room in the most desirable location.

Serena and Raphael got back into the front seat, and Siri proceeded to give us directions in her newly minted Australian voice. She sent us down a closed freeway exit, and just as I was checking Waze for a better route, I felt a jolt and looked up to see a car slam into us, drive down the street, and stop.

"I didn't do anything, I didn't . . ." Serena said, immediately crying, clearly agitated.

"Is everyone okay?" I asked, and the kids assured me that they were. "Pull over," I commanded. I knew what to do; I have been around the block a few times when it came to car accidents.

The man from the car that hit us ran up to the driver's window, motioning to Serena to roll it down, and asked in a heavy Spanish accent, "Everyone okay? All okay?"

Again, the kids nodded yes.

"Good!" he said and ran off, got into his car, and drove away. "Shit!" I yelled out. "We need his information!"

The kids, having already recovered from the shock, spoke in unison. "He's probably illegal. Yeah . . . do you want him to get deported? Probably doesn't have insurance, and now you want him to be separated from his wife and children? That's not cool, Mom!"

"Of course not, but I just got the car fixed!" I was the last person to want someone deported or separated from family. Little shits!

It seemed like this trip was getting longer and longer. I'd lost track of time, but by now we could have driven to Sedona, the Grand Canyon, or even partway to New Mexico. Places I had wanted to take the kids. Reluctantly, I took over driving and got us to the treatment center and began the now somewhat familiar check-in process.

When I thought about this trip later, I remembered that I simultaneously felt both another surge of adrenaline and incredibly exhausted. Just whupped. Later, I fantasized that instead of driving on to drop off Raphael, I'd said to my kids, "Fuck it! Road trip! Serena, get out. I'm driving; we're changing routes."

I imagine that my kids would have looked at me like I was crazy, but they'd have gone along. After all, they'd seen me do wacky things like insisting on making a heart-shaped Valentine's Day cake when our blended family was an oozing mass of bloody dysfunction. They had seen me cry plenty. And beg and rage and laugh. But this kind of enthusiastic spirit of adventure at such a juncture in our lives would have been new to them.

I may have had no idea what I was doing, but I did know that my two kids were alive and together and that they'd never been to the Four Corners area of New Mexico. When I was just a year older than them, Chaco Canyon had changed my life. Wouldn't it be a better place for my son than one more treatment center (which often harbored opportunities for more drugs)? Besides, at the time, I felt I couldn't face taking the car in for yet another repair. And I thought that my son and stepdaughter needed some quality time together.

In my imagined alternate route, the kids would have been temporarily stunned silent. But then I think they would have just shrugged, looked at each other, and yelled out, "Road trip!" They knew crazy. And when to go along with it.

I pictured getting in the front seat, sending Raphael to the back, and Serena riding shotgun. I'd check to make sure everyone was belted in and then type "Chaco Canyon" into Google Maps. And Australian Siri would send us on our way with her command, "Proceed to the route."

When I was eighteen, living and working as an intern at Chaco Canyon National Monument among the ancient Anasazi ruins, running at night over high-desert plateaus, I felt utterly in the moment. I remembered when I worked strengthening my body and soul on the all-women backcountry trail crew a couple of years later. When Raphael was close to eighteen, I did contemplate sending him to a wilderness treatment center, but the cost was prohibitive (more than $30,000 for several weeks). But this was my road trip fantasy.

I had also worked in the inner Grand Canyon when I was seventeen, about the same age as Serena and Raphael were now, so I could picture taking them deep into the canyon, showing them the hidden warm pools surrounded by the vastness of the colorful rock walls. I dreamed we would reconnect as a family there, and the demons of addiction would release the hijacked soul of my son, their toxic presence floating far away down the river. We'd find a smooth, flat rock on which to dry out together in the sun, and all would be good again.

#CrayCray Mom

Over the years, I have erupted into distinctly unfunny states—crying violent tears, spewing Tourette-like curses, grabbing someone's leg, begging to be seen, pleading not to be abandoned. *Don't leave me. Don't hurt me.* And time after time, I disintegrate further as I cling to this panic. I experience *deshacer*—total undoing of self. Like molten lava pouring out of me. I have to stop this flow, but coming out from under the unnatural disaster of my life is not a linear process.

Raphael had been in the inpatient treatment center for thirty days, and the insurance company said his time was up, even though neither Raphael nor I felt he was ready. I was in this volcanic state then, barely over pneumonia and feeling the PTSD of running in and out of ERs hearing that my son might die soon. We were sitting in an office with Raphael's assigned therapist, who was preparing to discharge him. She had just informed me that Raphael wanted to go home with his father for the evening. I threw myself on the ground, begging him to come home with me. I watched Raphael's face fall in disbelief at his mother's wild, almost possessed convulsions, resembling a bride we once witnessed in a Baptist church "getting the spirit."

"What do you want from me?" I asked. "I could kill myself—will that make it better?" Raphael ran out of the office.

At the treatment center, kids lay about the living room area watching reality rehab shows. Raphael received daily therapy, ate healthy meals, went to an empowerment group, and had therapy sessions with his dad for the first time.

Occasionally, I also met with Raphael and his therapist. These sessions didn't go well. Raphael was furious with me. I was sad and afraid that I'd caused his despair, angry that he held me responsible for the times he felt his dad had abandoned him, not being willing to set a regular schedule, and refusing to be with him when Raphael didn't "act right."

That afternoon at the inpatient treatment center, the day he was to have gone home with me, Raphael ran from me—his molten mom. I was crazy with fear, fear of losing him, fear that he would always blame me for his addiction, and fear that perhaps it was true that it was my fault . . . no matter how many times I was told, "You didn't cause it; you can't control it; you can't cure it."

Not knowing where Raphael had fled to, I sobbed uncontrollably, ran out to the parking lot and frantically called the people at the new intensive outpatient treatment program Raphael was about to start. They had given me specific instructions to take him home with me, not send him with his father. I believed if I didn't follow their instructions exactly, I might cause him to relapse. I didn't know what the formula was to battle his addiction, and I was desperate for direction. Though the plan Raphael made with the inpatient staff was to spend the night with his father, I still hoped that he would come home with me. But they told me they had called his father, and I was no longer an option for that night.

I thought I'd hit bottom then, running in and out of the building, sobbing, while the staff, teens, and other parents stared at me. The horrified look on Raphael's face before he bolted said that I had finally gone too far. But I continued erupting. I ran around the treatment center and found my son huddled outside in the protective womb of the center's staff. I had to push my way in, asking permission to talk to him. Who were those people who felt they had to protect him from his own mom, I wondered?

Raphael stood away from me, seeking refuge from his crazy mother.

Suddenly, I wanted them to take me in. I wanted what Raphael had experienced for thirty days. I was a desperate child-mom, even though the staff could have been my children, age-wise.

"Raphael," I addressed him. No response.

He looked wary, scared, as one staff member held his arm around him and asked, "You okay, son?"

"Raphael, please come home with me. I didn't mean it," I said as calmly as I could, but he heard the shaking edge and knew it was a temporary calm. Children are trained to hear the possibility of eruptions. I know, having lived through the minefields of my own family. "Raphael, please, I'm sorry. I didn't mean it. I've just been so worried, so tired," I pleaded.

Underneath my panicked eruption was grief, fear, loss. I didn't feel that I could bear it if I lost my son, especially without ever recovering our close relationship. Without fixing things.

"No, no, no." He shook his head. "I can't go with you. I can't."

And then—just like that—the words tumbled out of my mouth as if I was watching them in slow motion, in a voice bubble, unable to take them back. "What do you want from me? I'll do anything you want. You want drugs? I'll get you your drugs of choice!"

The staff stared at me. This might have actually been a first in their adolescent treatment center. They led me out; another counselor held Raphael as he stumbled away.

One young staff member, far closer in age to Raphael than to me, put both arms around me. "Mom, come here, calm down, let me give you a hug," he said and held me the way I used to hold my son when he was younger and couldn't contain himself. "Momz, it's okay. Calm down. Everything is okay. You need to take care of yourself."

Later that evening, I spoke with the parent coordinator from the program. She was both an alcoholic and a parent of an addict. Both she and her daughter (who was only a year or so older than Raphael) had solid years of recovery behind them. She put her daughter on the phone.

"Oh, the threatening to kill yourself," she said. "My mom did that with me." The daughter explained, "We can't stand seeing you—our moms—so early in our recovery. You only remind us of all the fucked-up things we did. Just looking at you makes us feel guilty. We want to use, and we can't."

A week later, I continued to wonder, *Who is this mom who fell apart the way I did at my son's treatment center?* I attended a parent meeting and heard a mom say, "The doctor asked me what I might do if my daughter didn't stop using, and I said I knew exactly what I'd do. I would drive my car right off a cliff."

I had longed to create a safe, strong sanctuary for my family as an adult. Even my stepdaughter had admonished me over the years, "Carla, you know you can't make everyone happy." I certainly couldn't make her mother, the second person I married, happy.

Several years ago, my younger sister, Sheli, performed a solo show about being caught in the onset of the Sri Lankan Civil War, and she compared the experience to growing up in our childhood home. We all have different memories. Who got the black eye from being chased by Dad and running into the kidney-shaped coffee table with the tile mosaic? (The one my mom had filled in with little tiles to keep from going crazy.) My older sister, Jane, prefers to think of it as having been better than many childhoods; my younger sister holds more childhood traumatic memories; my older brother, Jim, doesn't talk about it. Was it only because we had different personalities, or did history and economics play a role too? I remember it all—the laughter, the fun, the love, the violent eruptions. I'm grateful for my spilling-out immigrant-like family that gets involved in everything, viewing each illness or celebration as one that we all will tackle together. A family meeting to solve each crisis. My mom always determined to fix it all. My dad's unyielding loyalty and his lifesaving sense of humor are what I cherished in the end. I can only hope that my son, too, will choose the good memories.

I remember myself as the fighter. The one who protected my two sisters from skinheads in Haight-Ashbury in the 1980s. Do they remember my fierce protection in those teen and young-adult years? Or do they remember only my bottomless despair as an adult when I've tried to make untenable situations okay?

"What was your bottom?" Raphael asked me later, when he was eighteen.

"That time. Offering to buy you your drugs of choice at an inpatient substance-abuse center." Raphael looked at me and nodded knowingly.

That was my bottom, but I had cried so many times before it, convinced that I had lost my son forever. Convinced that I could never make up for all the suffering—the loss of stepsister and home, the war zone with his stepmother, and the rage and absence of his father. My own craziness in response. Desperation to control the uncontrollable.

A mother wants to fix things—to take her baby in her arms and rock and nurse him until all is okay. Even when he's eighteen, this is what I thought when he fell asleep, head on my lap, in yet another waiting room. A year after my bottom, I sat on top of Halaeakalā, a volcano on the island of Maui in Hawaii. My son was living in the young men's recovery house, had achieved six months' sobriety, and had just graduated from high school. I remembered the volcano that had erupted inside of me.

Molten lava had spilled out and threatened to carry my son away. The volcano was calm now.

Mamacita and Princesa

My son and I were visiting friends in the hills of Echo Park, where I imagined we might take refuge when we fled the scorched earth of our family's unblending. Our friends were offering us a kitten, which only sort of made sense, given our uncertain living situation. My dad was nearby in Verdugo Hills Hospital and almost dead. He had arrived in Southern California from Seattle to get out of the rain, but it rained continuously after he got here, and he got pneumonia.

Maybe a sweet kitten would fix our thrashed hearts.

Our friends had just adopted a mother cat, Mamacita, and her kittens were running underfoot, nursing way past vet-recommended time. My son had nursed the same way.

The kitten ignored us, ran up to Mamacita, latched right on, sighed, and went to sleep. He happily moved his little kitty lips as he slept.

Mamacita left her sleeping kitty and came over to us, purring and cuddling into our lives. Cats rub up to you and mark you with their scents, claiming you. Our friends decided to give us Mamacita; we were clearly in need of her maternal instincts.

The first day Mamacita came home with us, Slurpy, our shelty shepherd, herded her, and Max, the Labrador, retrieved her. When I walked in, Mamacita was a slobber ball, emitting a toxic-smelling odor. (I learned that cats spray this liquid from their anal glands, kind of like skunks, when they are frightened.) I grabbed her and ran to the vet.

At the vet's office, Dr. Tyson asked, "Who is the alpha in the house?"

I answered, "We're in transit . . ."

"I remember you now." She looked at us while Mamacita began to emerge from her temporarily subdued state, purring and rubbing up to Dr. Tyson.

"Yes, we were two moms, two kids, two dogs," I continued, "but now . . ."

I guess Lizette had been the angry alpha. Now she and Serena were gone, leaving us temporarily caring for the two dogs. Unhinged, roaming, chewing up whatever came in their path, the dogs looked as lost and bewildered as we felt. Losing my stepdaughter, Raphael's stepsister, had left us gutted; Raphael didn't understand why Serena couldn't still live with us.

"My dad died when I was about Raphael's age. I didn't want to talk to anyone. My cat was my lifeline," Dr. Tyson told us. "Mamacita is amazing. I just feel she chose you. Your son needs her."

She advised us how to manage the dogs and the cat together and sent us home feeling Mamacita was our beshert (Yiddish for "destiny, soul mate"). When I thanked her for the counseling session, she said, "I became a vet to deal with animals, not people. Turns out the owners need me more."

Mamacita sat on Raphael's head and purred. "She's a motor," he said, moving her gently off. A big, straggly cat security blanket with deep-seeing orange eyes, she curled up on one side of me, my son on the other.

Serena came over one day and cried nonstop. "Why can't I stay here with you guys?" Mamacita climbed on her lap and licked her tears away.

In the mornings Mamacita went out on her neighborhood walks. Having roamed the Echo Park hills, she was desperate to explore our barrio.

One night she didn't come back. The following morning, she staggered in appearing lobotomized.

She smelled awful. Not knowing any better, I tried to bathe her. Afterward, she stayed curled up in a blanket and, like a cartoon cat, left an exact cat shape frozen into place with wet stink. I carried her into the vet the next day and was told that her innards were crushed. "She came into your life when you needed her; now you have to let her go," Dr. Tyson counseled.

Later, a neighbor told us, "I saw your cat. She was attacked by two coyotes. She put up a fight!"

"That's my girl," Raphael said.

I remembered our therapy cat years later, when seventeen-year-old Raphael struggled with drug addiction. Unable to stop him from using, I decided to look for another. I wanted a cat that would just sit on my lap and purr, a "senior for a senior," as they advertised at the Humane Society. Raphael insisted we needed a fun cat. We ended up with a one-year-old rescue whom Raphael named Princess Leia; she was nicknamed D'Princesa. She'd been a teen mom, and I hoped she'd be a replacement for Mamacita.

As with trying to replace people, you can't make a cat be someone she's not. Unlike Mamacita, Princesa was not a cuddler. Like most cats, she ruled. She chewed on books, cords, and our toes, and she leaped frenetically over my body when I lay in bed. Whatever Princesa wanted, I gave. A petite, short-haired cat, she gained weight quickly. Regal like her name, with velvety white fur and spots of brown and orange, she would fix her steely green eyes on me.

Two months later Raphael left home to live in a young men's recovery house, and I found myself alone for the first time in twenty years. Princesa banged on my bedroom door, demanding I get up. She stared into my eyes, insisting I could do better, and chewed her way through our house until I played with her.

Some people see cats as finicky and purely self-absorbed, calculating in their affection, while others find cats to be therapeutic and say that they ask for little other than to be nearby. Much seems to depend on the nature of the particular cat, a bit like people. Mamacita seemed to be the epitome of the all-giving Earth Mother that I'd perhaps aspired to be, but my maternal strength was badly battered when we met her. And Princesa? Well, because it was all about her, she taught me how to set boundaries. I stopped allowing her to sleep with me, since she was youthful, nocturnal, and restless and knocked the eyeliner and other makeup off my vanity at night. She would shuffle it into hidden corners, perhaps hoarding it for a secret kitty makeup party.

My experience is that the cats we need come into our lives. Mamacita mothered us into resilience. Princesa arrived to make sure an empty nest and the fallout from addiction didn't send me permanently under the covers.

Graduation Day at Addiction High

June 18, 2014. Eight young men in royal blue caps and gowns pose holding high school diplomas. Our boys. They have reached a milestone that I had not expected to see happen this spring—not in my son's case, at least: they finished high school. An independent study program in Torrance, California, allowed them to meet with a teacher once a week, working online from the young men's recovery house where they live. A cake decorated with their faces sits in front of them—eight young addicts.

"I never thought I'd graduate on time," says Raphael as part of his short speech at the graduation celebration. "But here I am, thanks to the support of all my brothers in the house." Less than a year before, he was taking eighty Robitussin caplets at a time.

"The house" is the "Renewal Recovery House," a home for young men "on the path of recovery from drug and alcohol addiction." The large, custom- built, immaculate home in the South Bay area of LA is decorated in a masculine Old West motif, with a wagon-wheel chandelier and a black-and-white photo of Indian chiefs. Two large, honey-colored Labradors lounge on the patio. They have seen a lot of boys come and go.

The young men sleep in bunk beds four or six to a room. Many of them have been through several treatment centers, wilderness programs, and legal actions because of their addictions. Each one has a different story. But their parents will tell you—same as I will—that their sons once had bright eyes and big dreams and were small enough to hold in their arms.

♦

Only a year before, I was dashing off to the emergency room; it had become such a frequent occurrence, I went on autopilot. Charger? Check. iPad? Check. Book, sweatshirt, snacks? Check, check, check. Too often I had been stranded following the 911 calls, arriving at the ER in the middle of the night, emerging only at dawn. During one long night, I told Raphael to move over, closed my eyes for a moment, and scrunched down next to him on the gurney in the ER hallway. Sometimes my son came back with me. Sometimes Raphael headed out for the 5150 mandatory seventy-two-hour hold in a hospital adolescent psych ward, after they decided that his pattern of drug abuse posed a risk to his life. While the social workers evaluated him, Raphael had joked about rating his favorite hospitals on Yelp.

I hadn't been thinking about whether Raphael might not graduate from high school when one evaluating social worker in the ER told me, "Your son says he doesn't have much more time. It's curious—he lacks affect."

"He must mean until he turns eighteen," I told the social worker.

"No, he means until he dies from what he's taking," the social worker said. "If he were eighteen, I would just send him home to kill himself."

This thought had put me out of my mind. I was shell-shocked, pleading, angry, bereft, wondering if *I* should try using. Desperate not to lose my son's love, not to lose him to addiction, I had even threatened to kill myself if I couldn't stop him—something I later heard expressed by other mothers as we recounted the insanity of trying to control the uncontrollable. I relived and regretted every decision, every trauma, every battle I had fought for him and lost.

I was reading all I could about addiction. Books by addicts such as Nic Sheff's *Tweak: Growing Up on Methamphetamines* and *We All Fall Down: Living with Addiction*. Books by their parents, including *Beautiful Boy: A Father's Journey through His Son's Addiction* and *Clean: Overcoming Addiction and Ending America's Greatest Tragedy* by David Sheff. I stepped up my program, attending my own twelve-step meetings—Al-Anon, for the families of those affected by drugs and alcohol. And I found compassion again.

Then, one more time, I came home to see my son's eyes rolled back in his head. I called 911. But I knew this time was different.

I told him I couldn't let him live with me anymore; I could not protect him from this disease. I said, "I love you right up to the moon and back," quoting the children's book we used to read over and over again, *Guess How Much I Love You*. "But I can't keep you alive here; you know that." We held each other tight.

It felt like the most loving moment that we'd had in years. We understood each other perfectly, even though it seemed as if the most vital part of me was being ripped away.

A mother of a young man who was with Raphael in another treatment center had called me repeatedly over the previous months, urging me to look at the Renewal Recovery House, where her son was now staying. I visited the place and spoke with some of the young men there. Through living and working together, they had found the strength and peace to live a sober life. It felt like home. The long-term program and tight structure seemed to provide the scaffolding these young men needed, along with a community of "brothers"—something my son had always craved.

I went to see Raphael at the thirty-day treatment center, and he (gratefully) chose to go to the Renewal Recovery House. The staff there asked him to try it out for only three months, but I hoped he would stay for the full eighteen. It wasn't easy being in "the House," as everyone called it. No one was allowed to just veg. And not everyone made it.

During the first months Raphael was there, though sober, he struggled with being fully present, honest, and participating in the program. He sat behind dark glasses, sleeping but pretending he was studying. The director of the recovery house suggested that he needed more serious consequences—incarceration or homelessness, things no mom would want to have happen to her son. But then he began to cross over to a new level of willingness—even desire—to make real change. He finished his schoolwork a full month before graduation.

◆

After my son left home, it took me a long time to figure out what I liked. The food in my refrigerator, the music on my iTunes—everything had revolved around Raphael for so long that I couldn't remember my own preferences. I hadn't lived alone for many years. Knowing I'd have to face my own demons at some point, I wanted to stay busy. But first I needed to catch up on some sleep.

My therapist had asked, "What are you doing besides work, Al-Anon, and visiting your son?" Not much, I admitted. She suggested I try improv or stand-up comedy. I guess my therapist thought I was funny.

So I signed up for a class in stand-up. At the end of the series, we performed at the Comedy Store in West Hollywood. It was a packed Sunday night, but I invited only a few friends; I was a bit terrified. Our instructor had promised that after getting up on that stage, nothing else in life would be as scary or difficult. I needed that. People were stoked and nervous in the green room. Out where the audience sat, it was dark and I tried to step out onto the stage with confidence, but I was just jumping in with my eyes shut.

"So, my son left home recently," I launched into my first set. "It was a really hard choice—Harvard, Yale, or the young men's recovery house. Yup, he's doing his gap year studying addiction."

Lots of laughs. Our instructor was right: I did feel different—fearless, at least for a moment.

But I woke up the following day feeling like shit. I had outed my son as an addict! He had given me the go-ahead, though, to write about him, about us, about addiction. And maybe other families would benefit.

I got asked back to do another set but declined.

Three weeks after my comedy set, I attended Raphael's graduation. As he walked down the field to receive his diploma, I sat in the stands with my family, full of joy. Later, we celebrated at his recovery house and then at the bowling alley with his recovery house brothers and their families. No drunken grad night.

After so many years of homework ruling our lives, of micromanaging, advocating, screaming, of pleading with teachers to understand my dreamy, intellectual, creative (distracted, unfocused, disorganized), beautiful son, he had graduated. Raphael did this without me standing over him. He had done it with the support of the other twenty-four young men in recovery. The next step was for him to get a job and eventually, if he stayed the course, to move out with a few of the others from the house. Maybe then college and beyond. But I was focused only on that day's celebration.

"I love the way you are so happy about your son's high school graduation," a friend had told me. "For most other kids it's just a step on the way to the next—it's all about where they are going to college."

I was thrilled that he was graduating, but mostly I was happy each time I saw that he was alive.

◆

Getting and staying sober holds particular challenges for young people. Two of the eight high school graduates later left the recovery house abruptly; one came back. Another young man walked out and lost an eye from an unexplained street brawl his first night back out.

These young men have lost years of their lives to addiction. Those who stayed in the house were far ahead of their peers in their profound work of self-examination—work I wish I'd done at that age.

Dealing with my son's addiction had also forced me to find a different way of living. "One day at a time" had finally become the only option— short of being placed on my own psych hold. Years earlier, before addiction took over, I used to tease and terrify Raphael by saying, "Maybe when you start college, I'll go back to school. We'll live in a dorm together and go out partying."

Raphael remained in the Renewal Recovery House after his high school graduation, and soon after that I did go back to school. At age fifty-four, I began my MFA in creative writing, something I had contemplated for more than twenty years but found daunting to pursue as a single mom. Coming face-to-face with my son's mortality had helped me realize that we need to seize our dreams today. Seeing Raphael with the other young men in the house facing their demons so unflinchingly gave me the courage to face mine. Not so long ago, I had been able to see myself only in the fetal position.

He was proud of me. I was proud of him. "That's sick, Mom," Raphael told me on hearing about graduate school. Urban Dictionary translation of "sick": Crazy. Cool. Insane. Awesome. The ultimate teen compliment, laced with love.

Paper Weights

In a story I once wrote about my own death, I imagined my son was a writer living in Brazil. He returned to the States to go through my stuff and sift helplessly through piles and scraps of paper, my hoarded, semilegible writing from childhood through menopause. He threw up his arms—what could he do? He couldn't read most of it, wouldn't want to if he could.

In my office I keep a tall file cabinet. All three drawers are filled with journals and writings dating back to my primary-school years; they are also scattered throughout my house. There are notebooks of all sizes and shapes—black composition books, a few of those annoyingly common Moleskines, scraps of paper, a three-ring binder or two, museum-decorated journals. A treasure hunt for my cat, who likes to chew paper.

I have thought that someday I'll read these mounds of scrawled paper. I read an article written by several poets who devoted considerable time to contemplating what to do with their writing detritus. It described people burning or even shooting their journals while they were still alive to make the decision. One poet entrusted her son to dispose of her journals after her death but was okay with him reading them first. Another said she decided to "store them in an attic where I don't have to run into them" after her Facebook community decried her post announcing the volumes' imminent destruction.

I might have to destroy my past before I ever reread it. I can't seem to organize any of it; random excursions into my filing cabinets have often sent me scurrying back to safety when I find that some of the same things cluttering my mind at age thirteen still do so today: debt, love, family, mortality, worrying. Or I am just bored with making the same mistakes and lamentations over and over again? Occasionally I find a gem worth saving, but more often than not, my search for that epiphany is fruitless.

My mom kept doing crossword puzzles for a long while, even when she spent more time staring into space, but she still had more answers than I could ever get. A grammarian, a librarian, she'd corrected our speech all of our lives. Sometimes her children and caregivers try to help with the crosswords and can't read a thing she writes. Often, she writes nothing, creates new words, or colors so hard she puts a hole through the paper. I am not sure what my mom thinks—or if she does—when she sits silently. I didn't grow up with silence.

But sometimes, I, too, could just sit staring into space, trying to understand it all.

♦

You spent years of your life trying not to get pregnant, and then—boom— you spend years trying to be pregnant, and then in no time, when you've barely stopped nursing and just started sleeping through the night, it seems it's perimenopause and menopause time.

You spent years trying to get away from your parents, and then you start liking them more (you always *loved* them). And then—boom—they are changing or changed or dead. Or they think you are their sister or mom.

You spent years longing for some time, just a little spare time for yourself away from your kids—a son and stepdaughter, born four months apart. Then—boom—they are ready to go, don't want you around, or some positive thing might happen, like college or sports or a boyfriend or girlfriend or a job. Or something horrible happens, like unblended families or drugs, and you fear you'll lose them or their love, or both, forever.

You go to the funeral and then sit shiva for a temple friend's son. He had hanged himself, and she had found him—twenty-two years old. At shiva, she hugs you and whispers, "We worry so about our boys."

And you consider this a gift amid a loss you didn't—still don't—believe you could live with. She knew about your son's struggles with addiction. But your son is alive. Yes, she was generous. The distance between your fears and her reality was mountainous but not remote.

And then you land—WOMP. Like in *The Wizard of Oz*, a tornado spun you about, your house plopped on top of a witch, and how did you get there? But all you know is that your son and stepdaughter are both eighteen, they both tell you they love you, and they both seem to be okay. They want to see you regularly, and it is all you can do to fit that in once or twice a week, because by then you are really busy again with your own separate life.

And in this short entry, you have summed up your entire life—something you imagine should have taken at least a day to compose, but you finished in a blink. And that, too, is something that happened. The writing of words that are unplanned, but sometimes misspelled or otherwise humiliatingly wrong when you submitted "a peace" instead of "a piece." It's the dreaded homonym disorder you named in the early stages of perimenopause. Back in the day, growing up in your house, your parents taught you to be very suspicious of anyone mixing up "too," "to," and "two." And ten years ago, you asked to be taken out and shot if you ever wrote, "Nice to meat you."

And yet you did—the evidence is in an old e-mail to the client who hired you; you assume he didn't see it.

And all you can do now is hope that you'll finish your book before you end up like your mom, watching the same movie over and over again. Though it won't be *Pride and Prejudice*, most likely. Nor will it be Mr. Darcy to whom you imagine you are married. But you might have to wear a diaper. And she doesn't really know what she is watching at all these days. And the good thing was that for awhile, when you were still very busy, it didn't take much time to talk to your mom—not like in the past, when you'd have to set aside close to an hour. After so many years of engaged, animated, and sometimes intrusive questioning, she had very little to say to you, or anyone, most of the time. Her mind was running out like the hourglass in *The Wizard of Oz*, but even today, you still don't know how long it will take. She is just placid, more accepting and inactive than she'd been all your life, and sometimes you miss her persistent interest in your well-being.

And one day, when you are fifty-four years old, you call her up and say, "Mom, I'm going back to school."

She answers clearly, your mom again for a moment: "That's good, honey, you've always been such a great writer." She ought to know; she used to get up in the wee hours to type your stories when you were too young, just as you did later for your son.

She doesn't remember when you last called, but she is always happy to say hello when you do. She asks where you are and if you need her to pick you up at the airport—even though she hasn't driven anywhere for years. You tell her you are home and not coming that day, not for a while. The conversation is over in less than a minute. She is ready to hang up. And that is that; she is back to *Pride and Prejudice*.

And you are back to your life, what is left of it, and there is an awful lot still left.

A Creature Apart

My mom was in the hospital. I had just returned from a trip to Brazil. Walking into Huntington Hospital and seeing all the characters swirling about transported me through a barrage of memories and images. How many times in the past had I emerged, blinking from the bright lights of the ER, into the dark or early morning dawn?

The duty nurse entered the room and said, "We gave your mom an Ativan last night for her agitation and BP up to 160," which is why she was still sleeping soundly. (I, too, took an Ativan the day before that. I also sometimes took one when agitated or stressed.) The nurse told me that my mom hadn't slept much the night before, after my brother left. Instead, she had remained awake, inert, with her eyes wide open, as she often seemed to do. *What is in her head?* I asked myself as she stared blankly, silent.

"We tried to turn her, didn't get her up to go to the bathroom," the patient care person said. "We bathed her at 11:30 p.m. She only resisted a little, a scratch." I wondered how they did it, but I found out later from the nurse: Ativan. "Then I cleaned her up again in the morning." The rectal tube was not spill proof at all.

At this moment, she was sleeping. She seemed somewhat peaceful. I sat in the vinyl armchair next to my mom's bed and wrote. It was unusually quiet in the hospital.

I had wished my older sister and brother-in-law would stop using the hospital-speak word "compliant" when asking if our mom could be put back on antipsychotics. *Is it all about compliance?* I had thought. My mom didn't want to move from Seattle to California, but all her children lived here, and she had been rapidly declining, making managing her care from afar difficult. Her only forms of protest seemed to be lashing out (physically and verbally) at her caregivers and refusing to take her prescriptions. Initially, I thought, *I am well-prepared to handle the powerlessness of dementia, having learned about this with addiction.* But as it has turned out, there is a lot of unexpected pain in not being able to stop my mom's topple down the rabbit hole.

At times I, too, have tried to be compliant. Good. Though many knew me as a rebel when I was younger, and internally, I still often rebelled. I went wild. All my life I had explained, justified, and defended. What if I just stopped?

Now, years later, I know in the quiet of my life that "compliance" did not capture the deep sadness—unspoken to me at the time—my sister felt about our mom's diminished mental state, which is a nicer name than what this looks like in real life. Rather, the plea for compliance stemmed from the desperation she experienced when, day after day, we had seen our mom behave in ways she most certainly would have abhorred in her former state.

Today it's not the word "compliance" that matters when my sister tells me that she did cry, that she wept daily after leaving my mom's assisted care, although we didn't speak of it at the time. I only saw the despair we shared and the guilt I felt at the decision to force our mom to leave her home where she'd lived for more than forty-five years. For not being able to visit her daily, as my older sister did. And I wasn't as accepting as I imagined—I wanted to hear my sister express her grief to me in a way I could recognize. I still struggle with forcing others to hear what I'm saying and to say what they are feeling in the manner I might.

Pretty funny for someone who finds it difficult to tolerate the use of the word "compliance."

♦

Being in the hospital put me in a PTSD state. It reminded me of the time I accidentally burned my foot and had to go to the ER before my first wedding. It was there, the ER—some ER—that I used to take Raphael when he was a baby, a toddler. Back then, the 911 calls were about breathing. He got a diagnosis of asthma, and they gave us a nebulizer. I learned to pack necessities like underwear and a toothbrush. Later, when he struggled with addiction, technology had evolved, and my bag included chargers and an iPad in addition to a journal and a book.

Constipation, a lifelong issue for my mom and my dad and the precipitating problem of my mom's hospitalizations, hit my son beginning in infancy. By preschool he knew about the importance of fiber (or "fiver," as he called it) and insisted on including it in preschool cooking projects. Like with my parents, his constipation became chronic. In fact, my mom had begun to smell like my son did when the pent-up poop leaked out in little amounts. The same misery. When Raphael was perhaps seven, he couldn't poop for a week, and then one night he couldn't get up from the toilet, and it looked as if he'd stopped breathing, so I called 911. The firemen came and carried him off the toilet. (He couldn't bend, so full up he was.) They carried him like he was a little prince of constipation, and we were taken to a small hospital in the San Gabriel Valley that had one doctor on duty. He did an X-ray and said, "I'll tell you what his problem is, I'll tell you. Your son is full of shit!" He showed me the X-ray and said he had no intention of dealing with it in "my ER." Raphael would have to see his pediatrician in the morning. By then, Raphael was more peaceful. The horrible pain, the urge to push, and the paralyzing fear were all gone, and he'd temporarily quieted. Later, my son's allergist would excitedly tell his students, "Take a look: This is a case of asthma induced by constipation!" This is why my mom ended up in the hospital so often: constipation, which often turned into other problems, like a stomach blown up so high that she felt as though she had a baby inside. And there was so much crossover between Raphael and my dad. Both were dreamy intellectuals, intense, passionate, and distracted. The family inheritance includes addictions to worry and anxiety along with constipation, allergies, eczema, and asthma. (These last three run together as family traits, different ones for different family members; some, like Raphael, got all three.)

The ER remains active and buzzing twenty-four hours a day. It exists as a creature apart, and those who live within its entrails inhabit another world. The ER at Huntington Hospital or at our HMO was where Raphael was taken time after time when he struggled with drug abuse. I sat beside Raphael's gurney after another overdose, a spectator and participant in the ER milieu, as the detritus of the world walked in and out of our eyesight and earshot. In that pre-remodeled Huntington ER, the patients were all on gurneys in the hallway, so we heard their every word. There was no such thing as patient confidentiality. A young woman on a gurney further down from Raphael was being seen for a possible brain injury. A Pasadena police officer stood by watching her, somewhat disinterestedly. "She's good to go," the nurse said to the officer. "You are free to book her." The discharge nurse gave the young woman, who barely looked eighteen, all the precautions and instructions relating to a possible brain injury. "Put ice on it, take Tylenol, and if the headache continues or if you experience shooting pain, you need to come right back," the nurse told her. I watched the police officer roll his eyes, and I wondered if the nurse realized how hard it would be for that patient to return to the hospital if she was booked in county jail. The nurse was polite but detached as she moved on to the next patient.

Another patient stood nearby, a homeless alcoholic addict who had been found naked and brought to the hospital. They had to discharge her, telling her to return to the ER once the DTs started. She could be readmitted then, another nurse, Tony, explained patiently, repeating the instructions, making eye contact. "Do you understand?" he asked the patient, who nodded, eyes glazed. A hospital social worker gave her a fresh set of clothes, and she left.

"Nothing else you can do?" I asked them.

"Oh, you heard?" Nurse Tony said. "No, it's the system. Nothing we can do until later, when she starts shaking and going into withdrawals." He addressed the audience around him (me, the social worker, another nurse). "Now, this is very interesting. Here's a mom whose son is taking one hundred Robitussin caplets—potentially lethal dosages—and yet she worries about this homeless woman."

At that time, I had endless space for worries, enough for the world.

Nurse Tony had been working in the ER for twenty-four years, but he still made his way from patient to patient, working his magic, seeing what impact he might make in the time he had with them. And to think that I thought him a cynic when I heard him giving the rundown of the evening's patients to the staff coming on: "This one, he's a Robohead.This woman, 200 pounds, smoker, diabetes, abused by parents. She'll be back later for sure."

Each patient got what he called his "bullshit Tony talk." They were like TED Talks, only his audience members all lay on gurneys.

He came right up to Raphael and started asking questions like, "So tell me about yourself? Where's your dad in all this? What made you start wanting to take this stuff? How'd you first get into drugs?" He ended with showing Raphael and me pictures of his beautiful family, hoping they might inspire Raphael to want what he had. He showed him one family photo, then random shots of his life: a close-up, mowing grass, bright sun surrounded by trees, a spider crawling in water, and more pictures of his family. His wife was dark and lovely and clearly the other half of his energy. His olive-skinned, delicious, wild and curly-haired children were hanging onto their mom and smiling into the picture—natural, not posed. Their loving, intact, happy, healthy family—it was so heartbreakingly clear we didn't have that.

Tony told Raphael that he used to be a "skate rat." Then he said, "You are free to change yourself, to say, 'You're right, Tony, I can.' Think of this: Do you want to remember yourself as dead with a hundred Robitussin?" Raphael just smiled, as if helpless to contemplate his agency in the decision about how he would live or die.

◆

Years later, sitting by my mom's bed in the same hospital, I didn't feel that I had much room for any more worries—little psychic space left to accommodate ER visits and trauma. My chest felt as though it might explode. As my mom slept soundly (I now knew why—Ativan—and I was glad she was still asleep), I tried to meditate.

Breathe in, breathe out. Breathing in, I calm my body. Breathing out, I smile. I heard groans next door. They almost matched my rhythmic breathing. I remembered my own groans, other ER visits, county hospital—more than I cared to revisit. *Breathing in, I calm my body.*

I left to go to the bathroom. Although I knew that the previous night's nurse might sneak out before I got a report, I was powerless because obeying my body's signal was my priority. Even though I knew that if it were my older sister, she'd get that report first. But I'd made myself wait too many times to take care of the basic needs. So now I tried to make peeing and pooping within fifteen to thirty minutes of when I felt the urge a priority.

Six months before this, returning from another trip, I had contracted a severe urinary tract infection. I peed bright red blood and felt perhaps the worst kind of pain. I went to this hospital's ER, where I was given morphine. A week of hardcore constipation followed. So I thanked God, as I shit and pissed, for the gift of my body functioning. Unlike my mom's body, which blew up like a hard, full balloon with explosions happening inside, the gas refusing to come out—the body not working the way it was built (initially attributed to a condition called ileus). Now she said little, mostly baby talk. Sometimes she would insist loudly, "I, Princesa!" (unrelated to our cat, whom she'd never met) as she protested another invasion: pills she refused, exams, all the caregivers and medical providers who surrounded her, whom she was certain existed to poison and imprison her. Or the bad, abusive man whom she alone saw. The one she believed she had married after my dad died. My mom seemed to have developed a thing for bad boys. At one time, she thought she was married to Mr. Darcy from *Pride and Prejudice*, another time to Agent Booth from the television show *Bones*.

Another nurse entered and gave her six little shots in her hand, which was swollen and bruised from an IV. Before she injected her, I warned the nurse, "She won't like that; you might need some help." My mom screamed in pain, eardrum-shattering shrieks, as loudly and as shrilly as she could manage.

That scream chilled me. I knew it to be my scream and my younger sister's scream as well. What do we hold, we two younger siblings? Where did it come from? That primal, razor-sharp scream that must come out, cutting through all the layers of false normalcy that might still surround us? I was afraid. Afraid that the trauma would suck me up, cause me to be lost again in the churnings of the medical crisis system. I was dragged into the murky, dark swamp—the quicksand where the despairing of the world resided. When I was about seven, my Grandpa Sam told me to hold his hand so I wouldn't fall in as we walked the rocky perimeter of a little pond in a park near Lake Washington. He slipped, fell in, and pulled me down. I imagined our parents were unable to keep us safe as well. From their own unsteady footing, they, too, dragged us into the swamp. Now it was our turn to care for our parents, and we did it with grace at times; we knew they had meant well. But on that day, I had gone past that, I was tired. I wanted to lie down, to rest peacefully, as my mom seemed to be doing.

Outside the ER a man sat in his wheelchair, shoeless, wearing holey, dirty socks. Bumpy gray stubble dotted his face. He didn't look like anyone would claim him, but he sat there on the curb near where the security guard sometimes stood.

This was the same ER that I had come to for injections when I was getting inseminated with anonymous donor sperm. I remembered watching the wounded of the world pass through: people wearing articles of clothing wrapped around head wounds; babies lying limp, sweating and exhausted, trying to vomit with nothing left in their wracked stomachs while their moms rocked them, eyes glazed; and the two infant seats dropped off for the babies who no longer had parents.

That day as I meditated, I remembered my gratitude for being allowed to carry and give birth to a baby, my then-nineteen-year-old son. For his having been kept alive and receiving help to break the cycle of pain. His recovery ultimately carried me along to work on my own recovery. I gave thanks for my nineteen-year-old stepdaughter, Serena, coming into my life when she was seven. I still struggled with prayer and acknowledging the idea of a Higher Power or God, but I now admit that I did do it and still do—pray.

◆

My children had survived. They had grown. They brought hope to me with their existence like the mint in the planter outside my apartment, which insisted on living when everything died around it. The roots were there, and with much love and the water that my girlfriend gave the mint, it always sprang up yet again.

My children's insistent ability to thrive despite it all buoyed me up, just as we gave our parents a spot of joy in their suffering years. With them, our children, it's like falling in love over and over again. The vulnerability and the potential for loss never go away, but neither does the love.

I didn't know how many more trips to the ER were in store for me. A couple of months after sitting with my mom in the hospital, I visited a friend who managed a bed and breakfast at a hot springs in Boulder, Montana. Intending to go on a retreat, soak up some rest, recover, and get some writing time, I instead ended up in urgent care at the hospital in Helena being told that I had pneumonia. Afterward, I took the longed-for rest without guilt, lounging about the hot springs, writing again as I started to feel better. Coming back to my life in California, I had to remind myself over and over again that I didn't need to have pneumonia to be able to love and care for myself. And little by little, I began to repair and to write my story.

Singing Mommy Returns

Raphael is thirteen years old, and we are getting ready for his bar mitzvah. All year long I have been trying to break up with Jessica, the unavailable girlfriend, who is still living with her long-term boyfriend from Zimbabwe. My friends worry about him coming after me, and I worry about my sanity and about Raphael getting the wrong idea of what constitutes a healthy relationship. Raphael plays me his latest hip-hop picks, including Talib Kweli's "Get By," Nas' "I Can," and Tupac's "Dear Mama." All these songs give me a strange energy to persevere, and I believe that I can beat back all the legal and financial hellishness I am going through. Raphael knows I fantasize that he will someday write an ode to his single mom, like Tupac did and Boyz II Men with their "A Song for Mama." For his bar mitzvah, he composes an alternative version of Tupac's "Dear Mama," thanking me for putting on the big event. And at the reception he performs his parody, "Dear Carla," with his good friend, asking for audience participation.

Music brings us back together again when Raphael is seventeen. We have mostly been at battle with each other and at battle with a ruthless adversary: the drug addiction that threatens to swallow him up. On Saturdays, mutually pissed off, we walk from our apartment in South Pasadena to a music lesson (Raphael charging ahead of me whenever possible). There, in separate rooms, we escape to other worlds. I belt out "Don't Let Me Be Misunderstood," written for Nina Simone, and "Same Love" by Macklemore and Ryan Lewis, singing Mary Lambert's part, which comforts me with the words about her partner (a woman) keeping her warm. "Same Love" was a song that Raphael introduced me to, as he did with so much contemporary hip-hop music. (I introduced him to the Roots and Lauryn Hill, among others.) Inside the brightly colored music room, belting it out, I remember those days Raphael and I sang together when he was little.

"You emote really well," my voice teacher tells me.

"It's the only place I feel it's safe to do it," I say. Meanwhile, Raphael works on guitar—practicing Eric Clapton's "Cocaine"—with another teacher. Music temporarily abates our stalemate of anger and despair, allowing us to breathe and laugh together again. My voice teacher and I tease Raphael with the possibility of us doing a dual recital: a mom and son duet. He is horrified and ignores us. Raphael and I leave the music school and walk home, temporarily safe in our love for each other, enjoying an uneasy truce for one more day.

The next year, while Raphael is at the Renewal Recovery House for young men in recovery, we go to Beit T'Shuvah, a recovery synagogue in Santa Monica, for Yom Kippur services. The synagogue is filled with tattooed young people of all persuasions, a "rappin' rabbi" (another Afro-Jew), a rocking band, and a soulful choir. And I remember how some other versions of these Jewish melodies used to calm me. This service feels like a cross between a Southern Baptist church service and an AA meeting infused with Judaism. Tears glide down my cheeks. I feel grateful that I am not bone-dry, cried out, as I stand close to Raphael and one of his "sober colleagues." Gratitude, strong words, music, swaying bodies, euphonious music. Euphoria. Other than his bar mitzvah, this might be the one service Raphael has been able to sit all the way through.

A year passes, and Raphael is ready to graduate from the Renewal Recovery House program and move out. We go to Seattle for my brother's wedding. I bring my sober girlfriend, and Raphael brings his good friend, a sober companion from the program. Both he and Raphael are newly out in the world enjoying a sober social life, sober house parties, and dating for the first time in over a year and a half. They are on fire with young man angst. It is also Seattle Pride weekend and the anniversary of the landmark Supreme Court decision on same-sex marriage. Raphael's friend has just come out to the twenty-three young men in their recovery house. We walk around together for two days, listening to Sam Smith and the Weekend, and I just want to hang onto these moments of joy with my girlfriend and these beautiful young men.

Nine months later, I am with my mom at her assisted living facility. She lives in the memory care unit, called Connections. They are having "Singing Time," and a young mom comes in to lead the group wearing her baby on her back. I play a little hide-and-seek with her baby. We sing "I've Been Working on the Railroad," and I am reminded of my version from when Raphael was still nursing:

I've been feeding baby Raphael, all the live-long day.
I've been feeding Baby Rafi just to pass the time away.
Can't you hear the baby crying, rise up so early in the morning
Mama won't you nurse, Mama won't your nurse?
Mama won't you nurse right nowowowww!

Music still brings me comfort.

Some Markers as My Black Son Gets Older

1. While I am pregnant with a Black son, do I really think about what it means when I hear the statistics being passed around that one in three African American men will be incarcerated? I just think of us being a "We Are the World" family: multicultural, Jewish, African American, LGBTQ. I dream of rainbows.

2. Every year around Martin Luther King Jr. Day, while he's in preschool and early elementary school, Raphael gets worked up. "But why? Why did that man kill him?" His "Auntie Nana" (my friend María Elena) comes up with an answer: "It was fear. He killed him out of hatred created by fear."

3. I pick Raphael up from a friend's home; he is seven years old. The mom greets me with, "Something happened." Her ten-year-old nephew—who, like her and her son, is of Armenian descent—told Raphael that he didn't like Black people touching him, using a racist slur, when Raphael's hand brushed against his. Furious and devastated for my son, I ask Raphael, "What did you say to him? Did you tell him your mom would kick his ass?"

   "No," Raphael replies. "That's not what Martin Luther King would do. He'd fight back with words and talk and talk."

4. We attend a weekend for multiracial Jewish families in the Bay Area called Camp Tawonga. One family, made up of two moms—Jewish and white—tells a story: They live in Albany, a small town next to Berkeley, predominantly white at the time. When their Black son was around ten, they introduced their family to the local police department and explained, "This is our son. We live here in the community." They had heard of kids being pulled over for "walking while Black."

   It is chilling to think that my little boy could someday be seen as a potential perpetrator.

5. An African American friend, the mother of one of Raphael's schoolmates, tells me, "I'd cross to the other side of the street if I saw a bunch of Black teenagers coming towards me."

6. The book *The New Jim Crow: Mass Incarceration in the Age of Colorblindness* by Michelle Alexander comes out. Police shootings of young Black men are seen more often and by more people, captured with the use of cell phone video cameras and posted all over social media.

7.   I teach some writing workshops in the juvenile detention facilities in Northern California. Many of the youth (all African American or Latinx) are lifers and great writers. I walk in and see a boy, perhaps twelve, my son's age, beautiful, talkative, eager to write. I see a girl, thirteen years old, in for armed robbery (she accompanied her boyfriend). She is pregnant.

8.   We move to a condo in a somewhat less diverse, more affluent part of Pasadena than where we previously lived. My son is almost thirteen, getting taller, but he and most of his friends don't even have armpit hair yet. I become more aware that many people look at groups of young Black boys and react by crossing the street. Afraid of our young sons.

9.   We live close to the Rose Bowl parade route; it is New Year's Eve, and my friend comes over with her two daughters. They plan to go out and throw eggs at the cars, as is the custom, they tell me, the night before the Rose Parade. Raphael goes with them. I stay in. They come back under an hour later looking sheepish, subdued. "Tell them what happened," my friend says. My son is silent. Her daughter says, "The police grabbed Raphael." Apparently, a lot of people were throwing eggs, but two policemen came by and went after the only Black kid, my son, whose hand was up, poised to throw his first egg. The policemen, huge, one on each side, asked, "Where's your mom?" My friend explains, "I told the police that he was with me," but I think the damage is done. My son sees that he is the one picked out of the crowd for the color of his skin.

10.   It is my son's thirteenth birthday party. We go to see a movie about Jews hiding from Nazis in the woods. Later, at our place, the school counselor joins us, and we play a somewhat raucous game of Spoons. Afterward, she tells a scary story to the group of mostly Black boys, about a lynching and castration. So Raphael, my Afro-Jewish son, gets to hear about two ways that his people were brutalized, annihilated.

Suddenly a loud bang on the door: the police checking out a noise complaint. "Yes, the school counselor gets noisy when she plays Spoons," I tell them. The cops look surprised to see that it is only kids and me and the school counselor. They wish us well and tell us to keep it down. Apparently our (white) neighbor had called them.

Later, she complains to our leasing agent that she felt threatened, that she saw (Black) boys looking in her window. I write the neighbor a long letter, send flowers. The neighbor gives the flowers back. Says that she only wants to return "to how things were before" we moved in.

11. A friend tells me that her church hosts a program together with the Seattle Police Department to teach African American youth how to "behave" with police to "avoid problems." I wish that there were something like that in LA. Raphael gets cautioned by his friends' Black dads, "Don't make those hand motions, looks like gang signs," and is encouraged not to walk around wearing hoodies or other clothing that might encourage police to be even more likely to pick him out in a crowd.

12. Raphael's bar mitzvah is attended largely by African American and Latinx friends who say afterward, "I want a bro mitzvah." There is gospel music at the reception, and a story runs in *La Opinión* about it being "the real LA." The reporter translates Raphael's poems into Spanish.

   Raphael's eighth-grade school group is diverse. His Arab friend gives the two Jewish kids hearts with "I love Jew" on Valentine's Day. Raphael signs off his texts as "Afro-Jew without a 'Fro." These kids consider themselves post-racial. Still, I ask Raphael's dad to give him "the Talk" more than once.

13. We move to an apartment in South Pasadena (wealthier, whiter, though with a substantial rental population, like us), where Raphael starts high school. He notes that the number of textbooks each kid carries around corresponds to their ethnicity. In his estimation: "Of course, the most go to the Asian kids, perhaps eight books," and "The African American kids have the least; see, I only have four."

14. At about fifteen, Raphael starts smoking pot. One day, he is with a bunch of white friends; they all run when the police come, but my son stops, hands up. A police officer has a gun pulled out. Raphael knows not to run.

15. I research a story my son has told me about how the few Black kids at South Pasadena High School found themselves coincidentally all wearing the color purple one day. They walked around together, and then they were called into the office of the vice principal, who admonished them that other kids were afraid and saying, "It's a gang." And that perhaps they were chanting, "Black Power" too? I publish my article in *South Pasadena Patch*, which I title "Walking While Black in South Pasadena: Is That a Problem?" Some readers write in defensively: "Perhaps those kids were up to no good."

Others write, "Welcome to my world."

16.   Raphael is in an outpatient substance-abuse treatment program at our HMO. The social workers are all white, and the young people in treatment are all kids of color. They encourage the parents to call the police "as necessary" when our children are truant, steal from us, and continue to use drugs. As is the case in many treatment centers, these social workers suggest that legal consequences, including incarceration, may help drive our kids into recovery. Although desperate for Raphael to stop using, I find the prospect of my Black son being incarcerated chilling, and I wonder if there is a disconnect among the social workers, who are perhaps unaware of the mass incarceration of Black men. For our children, being caught in the juvenile justice system seems to promise only an entry into the so-called school-to-prison pipeline, not to offer treatment or support.

17.   Trayvon Martin, a seventeen-year-old unarmed Black student, is killed by George Zimmerman, a neighborhood watch captain, and the Black Lives Matter movement is launched. On its heels comes the slaying of unarmed nineteen-year-old Kendrec McDade by two police offers in Pasadena. Raphael and I join the protest in front of the Pasadena City Hall. We listen to Kendrec McDade's father speaking about how difficult it is for him and his wife to talk to their other children about what happened, about the need to hold the police accountable. We see Kendrec's mother fighting tears as she holds up a picture of her son. I look at my sixteen-year-old boy and imagine the unspeakable.

18.   I read the book *Citizen: An American Lyric* by Claudia Rankine and realize that no matter how much I think I get it—what it means to live as a Black person in white society—I don't. Empathy, concern, commitment, awareness: yes, I have all that. The reality of living in a particular shade of skin, though, is irreplaceable. I don't have that experience. But being the mother of a son who, because of the color of his skin, is at overwhelming risk of being harmed, assaulted, incarcerated, killed, or otherwise impacted physically and spiritually, that is something I do get. I get that all day, every day.

19.   Raphael obtains his license and is driving but hasn't changed the out- of-state registration and plates for the car given to him by his grandmother. I call him after the most recent shooting of a Black man, Philando Castile, by a police officer during a traffic stop for a busted brake light. We see the footage as he lay dying; his girlfriend

captures the moment on tape. She is in the back seat of the car with her four-year-old daughter. On recordings made public, she narrates what happened. "Oh my God, please don't tell me Officer that you just did this to him. Please don't tell me he's gone. You shot four bullets into him, sir." It is devastating.

20.   I say, "Honey, you know you are a new driver, you're young, you're Black. You don't need to add to the list of reasons they'll pull you over." I know I'm repeating myself. I don't wait for an answer but go through it again. And of course, he's been given the Talk before, but I'm not sure it has sunk in.

"It's okay, Mom, I get it."

21.   On NPR I hear a segment about the Talk families must give to their African American children. One parent relates that his four-year-old overheard them discussing the shootings of Black men by cops and asks if he should wear a bulletproof vest. And I wonder for the first time, *Would I still do it if I knew it would be this hard?*

Yes, I know I would still have this son.

Letting Go

I took my first shaky step and saw my eight-year-old son opposite me on the same thin tightrope one hundred feet above the ground, taking a step in my direction. "Raphael! Are you okay?" I asked, panic edging my voice. Raphael looked directly at me from what seemed like an insurmountable distance across the tightrope. He stood still for a moment, balanced.

"Mom, I'm okay. You need to just think about yourself now."

I saw my son's intent gaze, long eyelashes, café au lait–colored skin, the face like my father's, the face I knew better than my own. I was barely holding steady, and I realized that in order for me to make it across and hug him briefly, as we had been instructed for this trust-building exercise, every last part of me needed to be focused. I had to let go of my concern for him and be fully present in my own moment in order to reach Raphael. We were on a challenge ropes course at Camp Tawonga, near Yosemite, during a special family camp weekend for multiracial Jewish interfaith families. I'd tried a couple of different family camps, and it was hard to find one that fit our family: LGBT, *keshet* (rainbow), interfaith, biracial, single parent. I was hoping for spiritual renewal, to find kinship, perhaps some answers, by connecting to similar families—or maybe just some rest while Raphael spent time with his father or other kids. For much of the weekend, Raphael was clingy, not wanting me to be far away, often not wanting to participate in the camp activities. So when he had enthusiastically demanded we do the ropes course, I knew I had to go along.

We had on harnesses, but for me, it was still terrifying. I'd stepped up only because Raphael had asked that of me, knowing that this exercise was not something his dad would ever participate in—the height, the tightrope. Larry had agreed, warily, to travel with us for this family camp weekend. We still sometimes attempted to be a family, though not together as a couple. Perhaps he, too, was hoping to find families like ours to look to as models of coparenting. He was standing alone down below, looking up at us.

Raphael and I walked toward each other. I made myself be utterly present; otherwise, I'd have fallen. My worries slipped away—finances, mother-son tug-of-wars, ongoing tension with Larry. The uncut umbilical cord propelled us closer, step by step. With one big step, we met in the middle, hugged, and somehow found the coordination to move as if in one graceful motion, edging past each other to the opposite side and then meeting down on the ground. We hugged again, longer. "I love you," we said to each other.

◆

It is October 9, 2015, about eleven years after the ropes course at Camp Tawonga. In the near future, Raphael will leave the recovery house that he has been in for almost two years. He's excited, following the plan of moving out to an apartment with two other graduates of the recovery program.

I am suddenly terrified. The Renewal Recovery House will still exist as a place to go for support, but in reality it's time for Raphael to live his own life. He's only nineteen, soon to turn twenty, and I'm fucking scared. I have spent the last three weeks spinning out of control myself, worried perhaps I won't graduate from school, the long-awaited book and MFA maybe not completed. Perhaps I won't be able to support myself as I get older. Perhaps I'll lose my mind like my mom. Seeing my mom as we knew her vanish adds to my sense of shakiness, of the utter lack of control, as I prepare for Raphael to go out into the world.

My mom has talked about fairies that might come rescue her from her assisted living residence, which she calls "prison," and take her home to the Bronx, where she hasn't lived for more than sixty years. Recently she was questioned by a social worker to determine if she still had dementia and still qualified for her long-term care plan. "I can't tell you how old I am. But I can tell you this: I do exist," she said.

◆

When I was fifty-one, I decided that I needed to make a visible statement, get a tattoo. *Hineni*—"I am here." I had the Hebrew word tattooed on me. My brother, in his Mr. Spock–ian way, said, "'I am here?' Is this a map?" I have a *hamsa* hand (to ward off the evil eye) on my back, and *"Hineni"* in Hebrew letters is inscribed below. Very tiny Hebrew letters, because, after all, I don't want to be a target for anti-Semites and white supremacists.

For years I had contemplated getting a tattoo and gone over what I'd want and where. I researched the Jewish ban on tattoos and found out that it is an urban legend. In fact, in Israel a very high percentage of people ages nineteen to forty have tattoos. And you *can* be buried in a Jewish cemetery with a tattoo.

I went to a tattoo artist who turned out to know me and my son from a co-op preschool that our kids went to in Sierra Madre many years earlier. Her tattoo parlor was called Shangri-La, and it looked like that: vines of bright scarlet, purple, and orange bougainvillea intertwined with Provence blue morning glory and sweet-smelling jasmine. The studio was in her backyard, and it felt as if I was walking into another dimension. After I approved a sketch of the tattoo based on my ideas, she started her work, turning her needle, which buzzed quietly into my skin, while she explained that the natural endorphins would kick in after a bit of pain. At first I did feel jabs of intense pain. (I'd asked a woman getting a tattoo in Old Pasadena which hurt more, getting waxed or getting a tattoo, and she had said, "Oh yeah, waxing is worse for sure.") The pain was sharp enough that I gasped, and to distract myself I asked the tattoo artist to tell me how she had decided on her profession. She'd been trained as an artist and illustrator. Her dad, a biker, also a rocket scientist, suggested tattooing to her as a way of making a living.

And then, miraculously, those endorphins did kick in as she was asking me about myself. I told her all about me, about the recent episode of getting my nose broken by a sheriff's deputy when I couldn't immediately find my Metro ticket and about losing everything because of my marriage breaking up. (I didn't yet know what more I might lose—or have the potential to lose—because of my son's addiction.) But at that point I'd decided I had survived. By the time I was saying that I was now okay ". . . and that's what happened," she'd put the finishing touches on my tattoo.

♦

In the past three weeks, I've been thinking that now I have the freedom to go off the deep end because my son seems to be doing beyond well and my stepdaughter has stopped talking to me—and everyone else—for a bit. So I feel free to obsess, agitate, and generally neglect my own well-being. I've thought about using heroin—for real—for the first time. I've self-harmed. I dug a hole in my leg with my fingernails as I tried to feel, to give form to the pain that wracked me following an argument with my girlfriend. My first cutting incident at age fifty-six. Is there a support group for older-onset cutters?

I'm glad that the black-and-blue mark, the jagged scar, remains so I can remember. I did that. I went there. I knew I was bleeding inside, and I wanted the red, the injury, to be visible. Then perhaps the pain would stop, and I would be seen. But perhaps I'm seen only as insane. I'd also contacted my old ex, Jessica, via text, and then I'd cut it off, seemingly for good. She's my heroin, and I have to stop.

Moreover, I started looking at violent Internet porn, something I've got control over, unlike my dreams. Throughout my life, I've often dreamed of being raped and of having an orgasm while still resisting. It reflects the real-life complications of my sexuality. How many times in my life have I been aroused by what seems to be something or somebody so wrong, and yet some kind of twisted sexual friction is created? A Pavlovian response that I imagine began when I was around eleven or twelve and was sexually abused by my piano teacher.

We'd recently moved to the hated suburbs outside of Seattle—Bellevue—from the inner city, where I had been Sammy Boy. Now my siblings and I were outcasts in WASP Land, surrounded by families who looked nothing like us. In those days, we stayed out all afternoon and evening playing increasingly complicated games with the local kids. I tried to teach them about spying, starting a gang that was a cross between the Sharks and the Jets in *West Side Story* (which I had memorized in its entirety) and the kids from my old rough playground.

There was another piano student, a girl from the neighborhood. She was developing already, popular with the sleazy guys for her breasts and willingness. She and I would walk into the woods with our nineteen-year-old piano teacher, whose face was cratered with bright, inflamed pimples. I can't remember how we first began these walks to the woods, the same woods the older kids would sneak out to late at night to play spin the bottle and smoke pot. Did we not think it odd that our piano teacher wanted us to go back into the woods alone with him? Did we do this before or after our piano lessons? We walked down the path among the pine and Douglas fir trees, and it was probably already dusk. It gets dark early in the winter in Washington, and we must have walked back there, on the trail behind our neighbor's house, in the fading light, surrounded by moist, lightly rained-upon ground. The hammers of the workmen who were building a Jewish temple could be heard in the distance, but they would soon cut out for the day. Did we take a flashlight?

I remember once out there sitting down with him, and perhaps one of us asked about the lump in his pants. Or did he guide one of our hands to it? Or did he just start talking about what he called his "handkerchief" as he moved our hands, and we felt it through his pants first? I began to get a funny sick feeling in my stomach. "Touch it, it's soft," he told us. He placed our hands on his pants where the crotch went from being soft and full to feeling much harder after our hands were guided by him, back and forth, and then he pulled "it" out—a big, wide, fleshy penis. It seemed enormous and swollen, reddish purple, not exactly unlike the color of the large pimples that covered his neck and face. I imagine he touched us, too, because I remember starting to wonder, to even be curious about what it would be like to have that penis inside me.

"It would bust you wide open, so we have to wait," our piano teacher had told us. We returned various times to the woods with him, repeating this pattern. Some days we stayed out there kind of late, till almost dark, dinnertime, but I always made it back before my dad came looking for me.

I can't remember what happened exactly that last time, only the sound of my dad entering the woods, his flashlight, annoyance in his voice as he called out for me, and the sudden rush of shame and fear as the three of us stood up and walked quickly out of the trees. I'm guessing I was sexually aroused, because I sense that that's when those dreams and those feelings started. And thinking about the possibility of having been aroused as a child when I was being sexually abused, a memory that makes my stomach churn even now as I picture the bright, blistery pimples on the piano teacher's face, offers a clue as to why I might turn to something completely wrong like the violent porn I had begun watching and kept watching until someone more knowledgeable than me said, "Stop—it's an extremely difficult addiction to break." After the postmenopausal drought of libido and the despair I had been feeling but not understanding, my body was beginning to respond to the rough, sometimes even brutal, sexual images, almost like to a drug. Many of my previous years of being sexual with the "wrong" person, of being driven by those intense pulsating hormones and endorphins that immediately turned to shame after an orgasm and resulted in so many fucked up, dangerous, near-rape and actual rape experiences—these had become coupled with my inability to keep feeling sexual with someone who felt safe. My feelings quickly changed to shame and inertia, and then I'd rather just sit and watch videos, eat, ruminate, or anything else other than try to rouse my shut-down body.

The one thing that has held solid for me now for so many years is writing, and I finally thought I'd made the space to concentrate on it. But for awhile, I found myself focusing on everything else but the writing. I was yanked away by the rip currents of my mom leaving us, no longer being the mom we knew. Moving close to her children in Southern California from where she had lived more than forty-five years in Washington propelled her into a much more advanced state of dementia.

Now we have to wipe her butt, get her to take her medication, and leave her in a ritual as painful as that of leaving a pleading toddler.

I have simply been thrashing about. I still long for things I don't believe I have—complete freedom to write and the belief I'll be okay. In reality I could decide to believe that I have that kind of choice and abundance. Then again, I might never write another intelligent word or a decent story that anyone will read. Over the years, I've painstakingly eked out some writing here and there while attending to the more urgent needs of others: son, stepdaughter, work, aging parents. After witnessing how fragile life could be, watching my mom start to lose her mind and my son almost lose his life, I decided I couldn't put off seizing my time to write. But it's hard, this business of focusing on and believing in oneself.

◆

I held an image for many years of sitting in the woods, head leaning against a long-haired woman. She was comforting me, perhaps stroking my hair and singing, and our child was in my lap. I held tight to this image as I lost baby after baby and endured rage after rage from partners and suffered my own rages and bouts of craziness, flailing about in my desperation to "be seen." (And what the hell does that mean, anyway?) What was that urgent despair that demanded I carry a baby, be a mother, create this safe haven, this nurturing and nurtured family? That I didn't actually create, or rather what I did create was so distorted, it didn't look like that safe home in nature. But I did create something, something solid, a strength my kids know exists. They know I'm there day after day. My family and my friends know that in my so-very-imperfect mode of being in the world—messy, interrupting, inconsistent at times—I'm a person who loves and is unsinkable, solidly loyal. Now it's time to look that love in the mirror.

◆

I have felt secure enough in my son's recovery, his sobriety—almost two years now—to believe that I was free to go back to my old ways, the self- torture, rumination, all the anxiety I was raised with by my family, in particular my dad. Instead, I discover I must be vigilant. Lack of gratitude will cause life to simply slap the shit out of me. If I don't enjoy, or at least appreciate, every moment I have on the earth with a living, vibrant, life-loving son out in the world, well, I'll get so kicked in the butt. Even if I can't always sing with gratitude, I need to stop this genetically ingrained journey to the hellhole of regret and worry. And when I remember Raphael staggering about, eyes rolled back in his head, saying he didn't have much more time, then I need to also remember how lucky I am that he *does* exist, that he's found a spirituality, a core of inner strength, and a support system that I could not create alone for him. And his life is just beginning!

I want there to be some kind of letting-go ceremony. "It all happened too quickly," my friend Rose says, lamenting the absence of her two sons finally gone off to live their lives—university and beyond. I remember my son saying to me so long ago, walking that tightrope course we did together, "Mom, I'm okay; I will be all right. Worry about yourself now."

I'm not so sure I'm ready to let go. I'm not so sure I'm ready to worry only about myself.

When Sammy Boy and Mrs. Kumata Wore Paisley

In 1968 I walked down my street, 34th Avenue in south Seattle, carrying a sign that said, "Make Love Not War." I was nine years old, in fourth grade, going with my dad to protest marches against the Vietnam War. My older siblings walked with me to our elementary school, John "Manure" (Muir). Fourth grade, taught by Mrs. Kumata, is the class I remember most— turns out it was also her first year of teaching and her favorite. She held a class reunion when I was in my twenties, the only one I have ever attended. I am fifty-six now—forty-seven years since fourth grade.

I look back to see what was happening in 1968–69.

April 4, 1968. Martin Luther King Jr. is assassinated at the Lorraine Motel in Memphis. I remember sitting with my mom and a neighbor while they cried, watching the reporters announce the shooting over and over again on television. Discussing Martin Luther King's life and legacy. And everything that followed—politicians' speeches, riots, funeral.

June 5, 1968. Robert Kennedy is killed at the Ambassador Hotel in Los Angeles. Same: watching, crying.

Just the year before, an estimated 100,000 young people have shown up in San Francisco for what will come to be called the Summer of Love. These dreamers, poets, artists, musicians, radicals, and more aim to transform and connect people around the world and protest the Vietnam War with peace and love.

One year after the Summer of Love, there are student revolts across the world. Protesters attacked by police in France's Bloody Monday, Mexico City's Tlatelolco massacre, Bloody Thursday at People's Park in Berkeley. The Troubles in Northern Ireland. In the United States, the Black Panther Party is a strong presence. The Vietnam War escalates—so do demonstrations. At the Democratic National Convention in Chicago, police officers beat protestors unconscious.

I remember mock elections in class. I was Eldridge Cleaver, a Black Panther leader. Larry Rock, one of the African American students, was assigned to play George Wallace, the racist white governor of Alabama. Though adamant that he did not want the part, he played it in character with his version of what he considered a strong Southern "cracker" accent. "I'm George Wallace, and I'm a liar," he stated and told his classmates not to vote for him.

Just four years after the Civil Rights Act passed, I remember writing to officials in Louisiana, Mississippi, and Alabama: "Is it true that it's illegal in your state for me to marry my African American boyfriend?" (Being officially "Caucasian," though never viewed as such by most white folks, since I was a Jew.) They mailed me back a copy of the actual law forbidding Blacks and whites from marrying.

Musical explosion: the Jackson Five debut, the Grateful Dead, Woodstock, the Beatles, Aretha Franklin, and my all-time favorite, "My Cherie Amour" by Stevie Wonder. Dance parties!

And ugh—Richard Nixon inaugurated as president.

♦

I decide to go back and interview Mrs. Kumata about that year that meant so much to me. She tells me, "I felt it was very important to get along because at the time there was just so much strife. I wanted the kids not to feel that in the classroom. That was a big goal of mine."

We lived in a somewhat rough part of Seattle. Teachers were not afraid to discipline the bad kids. Kids were tied to chairs; mouths were taped shut. In second grade, Mrs. Stedman ripped the tape off one kid, taking part of his lip.

In fourth grade, we marched up red wooden stairs into Mrs. Kumata's huge, beige portable classroom filled with wooden lift-top desks.

Mrs. Kumata says, "We had the nicest boys in class. Everyone got along so well—no real fighting in our classroom—but the rest of school was rough, too many kids! Fourteen portables covered the playground, more than a thousand kids."

The kids I played with at school were of all different skin colors and ethnicities. I was Sammy Boy, strong and tough on the playground, the only one in my Brownie troop who wasn't Black. But Mrs. Kumata assured me, "You are something; you're Jewish."

I have wondered why that year was particularly memorable and if some of the other kids from our class felt the same way. So much of who I aspire to be now seems to be who I was then.

"It was a scary time, but you were the smartest and best class I ever had," she says. "All the riots were going on around the country. It was a tough place to teach and to go to school."

Mrs. Kumata kept me after school when she found out we were planning to take out the class bully, Marvin. My friend Norris's mom had gotten wind of the action too and took him home early. But the other boys went ahead, four or five of them. Everyone got suspended. They all ended up with black eyes—all except Marvin. At our class reunion, I had learned that Marvin was in prison for rape. He is still in prison. Rumor has it he found Jesus.

Mrs. Kumata recently sent me our class picture. A sea of multicolored faces. She wrote down almost all of my classmates' names. I'm standing right next to Mrs. Kumata with an almost identical classic sixties A-line dress. "I also see you and I had an eye for the fashion with our paisley," she wrote me.

I got in touch with Norris Washington to ask him about fourth grade. He replied, "It was the year I remember most, the first year I really enjoyed school, became more comfortable with friends, played kickball."

Mrs. Kumata's classroom style seemed to play a pivotal role for him, too—though together we remember little beyond the mock elections, creative writing, getting picked to take a special intelligence test. And this: in a place where classmates came from a wide variety of cultures and economic backgrounds—from huge houses overlooking Lake Washington to the projects on Rainier Avenue—everyone got along. "I met people who were wealthier and grew up in an intellectual tradition," Norris said.

Two other things stuck out for Norris. "Pilots—Seattle got their first professional baseball team! Lasted one year." And this: "Coming home from the drive-in movie, my father turned on the radio: Bobby Kennedy shot. My dad said, 'Oh, my God, they are killing them now . . .'"

♦

When I introduced Norris to my son, he said, "Your mom was my hero; she was courageous."

"How so?" I asked.

"The way you interacted with teachers—asking questions, being the leader. I was extremely shy back then. You were always kind of like, 'Let's go do this.' [Try to beat up the class bully?] We said, 'Great'; it was bound to be an adventure."

Snow days created a glorious battlefield where I could wear my tapered pants. Life seemed wide open. I was fearless, an athlete, an activist. In Mrs. Kumata's classroom, a strong-nosed, skinny-legged, knob-kneed, adventurous, independent Jewish tomboy was cool.

♦

When I was in fifth grade, my family moved to Bellevue. To us kids, Bellevue was a scary place full of white, ultra-suburbanite snobs. By sixth grade, I was last picked for sports; Sammy Boy remained buried somewhere back in south Seattle.

Many years later I look at a picture of me standing on our porch in the Mount Baker neighborhood of Seattle and playing the trumpet, belting out "Tijuana Taxi," made popular by Herb Alpert (a Jew) and the Tijuana Brass. The question of Sammy Boy comes up for me frequently. Where did he/she go?

Back then, being so comfortable in my skin, strong, rebellious, someone's hero—that person became a stranger and then came back throughout my life. That person *is* me, the same person who was willing to play rugby in college (even as a poor athlete) and willing to consider playing rugby again at age fifty-four, thinking it might save my life. Thinking that if I can do this, I can do anything—I can survive my son's addiction and the knowledge that I am ultimately powerless over whether he will live or die.

Now, after my son is two years in recovery, I'm suddenly filled with fear and uncertainty as I turn the lens back on me. I often look back and wonder, *Who is that person who did stand-up comedy a year-and-a-half ago, who applied for and started graduate school at age fifty-four?*

That's me, Sammy Boy, the same person who got flown into Simpson Meadow to be on (perhaps) the only all-women backcountry trail crew for the National Park Service when I was twenty years old. It was me on the lifeboat in the middle of the Mediterranean Sea, ready to die but resolving to go back and have a baby. And me in my early fifties, being told by my civil rights attorney about testifying after a sheriff's deputy broke my nose, "You're stronger than you think." I had said that I didn't think I could face it, knowing how the bashed get bashed and the victims get revictimized in the criminal (in)justice process. He must have seen that scrappy Sammy Boy who stays dormant—buried even—but refuses to die.

Sammy Boy will resurface time and time again. Lost and found. What will emerge temporarily from hibernation and what has stayed with me throughout my life is some grain of humor at the #CrayCray Mom, some words that find their way out, the rashness, the tenacity, the intrepidity of survival. Laughter. Connection. My words or yours, a book I've read, a book I am writing.

Gratitude and Debts

To my thesis mentor, Kathryn Rhett—brilliant, rigorous, compassionate, and supportive—who helped me envision and craft this manuscript. I'm also grateful to my readers: Natalie Kusz and Jon Pineda. To the writers and faculty, including Francisco Goldman and director Fred Lebron, at Queens University of Charlotte's MFA in Creative Writing (Latin America).

To the Northwest Institute of Literary Arts/Whidbey Writers Workshop, Ana Maria Spagna and Larry Cheek, and to the Vermont College of Fine Arts Postgraduate Writers' Conference, director Ellen Lesser.

To the talented, attentive, and gracious Thelma T. Reyna, Chief Editor and publisher of Golden Foothills Press—thank you for believing in my memoir!

To my insightful, scrupulous, and supportive editor, Diana Rico— thank you for walking me back from the cliff more than once and for making this book all that it is.

To all the other writing instructors, mentors, and role models who helped give breath to this book—you know who you are, but to name a few: Katya Williamson, Gerda Govine Ituarte, Rebecca Walker, Maestra Gaona, "Mrs. Kumata," and Joyce Maynard (who was one of the first to suggest that I write a book-length memoir). There have been many, and the author offers gratitude to those not listed; you are remembered.

To the editors who have helped get earlier versions of essays in this book out in the world, including: Meg Lemke (*Mutha Magazine)*, Jennifer Niesslein (*Full Grown People*), Michele Raphael (*Angels Flight | literary west*), Kevin Uhrich (*Pasadena Weekly*), Michael Sedano (*La Bloga*), Marcelle Soviero (*Brain, Child* and *Brain, Teen)*, Sara Finnerty (*Entropy*), Brendan Spiegel and Erika Hayasaki (*Narratively*), Chelsey Clammer (*The Nervous Breakdown*).

To the members of my Pasadena Writing Posse, Bocajapa Writing Group, and "Queenie's" MFA alum. support crew.

To Shuly Xóchitl Cawood, Seth Fischer, Tisha Marie Reichle, Kahaliah Reed, Melissa Chadburn, and Sehba Sarwar for reading my manuscript and providing notes.

To the Women Who Submit members and founders for all their support and encouragement.

To all the amazing authors whose work came before mine, providing inspiration and courage.

To everyone I've written with, workshopped with, and pushed through the work of excavating our stories with. Your names are here too.

To family and friends who have encouraged me and supported my writing, including María Elena Fernández, Karen Chester, Gale Cohen, Anne Roise, Kerri Kumasaka, Denise Diamond, Barbara Klare, Samantha Updegrave, Manuela Gomez, and many, many more.

To these busy and talented authors for your generous words and support of my book: Lillian Faderman, Hector Tobar, Sue William Silverman, Marcelle Soviero, Ariel Gore, Kathryn Rhett, Melodie J. Rodgers, Aimee Carrillo Rowe, and Shonda Buchanan.

To Katie Scrivner for brilliant editing and steadfast friendship. This would not be a book without you.

To Samantha, daughter of my heart.

To my loving, loyal, and generous siblings: Jim, Jane, and Sheli/Zoe, who had my back every step of the way.

To my father for his dogged support of family.

To my mother for typing up my stories when I was little and for always reminding me that I am a writer.

To Milo for believing in me and supporting me throughout the process. I couldn't have pushed this book out without you. Thank you for your love and support. Always. You are lovely and amazing.

To my son: My dearest one, my sweet, beautiful, and brilliant son, you've always helped me be my best. Thank you for encouraging me and supporting me and allowing me to write this story that includes so much of you. You've inspired and delighted me. Your wonderful sense of humor has kept me laughing throughout our lives together, even in some of the most difficult of times. You've made life so beautiful.

Acknowledgments:
Prior Publications

The following essays in this book have been individually published previously (some in different versions and with different titles), as follows:

"Simpson Meadow" in *Hashtag Queer: LGBTQ+ Creative Anthology*, vol. 2 (Qommunity, 2018).

"Heartbeat" in *PaniK: Candid Stories of Life Altering Experiences Surrounding Pregnancy*, compiled by Melissa Ferina (Lulu.com, 2011). A longer version of "Heartbeat" was published in *Mutha Magazine*, March 20, 2017.

"Singing Mommy" in *La Bloga*, May 12, 2012.

"Donor X" in *Mutha Magazine*, April 18, 2016.

"We Have Pets" in *Mutha Magazine*, October 14, 2015. Also included in the anthology *Unspoken: Writers on Infertility, Miscarriage, and Stillbirth*, edited by Whitney Roberts Hill and Elizabeth Ferris.

"Love in the Time of Foreclosures" in *Angels Flight | literary west*, March 30, 2016.

"The Year of Eating Banana Splits" in *Hashtag Queer: LGBTQ+ Creative Anthology*, vol. 1 (Qommunity, 2017).

"One Day on the Gold Line" in *Pasadena Weekly* (cover story), August 30, 2012. Also published in *Magnolia: A Journal of Women's Socially Engaged Literature*, vol. 3, September 10, 2013.

"Feed Me, Fund Me, Leave Me Alone" in *Brain, Child Magazine*, May 23, 2016.

"If This Is So, Why Am I?" in *The Nervous Breakdown*, February 26, 2018. Also selected as a Notable in *The Best American Essays 2019*.

"Stand Up Mom" in *Brain, Teen*, December 2017, and *Brain, Child*, May 20, 2018. (Title in book is "#CrayCray Mom.")

"The Cat, the Kid, and the Mom" in *Entropy*, April 4, 2017. (Title in book is "Mamacita and Princesa.")

"Graduation Day at Addiction High" in *Narratively*, December 9, 2014. Selected by *Longreads* for "Five Stories about Addiction," December 14, 2014.

"Things That Happened as My Black Son Got Older" in *Mutha Magazine*, November 13, 2017. (Title in book is "Some Markers as My Black Son Gets Older.")

"Letting Go" in *Full Grown People*, May 12, 2016.

"1968: Sammy Boy and Mrs. Kumata Wore Paisley" in *Angels Flight | literary west*, September 4, 2017.

About the Author

Writer. Teacher. Mother. As a writer, Carla hopes to help readers feel less alone and more resilient. As a teacher, she strives to help others tell their stories and hone their craft while experimenting with new forms. The journey of motherhood informs much of her writing.

Carla was selected as Co-Poet Laureate for Altadena, CA 2022-2024. Her chapbook, *What Is Left*, was published December 2021 by dancing girl press. A Pasadena Rose Poet, a Pride Poet with West Hollywood, and a former PEN in the Community Teaching Artist, Carla teaches creative writing to high school and university students and has taught incarcerated youth. Carla holds an MFA in Creative Writing from Queens University of Charlotte (Latin American program) and a bachelor's degree from the University of California, Santa Cruz. She also studied at the Universidad Autónoma de México.

Carla's work on blended/unblended, queer, biracial, and single parent families has appeared in a variety of literary journals and anthologies, including: *Narratively, Longreads, Brevity Blog, MUTHA Magazine, Brain/Child, Entropy, The Rumpus,* and *The Nervous Breakdown*. Her essay "If This Is So, Why Am I?" was selected as a Notable in *Best American Essays 2019*. (This essay is included in this book.) Also, "Mother's Day Triptych" and "This Is What I Want You to Know" were selected as Notable Essays in 2020 and 2021, respectively. Her story, "Graduation Day at Addiction High," which originally appeared in *Narratively*, was also chosen for *Longread's*, "Five Stories on Addiction."

Carla was named a Carrizozo Artist in Residence in New Mexico. She lives in Pasadena with her beloved partner, Milo. To learn more, see carlasameth.com.

 ## National Award-Winning Indie Literary Book Press

Our indie-published books have earned over 22 national book honors. Visit our website to see our poetry collections, anthologies, fiction, and non-fiction books at www.GoldenFoothillsPress.com .

Our authors are available for literary events; book signings; classroom presentations in high school and college; book clubs; civic organizations; panel presentations; and as guest speaker or workshop presenter on varied topics. Contact our press to arrange these special events.

Over 150 distinguished authors from across the United States have been published by our press since its founding in 2014, including Poets Laureate, Pushcart Prize Nominees, national and international book award winners, and recipients of many other regional and state honors. Visit our website to see listings of all our publications. Thank you for your supportiveness.

Contact Chief Editor/Publisher
Thelma T. Reyna, Ph.D.
www.GoldenFoothillsPress.com
goldenfoothillspress@ yahoo. com
Phone 626-710-0531

9 781737 248118